Quiet enjoyment

Arden and Partington's guide to remedies for harassment and illegal eviction

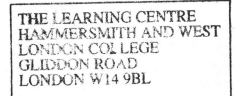

Andrew Arden QC founded **Arden Chambers** in 1993 to provide a centre for specialist practice, primarily in the area of housing law, together with local government and property. The set has been described in *Chambers and Partners* as 'a trailblazer ... extremely well-regarded and strong in its niche areas of local government, property and housing' and in *Legal 500* as 'a pre-eminent set for housing law'.

Andrew Arden QC is head of Arden Chambers, London. He has appeared in many of the leading cases in housing law over the past 30 years. He is author or editor of the principal practitioner texts on housing law, including the *Encyclopaedia of Housing Law, Housing Law Reports, Journal of Housing Law, Arden & Partington's Housing Law*, the *Manual of Housing Law* (Sweet & Maxwell) and *Homelessness and Allocations* (LAG), and of *Local Government Finance Law* and *Local Government Constitutional and Administrative Law* (Sweet & Maxwell).

Rebecca Chan is a barrister and member of Arden Chambers. She practises in all areas of housing and local government law. She has written articles for *Journal of Housing Law* and *Solicitors Journal*. She speaks regularly at conferences and provides legal training courses.

Sam Madge-Wyld is a barrister and member of Arden Chambers. He specialises in housing and local government law. Sam contributed to the 7th edition of *Defending Possession Proceedings* and the 5th edition of the *Housing Law Casebook* (LAG). He is an assistant editor of *Local Government Finance* (Sweet & Maxwell). He has additionally written articles that have appeared in *Journal of Housing Law, New Law Journal, Local Government Lawyer* and *Judicial Review*.

Available as an ebook at www.lag.org.uk/ebooks

The purpose of the Legal Action Group is to promote equal access to justice for all members of society who are socially, economically or otherwise disadvantaged. To this end, it seeks to improve law and practice, the administration of justice and legal services.

Quiet enjoyment

Arden and Partington's guide to remedies for harassment and illegal eviction

SEVENTH EDITION

Andrew Arden QC, Rebecca Chan and Sam Madge-Wyld

Legal Action Group
2012

arden
chambers

This edition published in Great Britain 2012
by LAG Education and Service Trust Limited
242 Pentonville Road, London N1 9UN
www.lag.org.uk

© Andrew Arden QC 2012

First published 1980
Second edition 1985
Third edition by Sylvester Carrott and Caroline Hunter 1990
Fourth edition by Caroline Hunter and Siobhan McGrath 1994
Fifth edition by David Carter and Andrew Dymond 1998
Sixth edition by Andrew Arden QC, David Carter and Andrew Dymond 2002

While every effort has been made to ensure that the details in this text are correct, readers must be aware that the law changes and that the accuracy of the material cannot be guaranteed and the author and the publisher accept no responsibility for any loss or damage sustained.

British Library Cataloguing in Publication Data
a CIP catalogue record for this book is available from the British Library.

Crown copyright material is produced with the permission of the Controller of HMSO and the Queen's Printer for Scotland.

FSC
www.fsc.org
MIX
Paper from
responsible sources
FSC® C020438

This book has been produced using Forest Stewardship Council (FSC) certified paper. The wood used to produce FSC certified products with a 'Mixed Sources' label comes from FSC certified well-managed forests, controlled sources and/or recycled material.

Print ISBN   978 1 908407 14 6
ebook ISBN   978 1 908407 15 3

Typeset by Regent Typesetting, London
Printed in Great Britain by Hobbs the Printers, Totton, Hampshire

Contents

Table of cases

Table of statutes

Table of statutory instruments

Table of European legislation

Abbreviations

ASBA 2003	Anti-social Behaviour Act 2003
ASBI	Anti-social behaviour injunction
ASBO	Anti-social behaviour order
BA 1976	Bail Act 1976
CBO	Criminal behaviour order
CCA 1984	County Courts Act 1984
CDA 1998	Crime and Disorder Act 1998
CJA 1982, 1991, 2003	Criminal Justice Act 1982, 1991, 2003
CJPA 2001	Criminal Justice and Police Act 2001
CLA 1977	Criminal Law Act 1977
CPA 1974	Control of Pollution Act 1974
CPI	Community protection order
CPO	Crime prevention injunction
CPR 1998	Civil Procedure Rules 1998
CPS	Crown Prosecution Service
C(RTP)A 1999	Contracts (Rights of Third Parties) Act 1999
DPP	Director of Public Prosecutions
EPA 1990	Environmental Protection Act 1990
HA 1985, 1998, 1996	Housing Act 1985, 1998, 1996
HMOs	Houses in multiple occupation
HRA 1998	Human Rights Act 1998
HRA 2008	Housing and Regeneration Act 2008
IAA 1999	Immigration and Asylum Act 1999
IANA 2006	Immigration, Asylum and Nationality Act 2006
LASPO 2012	Legal Aid, Sentencing and Prosecution of Offenders Act 2012
LGHA 1989	Local Government Housing Act 1989
LPA 1925	Law of Property Act 1925
LRA 2002	Land Registration Act 2002
LTA 1954	Landlord and Tenant Act 1954
MCA 1980	Magistrates' Courts Act 1980
MCR 1981	Magistrates' Courts Rules 1981
NA 1996	Noise Act 1996
PCC(S)A 2000	Powers of the Criminal Courts (Sentencing) Act 2000
PEA 1977	Protection from Eviction Act 1977
PHA 1997	Protection from Harassment Act 1997
POA 1985	Public Order Act 1985

RA 1977	Rent Act 1977
R(A)A 1976	Rent (Agriculture) Act 1976
SCA 1981	Senior Courts Act 1981
SOCPA 2005	Serious and Organised Crime and Police Act 2005

CHAPTER 1

Introduction

1.1   This book is concerned with the rights of occupiers of residential property to live undisturbed in their homes and the legal remedies available when their peace is threatened.

1.2   Earlier editions addressed the rights of occupiers to protect themselves against unlawful eviction and harassment primarily from their landlords and – if a less frequent occurrence – from others seeking to force them out of their homes. In the last two editions, however, there was something of a move towards recognition that occupiers' enjoyment of their homes could also be disturbed as a result of anti-social behaviour from persons entirely unconnected with their landlords, for example, nuisance neighbours, gangs of youths who roam estates, drug dealers and stalkers, whose objectives were directed towards making others' lives miserable, and/or conducting themselves in an uncontrolled manner, rather than actually to make others quit their homes.

1.3   This expanded focus reflected a number of propositions: that eviction and harassment by landlords is itself a form of anti-social conduct; as noted, that anti-social conduct from any source could and did affect occupation of the home; and, that laws directed towards anti-social conduct were capable of catching both kinds of activity.

1.4   The extension of coverage to the Protection from Harassment Act (PHA) 1997 in the fifth edition was described in the introduction to the last edition as being, perhaps, the first step away from the book's primary focus, recognising that a landlord could as easily – and as disturbingly – commit harassment within that Act as harassment under the Protection from Eviction Act (PEA) 1977; indeed, it is now standard practice to plead both Acts. In truth, though, the coverage had always addressed an element of conduct not primarily directed at landlords, both insofar as offences of harassment and unlawful eviction under that Act are not confined to acts by or on behalf of landlords and insofar as, from the first edition, it was considered appropriate to include offences which a landlord could commit under the Criminal Law Act (CLA) 1977.

1.5   Housing law emerged from a number of different subjects; over time, having achieved recognition in its own right, it has gone in something of a circle, as other policy areas have impacted on it, eg immigration law, welfare law and, of course, the law governing anti-social behaviour itself. The last edition took a step which it described, presciently, as 'tentative', towards 'a broader concept of the peaceful occupation of residential premises' the book was 'intended to help protect ...'. Given the 'general trend towards (on the one hand) "social landlordism", with decreased security of tenure in the truly private sector ...' it was noted that '[h]arassment and unlawful eviction in their most obvious forms are probably no longer the main ways in which ... lives can be made "hell"'.[1]

1.6   The step was described as tentative for two principal reasons: first, that the measures adopted to tackle the broader problem of anti-social behaviour suggested that the subject needed attention in its own right (which it was of course already receiving elsewhere); second, that while occupiers could take proceedings themselves against the perpetrators of broader anti-social behaviour, it was often unrealistic for them to do so. To provide a full account of these measures would involve addressing the public authorities charged with dealing with the problem, rather than the occupiers whose advisers this book has long been intended to assist.

1.7   Of course, it can rightly be said that the provisions in PEA 1977 are likewise couched in terms which envisage action by local authorities; but the genesis of this book was the failure of authorities to use those powers, leading tenants to need to rely on their own advisers instead. In practice, that remains the case: authorities are much more inclined to use their powers to address anti-social conduct

---

1 In *Devonshire and Smith v Jenkins*, unreported, 28 April 1978, CA, Ormrod LJ said, describing the defendant's behaviour: 'It is fair to say in ordinary language that for some five months, Mr Jenkins made the lives of these people hell and I do not think it worthwhile elaborating on that good old English expression because it accurately describes the position of this household.' In a similar vein, judges talk of anti-social behaviour in its more modern usage: see *Hounslow LBC v McBride* (1999) 31 HLR 143, 146, per Simon Brown LJ ('monstrous reign of terror') and *Newcastle City Council v Morrison* (2000) 32 HLR 891, 899, CA per May LJ ('To call it anti-social behaviour would be so far to understate it as to trivialise the effect it must have had on the neighbourhood. It was much more like a reign of terror').

which affects a number of people, eg the residents of an estate, than they appear to be to address individual acts of eviction or harassment of a tenant.[2] Nor are the police often willing to become involved in disputes between occupiers and their landlords.[3]

1.8 In the event, the quest for a rigorously theoretical analysis of what this book should cover was becoming increasingly difficult and – with yet further new laws governing anti-social conduct on the horizon[4] – the decision has been taken not to continue to try to achieve it, with the risk that what seems to have proven over time to be a useful tool for tenants' advisers and representatives will lose its edge as it seeks to be all things to all people. Instead, a new title[5] will address broader anti-social conduct while this title will, as it were, revert to its traditional roots, although a new appendix A briefly mentions a number of statutory provisions not covered in the body of the text which advisers might also be able to pray in aid in cases of harassment and eviction.

1.9 The aim of this book remains to provide lawyers and other advisers with a practical guide to the law, so that the relevant legal issues may be more easily understood. In addition, particularly with assistance from non-lawyers in mind, it offers an outline of relevant court procedures and seeks to demonstrate how the legal system can be made to operate for the benefit of the occupier.

1.10 The book is divided into two parts:

a) civil proceedings; and
b) criminal proceedings.

Part I – Civil proceedings

1.11 Victims of harassment or unlawful eviction may be able to take civil proceedings, which are discussed in Part I. A civil court can award compensation for losses suffered, including any distress and discomfort caused. It can also grant injunctions requiring a person to act (or not to act) in a particular way. Accordingly, it can prohibit further

---

2 Only 38 prosecutions were brought in 2011.

3 See *Cowan v Chief Constable of Avon and Somerset* [2001] EWCA Civ 1699, in which the police failed to prevent an unlawful eviction taking place. The Court of Appeal held that the police do not owe occupiers a duty of care to prevent unlawful eviction.

4 *Putting victims first, More effective responses to anti-social behaviour*, Home Office, May 2012. See appendix A paras A55–A60, below.

5 A Dymond, *Anti-social behaviour: law and practice*, LAG, forthcoming.

acts of harassment or require an unlawfully evicted occupier to be re-admitted to his or her home.

1.12   Chapter 2 considers the various grounds under which civil proceedings may be started ('causes of action'). Certain causes of action are potentially available whoever is guilty of the conduct complained of, for example, nuisance, assault, breach of the PHA 1997, so that it is unnecessary to prove involvement by the landlord. Other causes of action are only relevant where the perpetrator of the harassment is – and can be shown to be – the occupier's landlord.[6]

1.13   The Housing Act (HA) 1988 provides a statutory tort of unlawful eviction of a residential occupier[7] but this should rarely be the only cause of action relied on in an unlawful eviction case. First, it cannot be used to obtain an injunction to re-admit the dispossessed occupier to his or her home. Another cause of action must be relied on to obtain an injunction. Second, if the occupier is re-admitted damages are unavailable. Third, it does not provide compensation for certain losses, for example, damage to the occupier's possessions. Advisers need to be aware of the full range of causes of action in chapter 2 to ensure that all their client's rights are protected.

1.14   Chapter 3 examines the available remedies: damages and injunctions. It includes a comprehensive digest of cases illustrating awards of damages for distress and discomfort.

1.15   Chapter 4 deals with county court procedure. A number of documents must be prepared and filed with the court before a case can be issued. These documents and how to use them are described and exemplified. Particular emphasis is placed on what is required to obtain an emergency order to enable a victim of unlawful eviction to be re-admitted to his or her home.

Part II – Criminal proceedings

1.16   In the course of an unlawful eviction, or a campaign of harassment, criminal offences may be committed: assault, criminal damage or obstructing a police officer. These are beyond the scope of this book. Rather, Part II focuses on the offences which are specific to cases of harassment and unlawful eviction.

---

6   'Landlord' is used to include 'licensor' throughout this book, unless a distinction is drawn.

7   HA 1988 s27.

1.17   Unlawful eviction was first made a criminal offence by the PEA 1964. Harassment was added as a criminal offence by the Rent Act 1965.[8] Both offences are now contained in the PEA 1977 and are described in chapter 5.

1.18   Chapter 6 considers the PHA 1997, which introduced the offence of harassment to combat a wide range of anti-social behaviour. Most activities which cause distress or anxiety to residential occupiers are criminal offences under this Act. A landlord – or anyone else – who has unlawfully evicted or harassed an occupier may equally be liable to prosecution under PHA 1997.

1.19   Chapter 7 considers violent entry to premises under the CLA 1977, an offence likewise directed more broadly than at landlords, but which a landlord evicting a tenant may commit.

1.20   Chapter 8 describes how criminal proceedings are instituted. In general, the purpose of criminal proceedings is to punish the wrongdoer, but the criminal courts also have powers to award compensation to victims. A criminal court cannot order a landlord to reinstate an occupier, although under PHA 1997 it is able to make a restraining order, equivalent to an injunction, to prevent the harassment within its scope.

Appendices

1.21   As noted above,[9] a new appendix A mentions other remedies which may be available to victims of harassment and unlawful eviction, including powers aimed at broader anti-social behaviour and other kinds of conduct, eg noise.

1.22   Not all occupiers have the same rights against their landlords. In every housing case, whether or not it involves harassment or unlawful eviction, the first step must be to identify the status of the occupier, ie, what sort of occupation rights and security of tenure they enjoy. This affects a wide range of rights and is a complex subject which

8   The offence was created in response to the Report of the Committee on Housing in Greater London (1965) (Cmnd 2605), more familiarly known as the 'Milner Holland Report', which revealed a shocking variety of abuses to which landlords were subjecting their tenants in order to obtain vacant possession of rent-restricted properties. The report came shortly after Perec Rachman had achieved notoriety in West London for the treatment of his tenants, giving rise to the term 'Rachmanism' to describe harassment and similar behaviour by landlords.

9   Para 1.8.

cannot be properly examined in this book.[10] A brief guide to the classification of occupation is, however, to be found in appendix B.

The relevant legislation

1.23   Throughout the book, frequent reference is made to statutory provisions. The four main statutes referred to are:
- the Protection from Eviction Act 1977;
- the Protection from Harassment Act 1997;
- the Housing Act 1988; and
- the Criminal Law Act 1977.

The relevant provisions are reproduced in appendix C.

Issues for advisers

1.24   Finally, it may be helpful to consider some of the issues that face those advising the victims of unlawful eviction or harassment, apart from the legal aspects of a case.

1.25   As a general point, advisers should always be sensitive to the fears of the victim and take primary account of his or her wishes, having advised of the possible courses of legal action.

1.26   In unlawful eviction cases, it is usually advisable to involve the local authority's tenancy relations officer at an early stage.[11] An inexperienced landlord may genuinely not realise the law and misunderstandings are often resolved swiftly by communication from the tenancy relations officer. Furthermore, if the tenancy relations officer becomes involved prior to the eviction itself, the fact that the landlord was warned about his or her conduct but chose to ignore the law may increase the tenant's compensation.[12] Finally, public funding may not be available to the occupier if he or she has not first sought to involve the tenancy relations officer.[13]

1.27   Any delay in an unlawful eviction case is likely to hinder a satisfactory outcome. It is essential to take action at an early stage if the

---

10   It is covered at length in chapter 2 of Arden, Partington, Hunter and Dymond, *Housing law* (looseleaf edition, Sweet & Maxwell).

11   The involvement of a tenancy relations officer and a solicitor in the same case are not mutually exclusive and should generally be regarded as complementary.

12   Exemplary damages may be awarded in unlawful eviction cases where the landlord has cynically disregarded the occupier's rights, see chapter 3.

13   Where the situation is urgent, however, failure to contact the tenancy relations officer should not preclude public funding.

occupier wishes to obtain an injunction re-admitting him or her to the property.

1.28   Whether civil or criminal proceedings are to be taken, the court can only make its decision based on evidence. The final hearing may be several months after the incident. Advisers should take a detailed statement of what happened at the earliest opportunity while events are still fresh in the victim's mind. In cases of continuing harassment, it is advisable for the victim to keep a diary of events which can later be referred to in court.

1.29   The victim of an eviction is often left without access to clothes, papers, money and items which (such as a rent book) may be essential for use in court proceedings. Although the police are often reluctant to assist at the scene of an unlawful eviction, they may be more willing to ensure that there is no violence when an occupier returns to the premises to try to retrieve possessions.

1.30   Advisers should be prepared to explain to the police what an occupier's rights are. It will be rare for even a senior officer to understand housing law. If there is a risk of violence and the police are reluctant to attend, the adviser should tell the officer that there may be a breach of the peace and remind him or her that the police have a duty[14] to prevent it.

1.31   Civil proceedings have a number of advantages over the institution of a criminal prosecution. For example:

- it is possible to get public funding;
- the victim only has to prove his or her case on the balance of probabilities;
- the court can award substantial damages to reflect the victim's suffering; and
- an interim injunction can be granted very quickly.

1.32   It is, however, generally not advisable for victims to start criminal proceedings themselves by way of private prosecution. In particular:

- public funding is not available to prosecute;
- the victim must prove the case beyond reasonable doubt;
- if the landlord is found guilty, any penalty is likely to be low; and
- although the court can award compensation, such an award is unlikely to compensate the victim for all his or her losses.

14 The primary duty of a police officer is the preservation of the Queen's peace: *Glasbrook Bros Ltd v Glamorgan CC* [1925] AC 270, HL at 277. If an officer reasonably apprehends that the action of any person may result in a breach of the peace, it is his or her duty to prevent that action: *Duncan v Jones* [1936] 1 KB 218, DC.

PART I

Civil proceedings

CHAPTER 2

Grounds for civil proceedings

continued

Introduction

2.1 This chapter concerns the actions which can be brought in the civil courts and the conditions that must be established in order to bring any of them to court.

Jurisdiction of the civil courts

2.2 Most civil cases are heard in the county court and *must* be started in the county court unless the value of the claim is more than £25,000[1] or £50,000 if the claim includes damages for personal injury.[2] With regard to other remedies, the general rule is that a county court has power to make any order which can be made by the High Court.[3] Accordingly, it may grant injunctions restraining the defendant from committing further acts of harassment or nuisance, or requiring a landlord[4] to re-admit an occupier[5] to his or her home. A claimant who incorrectly brings a claim in the High Court is likely to be penalised in costs.[6] A claimant wishing to rely on one or more of the causes of action discussed in this chapter should therefore bring county court proceedings.

Tracks

2.3 All defended claims must be allocated to one of three tracks. Claims are generally allocated to a track once the defendant has filed a defence. The three tracks are:

a) small claims track;
b) fast track; or
c) multi-track.

---

1 Civil Procedure Rules (CPR) Part 7 PD 7A 2.1.
2 CPR Part 7 PD 7A 2.2. Paragraph 9 of the High Court and County Courts Jurisdiction Order 1991 SI No 724 describes how the value of the claim is to be determined.
3 County Courts Act (CCA) 1984 s38 (as substituted by the Courts and Legal Services Act 1990). Note that the section does provide for the powers of county courts to be limited by regulation. By the County Courts Remedies Regulations 1991 SI No 1222, certain orders may not be made by county courts, but they are orders which are not generally relevant in illegal eviction and harassment cases and are therefore not considered here.
4 'Landlord' is used to include 'licensor' throughout this book, unless a distinction is drawn.
5 For instance, tenant or licensee.
6 Senior Courts Act (SCA) 1981 s51 (as amended).

Small claims track

2.4   The small claims track is designed to provide a relatively straightforward method of dispute resolution. The claim is heard by a district judge who may grant an injunction and/or damages.

2.5   Although the parties are entitled to be legally represented at the hearing, they are generally not entitled to recover their legal costs if they win, other than the costs attributable to issue of the claim.[7] If the proceedings include a claim for an injunction, some legal costs may be recovered.[8] Public funding from the Legal Services Commission is not available for small track claims.

2.6   For most claimants, it is therefore highly desirable to be able to argue that the claim should not be allocated to the small claims track, both to recover costs and to qualify for public funding. Fortunately, a claim by a tenant of residential premises against his or her landlord for a remedy in respect of harassment or unlawful eviction cannot be allocated to the small claims track.[9]

2.7   Although the Civil Procedure Rules (CPR) only refer to 'tenants', it is arguable that the word is not being used here in its technical sense and that the rule should apply to any other occupier of residential premises who is entitled to remain in the premises until the owner obtains a possession order against him or her.[10] It is hard to see how any other interpretation would make sense, for there are many tenants[11] who have fewer rights than some licensees.[12]

2.8   Where the perpetrator of the harassment has no – or no provable – connection with the claimant's landlord, it is more difficult to argue that a claim should be allocated to a higher track. The claimant will need to show that it is likely that damages will exceed more than £5,000[13] unless the claim includes damages for personal injury, in which case the threshold is only £1,000.[14]

---

7   The fixed costs are set out in CPR 45.2.

8   CPR 27.14(2)(b); currently the maximum amount allowed is £260: CPR Part 27 PD 7.3.

9   CPR 26.7(4).

10   Eg a licensee, or any other person entitled to rely on PEA 1977 s3, see below paras 2.109–2.115.

11   Eg assured shortholds; tenants with resident landlords.

12   Eg secure licensees, or someone with an irrevocable licence for life. See, generally, appendix B.

13   CPR 26.6(1)(a)(i).

14   CPR 26.6(1)(a)(ii).

Fast track

2.9 The fast track is appropriate where the claim is for less than £25,000,[15] the case is not likely to last more than one day and only one expert witness per party will be called and expert evidence is in no more than two expert fields.[16]

Multi-track

2.10 If the fast track is not appropriate, the claim is likely to be allocated to the multi-track.

Causes of action

Generally

2.11 To sue in the civil courts, it is necessary to show that a complaint falls within one of the categories that the law recognises as a ground for giving a remedy, known as a 'cause of action'. The facts in harassment and unlawful eviction claims can vary widely so that a number of causes of action may arise in relation to the events complained of. This chapter considers numerous causes of action, which should cover most situations that advisers may encounter. It is important for the adviser to identify all the relevant causes of action which may arise so that the claimant can obtain the remedies required.

2.12 The causes of action discussed in this book fall into two broad categories: breach of contract and tort. Additionally, in certain circumstances a claimant may also have a right of action arising under the Human Rights Act (HRA) 1998. Many of the causes of action are only relevant if the perpetrator of the harassment is the claimant's landlord or his or her agent. Claims for breach of contract can only arise where there is an agreement between the parties. This, therefore, will not apply to conduct which is not by or on behalf of a landlord. Likewise, some claims in tort do not assist a victim of harassment unless the perpetrator is the landlord or the landlord's agent.

---

15 For proceedings issued on or after 6 April 2009; for proceedings issued before that, not more than £15,000: CPR 26.6(4).

16 CPR 26.6(5).

2.13   Accordingly, the discussion of the causes of action is divided into three sections:
   1) Breach of contract:
      a) breach of covenant for quiet enjoyment;
      b) breach of implied obligation not to derogate from grant;
      c) breach of other contractual terms.
   2) Torts of general application:
      a) nuisance;
      b) breach of Protection from Harassment Act (PHA) 1997 s3;
      c) trespass to land;
      d) assault and battery (trespass to the person);
      e) trespass to goods;
      f) deceit;
      g) verbal threats;
      h) intimidation;
      i) breach of HRA 1998.
   3) Torts specific to unlawful eviction:
      a) breach of Housing Act (HA) 1988 s27;
      b) breach of Protection from Eviction Act (PEA) 1977 s3.

Breach of contract

2.14   Where there is an agreement between two persons, ie, a landlord and an occupier, and one party breaks that agreement or one of its terms, then there will a breach of contract for which it will usually be possible to sue. Breach of contract will, accordingly, not arise where the perpetrator is not acting for or on behalf of the landlord.

2.15   The general rule is that a claim for breach of contract can only arise between the parties to the agreement, ie, the occupier and the landlord. There are, however, exceptions to this rule. In some circumstances, a tenancy may be transferred, so that someone else becomes the tenant. Such persons can sue on the terms of the tenancy even though they were not parties to the original agreement. Examples are assignees to whom a tenancy is transferred by an agreement or persons who succeed to a tenancy on the tenant's death.

2.16   In addition, persons who are not parties to the contract can now seek to rely on the Contracts (Rights of Third Parties) Act (C(RTP)A) 1999. The C(RTP)A 1999 can only apply to agreements made on or after 11 May 2000. It will not apply to agreements made on or after that date if the parties did not intend the contract to be enforced by third parties.[17] Many modern tenancy agreements therefore now include a clause excluding the application of C(RTP)A 1999.

2.17   A person who is not a party to a contract can enforce its terms if either:

a) the contract expressly provides that a third party may enforce the term; or

b) the term purports to confer a benefit on him or her.[18]

2.18   The third party does not have to be identified by name in the contract. It is sufficient if he or she can be identified as 'a member of a class or as answering to a particular description'.[19] For example, if the tenancy agreement provides that the landlord should allow 'the tenant and his family' quiet enjoyment of the premises, a member of the tenant's family could seek to enforce that contractual term.

2.19   In many cases, however, members of an occupier's family or household will not be able to rely on the C(RTP)A 1999.

2.20   Usually, the appropriate person to be sued for breach of contract is the landlord, as the party to the contract. If, however, the landlord has acted through agents and the landlord's identity is unknown, the agents themselves can be sued by the occupier. If, ultimately, the landlord was responsible for his or her agents' actions, it well may be the case that the agents will add the landlord as a party to proceedings in any event.

Tort

2.21   Where there is no contractual arrangement between the parties, one person can sue another only if it can be established that a recognised tort (or civil wrong) has been committed. The same act may be both a crime and a tort but this is not invariably the case. Tort will usually be the basis for claiming in relation to conduct which is not by or on behalf of the landlord. A person may, however, sue a contractual party, such as a landlord, in tort as well as or instead of for breach of contract.

2.22   Whether or not a person may sue for a particular tort depends on the nature of the tort itself. Some torts, for example, nuisance and trespass to land, require the claimant to be in possession of the land affected by the conduct complained of. In the case of other torts,

---

17 C(RTP)A 1999 s1(2).
18 C(RTP)A 1999 s1(1).
19 C(RTP)A 1999 s1(3).

anyone who is the victim of the tort may be able to sue, for example, trespass to the person.

2.23   Usually, the perpetrator of the tort is the appropriate person to sue. Where a person uses agents to commit the tort, however, both the principal and the agent may be sued. For example, if a landlord uses agents to evict a tenant, both landlord and agents may be sued for trespass to land.

Damage

2.24   Generally, it is not sufficient to show that a breach of contract or a tort has been committed. Claimants must also show that they have suffered or are likely to suffer some harm or damage. (An exception to the rule that damage must be shown is trespass, whether to land, person or goods.) Damage, however, includes not only financial loss or physical harm but also shock, distress or inconvenience.

2.25   It is not necessary to wait for damage to occur. If it is anticipated that damage is likely to occur (or recur) then an injunction may be obtained from the court to pre-empt it. An injunction is a discretionary remedy and will not be granted for trivial matters nor where payment of damages (monetary compensation) is adequate. Acts of harassment or unlawful eviction, however, are so serious that the courts commonly grant injunctions.[20] Remedies are discussed in more detail in chapter 3.

Breach of contract

2.26   To claim for breach of contract, there must (normally) be a contract in existence. The exceptions are statutory tenancies under the Rent Act (RA) 1977 and Rent (Agriculture) Act (R(A)A) 1976, neither of which is a true tenancy (or contract) but a 'status of irremovability',[21] but each of which is subject – so far as consistent with the right of occupation – to the terms of the previous contractual tenancy,[22] which means that such statutory tenants can sue on them as if the tenancy was still in existence.

---

20 In *Handley v Halsall* August 1978 *LAG Bulletin* 189, CA, Lord Justice Waller was extremely critical of a county court judge who had failed to exercise his discretion to issue an injunction in an unlawful eviction case.

21 See appendix B, para B.22 below.

22 RA 1977 s3; R(A)A 1976 s10 and Sch 5 para 2.

2.27   Modern security,[23] however, operates by preventing the landlord determining the tenancy otherwise than by obtaining a court order, but that does not prevent the tenant bringing it to an end; where such a tenancy has been determined by the tenant, it will accordingly not be possible for the tenant to rely on breach of contract in order to prevent eviction or harassment, although some of the causes of action in tort will still be available and public sector tenants[24] will normally be able to rely on PEA 1977 s3.[25]

2.28   Furthermore, a landlord can still end some tenancies without a court order.[26] Or, in the case of a fixed-term tenancy which is not followed by an automatic periodic tenancy, the tenancy may simply expire by reason of time.[27]

2.29   It follows that the starting point will commonly need to be to establish whether or not there is a contract in existence at all, which will turn on whether or not it has been determined.

Termination by landlord

2.30   If a landlord – or licensor – is entitled (and wishes) to terminate the tenancy without obtaining a court order, he or she must first do so. A fixed-term tenancy will – as noted – expire by reason of time. To determine a periodic tenancy or licence, notice to quit must[28] be given to the occupier.[29] Unless the tenancy or licence is what is known as an excluded tenancy or licence,[30] then where the premises are let (or licensed) 'as a dwelling',[31] PEA 1977 s5 requires that the notice to quit must:

---

23 Secure tenancies by HA 1985 s82, assured tenancies by HA 1988 s5, introductory tenancies by HA 1996 s127, demoted tenancies by HA 1996 s143D, flexible tenancies by HA 1985 s107A: see appendix B.

24 Secure, introductory, demoted, flexible tenancies: see appendix B.

25 See below, paras 2.109–2.112.

26 Eg tenancies from resident landlords, tenancies excluded from security under HA 1985 because they are provided to homeless persons under HA 1996 Part 7: see appendix B.

27 See appendix B.

28 Theoretically, even a periodic tenancy can be forfeited, but this is so rare that it is not considered here.

29 In the case of certain tenancies (eg, assured, assured shorthold and secure tenancies), the tenancy cannot be determined by notice to quit and a notice complying with the relevant statutory provisions must (generally) be served before possession proceedings are commenced.

30 PEA 1977 s5(1B); see below, paras 2.118–2.126.

31 See below, paras 2.113–2.115.

a) be in writing and contain such information as may be prescribed;[32] and

b) be given not less than four weeks before the date on which it is to take effect.

2.31   In addition, the notice to quit must satisfy certain common law requirements:

a) the period of the notice required must be equivalent to at least one period of the tenancy;[33] and

b) the notice must expire on a day which is either the first or the last of a period of the tenancy.[34]

2.32   A landlord is not, however, required to serve a notice to quit if the tenancy is a tenancy at will[35] or if the tenancy has already determined, eg, if a fixed-term tenancy has ended and it has not been followed by a periodic tenancy, if the tenancy has been surrendered or if the tenant has served a notice to quit on the landlord.

2.33   The landlord must serve the notice to quit on the occupier. The general rule is that the notice must be served personally on the tenant. Many tenancy agreements include a clause allowing service of notices either by post or by leaving them at the property. In the absence of such a clause, however, the landlord must prove that the notice came to the occupier's attention.[36]

2.34   In the case of an excluded licence,[37] notice to quit does not have to be given in writing. Unless the agreement specifies a longer notice period, the landlord merely has to give reasonable notice.[38] What constitutes reasonable notice depends on all the circumstances of the

---

32   The current information applying to both tenancies and licences is contained in the Notices to Quit etc (Prescribed Information) Regulations 1988 SI No 2201.

33   Ie the four weeks' notice required by PEA 1977 s5 is the minimum notice period, which applies if the tenancy is weekly or fortnightly. If the tenancy is monthly, a month's notice is required. If the tenancy is quarterly, a quarter's notice is required.

34   If the tenancy commenced on a Monday, the notice must expire on a Sunday or a Monday. Sometimes the landlord may not know the period of the tenancy. Most notices to quit include a saving provision to avoid this, eg: 'I give you notice to quit [the address] by [the date] or at the expiration of the period of your tenancy which shall expire next after the expiration of 4 weeks from the service on you of this notice.'

35   *Crane v Morris* [1965] 1 WLR 1104, CA.

36   *Wandsworth LBC v Attwell* (1995) 27 HLR 536, CA.

37   PEA 1977 s5(1B); see below, paras 2.118–2.126.

38   *Minister of Health v Bellotti* [1944] KB 298, CA.

case. The period of the licence is relevant as is the length of time the occupier has been in occupation.

Termination by occupier

2.35 A tenant may determine a periodic tenancy by serving a notice to quit on the landlord. In the case of a joint tenancy, the service of a notice to quit by only one of the joint tenants will determine the joint tenancy.[39] As with a notice to quit served by a landlord, it must conform to certain formal requirements. The notice must be for a full period of the tenancy and must expire on the first or last day of a period of the tenancy,[40] and – again, unless an excluded tenancy[41] – it must be in writing and must be of at least 28 days' duration.[42] So far as concerns a licence, if excluded the notice need only be for a reasonable period and conform to any explicit requirements in the licence agreement;[43] if not excluded, then it must be in writing and be for at least 28 days.[44]

2.36 The landlord may, however, agree to waive any requirements.[45] Accordingly, the landlord may argue that the tenant gave notice orally, or that the parties had agreed a shorter period of notice than would otherwise be required. If the tenancy is a joint tenancy, however, all the tenants must be party to the agreement to waive the formal requirements.[46]

2.37 A tenant may also surrender a tenancy. An evicting landlord will often argue that the tenant has done so, and that when he or she took back possession, eg, changed the locks, he or she did so in the belief that the tenant had surrendered and abandoned the premises. Surrender, as a means of determining a fixed-term or periodic tenancy, occurs when the landlord and the tenant have explicitly agreed to bring the tenancy to an end, either by the execution of a deed or by operation of law if the tenant performs an act which is clearly inconsistent with the continuation of the tenancy and which leads the landlord to accept that the tenancy has been brought to an end.

---

39 *Hammersmith LBC v Monk* [1992] 1 AC 478, (1992) 24 HLR 206, HL.
40 See above, paras 2.30–2.34.
41 See below, paras 2.118–2.126.
42 PEA 1977 s5(1), (1A), (1B).
43 Eg written notice, minimum period.
44 PEA 1977 s5(1), (1A), (1B).
45 *Elsden v Pick* [1980] 1 WLR 898, CA; *King v Jackson* (1997) 30 HLR 541, CA.
46 *Hounslow LBC v Pilling* (1993) 26 HLR 305, CA; see *Wandsworth LBC v Osei-Bonsu* [1999] 1 WLR 1011, (1999) 31 HLR 515, CA, for a claim for unlawful eviction brought by one joint tenant where the notice to quit was invalid.

2.38   A common example of where surrender is claimed is when the tenant returns the keys to the property to the landlord. It will not be a surrender unless the purpose of handing back the keys is to end the tenancy. If the keys are handed back for another reason, for example, to allow access for repairs, there is no surrender. The act relied on by the landlord must show an unequivocal intention on the part of the tenant to end the tenancy. A mere indication by the tenant that he or she intends to move and is looking for other accommodation is not sufficient.[47] A tenant's departure does not necessarily show an unequivocal intention to end the tenancy,[48] especially if the tenant has not returned the keys and has left a partner in occupation of the property;[49] nonetheless, the tenant does not have to give up vacant possession for there to be a surrender if he or she has done all he or she can to indicate that the tenancy has come to an end, eg, by returning the keys.[50] If, however, the tenant's absence is prolonged, possessions have been removed and there are substantial rent arrears, an intention to end the tenancy may be inferred.[51]

2.39   The intention of the tenant is judged objectively on the circumstances as they appeared to the landlord; a tenant's subjective intention to return is irrelevant.[52] The circumstances as they appear to the landlord must, however, be unambiguous, so that where a landlord saw a note in the common parts addressed to 'those who have written graffiti on my flat' stating that he had left, there had been no evidence of a clear intention to give up possession.[53]

2.40   The landlord's act of acceptance must also be unequivocal. Where a tenant has left the property and indicated that he or she will not return, the tenancy will nonetheless continue unless and until the landlord takes a positive step to show that he or she has accepted that the tenancy has ended. Mere inaction (eg, a failure to re-take possession or collect rent) does not amount to such unequivocal conduct.[54] Examples of a landlord's unequivocal acts include re-letting

---

47   *Love v Herrity* (1990) 23 HLR 217, CA.
48   *Preston BC v Fairclough* (1982) 8 HLR 70, CA; although if the tenant has left permanently, his or her security of tenure will usually have been lost.
49   *Ealing Family Housing Association v McKenzie* [2003] EWCA Civ 1602, [2004] HLR 21.
50   *Sanctuary Housing Association v Campbell* [1999] 1 WLR 1279, (2000) 32 HLR 100, CA.
51   *R v Croydon LBC ex p Toth* (1986) 18 HLR 493, CA.
52   *R v Croydon LBC ex p Toth* (1986) 18 HLR 493, CA.
53   *Zionmoor v Islington LBC* (1997) 30 HLR 822, CA.
54   *Belcourt Estates Ltd v Adesina* [2005] EWCA Civ 208, [2005] 2 EGLR 33.

the property, changing the locks, closing the rent account,[55] moving his or her family or furniture into the property[56] or notifying the tenant that he or she deems the tenancy to have ended.

Contractual causes of action

2.41 Three contractual causes of action are considered:

a) breach of covenant for quiet enjoyment;
b) breach of implied obligation not to derogate from grant; and
c) breach of other contractual terms.

Covenant for quiet enjoyment

2.42 An agreement or promise by a landlord to allow his or her tenant 'quiet enjoyment' of the premises for as long as the tenancy lasts is part of every tenancy agreement.[57] It may be expressly stated in the tenancy agreement, if not, it is in any event implied into the agreement by law.

2.43 Many tenancy agreements express the right to quiet enjoyment to be conditional on the tenant performing his or her obligations under the agreement, for example, payment of the rent. Such a clause is of no effect, so that even if the tenant is in rent arrears the tenant is still entitled to quiet enjoyment.[58]

2.44 The covenant for quiet enjoyment is a covenant that the landlord will not interfere with the tenant's lawful possession of the premises. For there to be a breach of covenant, there must be a substantial interference with the tenant's ability to use the property in any ordinary, lawful way. The most obvious example of a breach of the covenant is where the landlord evicts the tenant by changing the locks. There does not, however, have to be dispossession or physical interference with the premises themselves. Interference with the tenant's comfort or the comfort of his or her family is sufficient.[59] Accordingly,

---

55 *Ealing Family Housing Association v McKenzie* [2003] EWCA Civ 1602, [2004] HLR 21.
56 *Artworld Financial Corporation v Safaryan & Others* [2009] EWCA Civ 303, [2009] L&TR 20.
57 Woodfall *Landlord and tenant* (looseleaf edition, Sweet & Maxwell), para 11.267.
58 Woodfall *Landlord and tenant* (looseleaf edition, Sweet & Maxwell), para 11.280.
59 *Southwark LBC v Tanner* (also known as *Southwark LBC v Mills*) [2001] 1 AC 1, (2001) 32 HLR 148, HL, approving *Kenny v Preen* [1963] 1 QB 499, CA. See also *Southwark LBC v Long* [2002] EWCA Civ 403, [2002] HLR 56.

acts of harassment which fall short of eviction may also breach the covenant.

2.45　In *Kenny v Preen*,[60] letters from the landlord threatening eviction, coupled with calls at the tenant's room, knocking on her door and shouting threats at her, were held to amount to a course of conduct which interfered with the tenant's right of quiet enjoyment. Cutting off the gas and electricity supplies has also been held to be capable of being a breach of the covenant,[61] as can be regular excessive noise by the landlord.[62]

2.46　The covenant has also been held to have been breached both where the landlord failed to comply with repairing obligations,[63] and where a landlord, while complying with his repairing obligations, failed to take all reasonable steps to minimise the disturbance caused during the works.[64]

2.47　The obligation is nonetheless limited. It is not an implied warranty as to the condition or fitness of the premises. It cannot be used to force the landlord to carry out improvements to the premises. In *Southwark LBC v Tanner*,[65] local authority tenants complained that the sound insulation between their flats was wholly inadequate with the result that they could hear everything their neighbours said or did. The tenants found this intrusive, inconvenient and often embarrassing. The House of Lords, however, held that there was no breach of the covenant for quiet enjoyment because the landlord had not caused the noise: the landlord was not obliged to remedy defects that pre-dated the grant of the tenancy; when the tenants took possession of their flats, they were deemed to have known that the walls were thin.

Obligation not to derogate from grant

2.48　It is an implied term of any tenancy agreement that a landlord must 'not derogate from' his or her 'grant'. A person who agrees to confer a benefit on another must not act so as to deprive him or her of that benefit. This obligation is primarily concerned with the situation where a landlord lets part of his or her land and retains the other

---

60　[1963] 1 QB 499, CA.
61　*McCall v Abelesz* [1976] QB 585, CA.
62　*Southwark LBC v Tanner* [2001] 1 AC 1, (2001) 32 HLR 148 HL.
63　*Gordon v Selico* (1986) 18 HLR 219, CA, *Mira v Aylmer Square Investments* (1989) 21 HLR 284, QBD.
64　*Goldmile Properties Ltd v Lechouritis* [2003] EWCA Civ 49, [2003] 2 P&CR 1.
65　[2001] 1 AC 1, (2001) 32 HLR 148, HL.

part for him or herself, for example, the common parts. The landlord must not do anything on the retained property so as to make the land which has been let unfit, or materially less fit for the particular purpose for which the letting was made.

2.49　　It is difficult to show that property is unfit. In one case, the top floor of a house was let and the landlord used the rest of the house as a hotel. It was held that, although the landlord's activities interfered with the tenant's amenities, the property was not rendered unfit, so that there was no derogation from grant.[66]

2.50　　The covenant obliges landlords not to take away any 'easements' that were granted (expressly or by implication) when the tenancy was created. Easements include rights of way, the right to use a parking place, or the right to use adjacent premises, often for storage purposes. The cause of action is therefore often applicable where the landlord has prevented the tenant gaining access to premises.

2.51　　Although limited in scope, if the landlord has retained part of the premises, acts of harassment or unlawful eviction could well amount to breaches of the implied obligation not to derogate from grant. This cause of action may therefore be of special relevance to tenants of resident landlords.

Breach of other contractual terms

2.52　　Wherever an agreement exists for the occupation of premises and the terms of the agreement are broken, there is a breach of contract for which the courts can give a remedy. There may be other terms agreed between the parties which are relevant to the case. For example, as a term of a tenancy, the tenant may have been required to provide a deposit. An unlawfully evicted tenant is entitled to its return.

2.53　　Terms are usually expressly agreed between the parties and may be set out in a written agreement. Certain terms are also implied into agreements by law as being necessary to give effect to the parties' intentions.[67]

2.54　　For example, in *McCall v Abelesz*,[68] cutting off gas and electricity was described as a breach of the implied term that the landlord would supply gas and electricity to the premises as long as the tenancy lasted.

66　*Kelly v Battershall* [1949] 2 All ER 830, CA.

67　*Liverpool City Council v Irwin* [1977] 2 AC 239, HL. The courts are only prepared to imply terms into a tenancy agreement in limited circumstances, eg, where something is so obvious that it does not have to be expressed in the agreement, or if it is necessary to do so in order to render the contract effective.

68　[1976] QB 585, CA.

A right to use furniture supplied in relation to, or a facility associated with, the tenancy, even though not actually spelled out at the outset of an arrangement, might be implied in all the circumstances.

2.55   It can be more difficult to establish a breach of contract where a right has been granted after the beginning of the arrangement and then taken away at a later date, unless the occupier gave something in exchange for the new facility (for example, paying more money or giving up some existing right), in which case it can be argued that there was a new contract or at least a new term in the original contract on which to sue.

2.56   As discussed above, a licensee does not have the benefit of a covenant for quiet enjoyment but it may be argued that a similar right is implied into the contractual licence where the licensee cannot otherwise be expected to use the premises for the purposes for which the right of occupation was granted. Thus, a covenant to similar effect as the covenant of quiet enjoyment has been implied into a licence agreement which gave a student the right to occupy a room in a hall of residence.[69]

Torts of general application

2.57   This section considers the following torts:

a) nuisance;
b) breach of PHA 1997 s3;
c) trespass to land;
d) assault and battery (trespass to the person);
e) trespass to goods;
f) deceit;
g) verbal threats;
h) intimidation; and
i) breach of HRA 1998.

Nuisance

2.58   A private nuisance is an activity or state of affairs existing on land which unduly interferes with the use or enjoyment of neighbouring land[70] or some right over or in connection with it. The nuisance must

---

69 *Smith v Nottinghamshire CC* (1981) *Times* 7 November, [1981] CLY 1520; 133 NLJ 13, CA.
70 *Arden and Partington's housing law* (2nd edn, Sweet & Maxwell) para 15-105.

generally arise from something emanating from the defendant's land.[71] It is not necessary for the claimant to prove that the defendant caused the nuisance; a land owner is liable in nuisance if he or she fails to take reasonable steps to abate it after he or she becomes, or should have become, aware of it.[72] The wronged person must be able to demonstrate that he or she has suffered loss arising from the nuisance, eg, physical damage to the land or injury to health.

2.59   Common examples include:

- excessive noise;
- bad odours;
- dust;
- smoke;
- vibrations resulting in damage to a neighbouring property;
- blocked drains resulting in an overflow of water; and
- leaks or overflowing baths or basins causing water penetration into the premises below.

2.60   In the context of residential premises, the nuisance most commonly complained of is noise, for example:

- loud music;
- parties;
- shouting and screaming; and
- noise from building works.

2.61   The tort of nuisance also affords a cause of action for interference with easements, for example, rights of way.[73] In the context of residential premises, such complaints often arise from parking disputes where a person blocks a right of way or prevents the use of an allocated parking space.

2.62   Apart from interference with easements, the essential basis for an action based on nuisance is unreasonable conduct. Some intrusion, eg, by noise or smell, is inevitable. The law proceeds on the basis that there must be some give and take. The task of the court is to strike a balance between the right of the defendant to use his or her property for his or her own lawful enjoyment and the right of the claimant to the undisturbed enjoyment of his or her property. The question for the court is whether the act complained of is one which would

---

71 *Hunter v Canary Wharf Ltd* [1997] AC 655, HL.
72 *Sedleigh-Denfield v O'Callaghan* [1940] AC 880, HL.
73 See above, para 2.50.

be considered a nuisance according to the standards of the average person (rather than one of undue sensitivity).[74]

2.63   Whether a state of affairs amounts to a nuisance can only be determined in light of all the circumstances, for example, the locality of the premises. Playing loud music occasionally for a short time in the early evening may be reasonable but if the music is played for a long time, or played in the early hours of the morning, or if the pattern of behaviour is repeated every day, then there may be a nuisance.

2.64   Acts of harassment (ie, by or on behalf of a landlord) may be a nuisance if they infringe on the claimant's enjoyment of property. In *Khorasandjian v Bush*,[75] harassing telephone calls made to someone's home were held to be actions capable of amounting to a nuisance because they interfered with enjoyment of the property.[76]

2.65   In a number of picketing cases, it was held that it is a nuisance to stand outside and watch a person's house with the intention of getting that person to do or refrain from doing something within his or her rights.[77] The principle in these picketing cases can be extended to anyone who deliberately hangs around a person's home in order to intimidate him or her. These cases were decided before the PHA 1997 and such acts of harassment are now more readily actionable under sections 3 and 3A of that Act.

2.66   In order to sue in nuisance, the claimant must have a sufficient right in land.[78] An owner of property or a tenant clearly has a sufficient interest because he or she has a proprietary interest. It is not, however, necessary to have a proprietary interest and possession is sufficient. Accordingly, all occupiers with possession can also sue in nuisance including for this purpose a licensee with exclusive occupation[79] or even a trespasser in adverse possession.[80]

---

74 *Robinson v Kilvert* (1889) 41 ChD 88.
75 [1993] QB 727, (1993) 25 HLR 392, CA.
76 The decision has subsequently been disapproved, but only as to who had the right to sue for nuisance: see below, para 2.67.
77 *Hubbard v Pitt* [1976] QB 142, CA.
78 *Hunter v Canary Wharf Ltd* [1997] AC 684, (1997) 30 HLR 409, HL.
79 *Hunter v Canary Wharf Ltd* [1997] AC 684, (1997) 30 HLR 409, HL.
80 *Hunter v Canary Wharf Ltd* [1997] AC 684, (1997) 30 HLR 409, HL; in the context of residential premises, a squatter is in adverse possession if he or she lives in the property as his or her home and has unequivocally shown his or her intention to exclude the world (including the true owner) from the property, eg by changing the locks to the premises: *Lambeth LBC v Blackburn LBC* (2002) 33 HLR 74, CA.

2.67   The licensee of a person with sufficient interest cannot, however, sue in nuisance. Accordingly, members of a tenant's family or household have no remedy in nuisance,[81] although in limited circumstances they may have cause of action arising from a breach of HRA 1998. In *Khorasandjian v Bush*,[82] the daughter of the owner-occupier of premises was held to be capable of suing in nuisance for persistent, harassing telephone calls but, on this aspect, the case was subsequently overruled.[83] Instead, she could now make a claim for harassment under PHA 1997 ss3 and 3A.

2.68   Whoever causes the nuisance can be sued, including landlords and their agents if they caused the nuisance. A landlord can, however, only be liable for a nuisance committed by his or her tenant if he or she has let the property to the tenant for the purpose of doing an act likely to cause a nuisance, or if he or she authorises the nuisance.[84] A landlord will nonetheless be liable for nuisance committed by his or her tenant if the acts of nuisance are committed on land in the landlord's possession, eg the communal stairway of a flat, if the landlord has become aware of the nuisance and has refused to take reasonable steps to prevent it recurring or continuing.[85]

2.69   Owners of land can, however, be liable for the actions of their licensees or trespassers. In *Lippiatt v South Gloucestershire Council*,[86] the authority was liable in nuisance for the actions of its licensees because it refused to take steps to remove them though they were using the land as a base from which to trespass on the claimant's land and cause a nuisance.

2.70   In *Baxter v Camden*,[87] a local authority tenant complained that the sound insulation between flats was wholly inadequate with the result that she could hear everything her neighbours said or did. The claim failed. The ordinary use of residential premises is not capable of amounting to a nuisance. The neighbours' use of the land could not amount to a nuisance because it was reasonable. As the neighbours were not committing a nuisance, nor could the landlord be held liable for authorising them to commit one. Nor may a tenant

---

81 *Hunter v Canary Wharf Ltd* [1997] AC 684, (1997) 30 HLR 409, HL approving *Malone v Laskey* [1907] 3 KB 141, CA.

82 [1993] QB 727, (1997) 25 HLR 392, CA.

83 *Hunter v Canary Wharf Ltd* [1997] AC 684, (1997) 30 HLR 409, HL.

84 *Smith v Scott* [1973] Ch 314, ChD; *Mowan v Wandsworth LBC* (2001) 33 HLR 616, [2001] LGR 110, CA.

85 *Octavia Hill Housing Trust v Brumby* [2010] EWHC 1793 (QB).

86 [2000] QB 51, CA.

87 Heard together with *Southwark v Tanner* [2001] 1 AC 1, (2001) 32 HLR 148, HL.

sue his or her landlord where the cause of the nuisance is a defect in the construction of the property which existed before the start of the tenancy and which does not amount to a breach of a repairing covenant.[88] A landlord, however, remains liable to parties other than the tenant if the nuisance arose prior to the letting and continues during the tenancy, if he or she knew, or ought to have known, of it.[89]

Breach of the Protection from Harassment Act 1997

2.71   The PHA 1997 was primarily introduced to combat the activities of stalkers but its provisions apply to all campaigns of harassment, including those by landlords. Harassment in contravention of PHA 1997 is an offence but PHA 1997 ss3 and 3A also provide a civil claim for actual or apprehended harassment, allowing the victim to seek an injunction and damages. (For a discussion of the elements of the offence, which also founds any civil claim, see chapter 6.) It is expressly provided that damages may be awarded for any anxiety caused by the harassment as well as for any financial loss.[90]

2.72   Actions under PHA 1997 ss3 and 3A inevitably overlap with other causes of action considered in this chapter, for example, breach of quiet enjoyment and nuisance. It may be of particular use, however, where the victim is not a tenant, as the right is not limited to persons with an interest in land, so that any victim of harassment can sue. Similarly, anyone can be sued for harassment, including landlords and their agents. It is also a more attractive cause of action than the tort of nuisance as a tenant may recover damages for all of his or her losses that were actually caused by the campaign of harassment rather than only those which were reasonably foreseeable (see chapter 3 on damages).[91]

Trespass to land

2.73   Any unlawful entry onto land, or unlawful placing of something on the land, constitutes the tort of trespass. In harassment cases, common complaints are the deposit of refuse in the complainant's garden or through the letter-box. All these acts constitute trespass to

---

88   *Jackson v JH Watson Property Investment Ltd* [2008] EWHC 14 (Ch), [2008] Env LR 30.

89   *Brew Bros Ltd v Snax* [1970] 1 QB 612, CA.

90   PHA 1997 s3(2); although damages are not limited to these two types of loss.

91   *Jones v Ruth* [2011] EWCA Civ 804, [2012] 1 All ER 490.

land. Driving a nail into the wall of the land of another has been held to be a trespass,[92] which could apply to a landlord who has nailed up a door or blocked up a lock.

2.74 An unlawful eviction will amount to a trespass to land if the landlord has re-taken possession of the property, which will include preventing the tenant from returning. In unlawful eviction cases, it is important to plead trespass alongside breach of quiet enjoyment as otherwise the evicted tenant will not be able to recover general damages for the anxiety, shock, discomfort or inconvenience of the eviction (see chapter 3).[93]

2.75 A trespass is committed as soon as the person enters on the land without permission, or fails to leave the land when requested to do so. A landlord might be invited in, perhaps to discuss something or to collect the rent, but then become so abusive that the tenant asks him or her to leave. As soon as the landlord has had an opportunity to leave but has failed to do so, the landlord becomes a trespasser. Likewise, even if the landlord originally had a specific right to enter the tenant's premises, he or she will subsequently become a trespasser[94] if the right of entry is used to do something that the right does not cover, or if he or she remains on the premises after the right has come to an end. Thus, a landlord who purports to enter in order to consider or carry out repairs, but who uses the opportunity to abuse or harass the tenant, would be trespassing.

2.76 Unlike most causes of action in tort, it is not necessary to show any harm in order to sue for damages for trespass. The fact that there has been a trespass is sufficient to give rise to a claim for damages (although obviously if there is no or little damage then the amount of compensation awarded may be small).

2.77 As in the case of nuisance, anyone with sufficient possession of the land can sue for trespass to land.[95] Accordingly, owners, tenants, licensees with exclusive occupation and even trespassers in adverse possession[96] may have a cause of action in trespass to land. Notably, it is the essence of tenancy that the tenant has the right of exclusive possession, ie the right to exclude everyone, which right extends

---

92 *Lawrence v Obee* (1815) 1 Stark 22.
93 *Branchett v Beaney* (1992) 24 HLR 348, CA.
94 *Hillen v ICI (Alkali) Ltd* [1936] AC 65, HL.
95 See above, paras 2.66–2.67.
96 Until the adverse possessor has acquired title to the property, however, he or she cannot exclude the true owner from the premises and the owner cannot be sued for trespass to land. If the owner enters, however, he or she must not use violence: see chapter 7.

(subject to any specific rights to enter, for example, to inspect – see above, para 2.75) to excluding the landlord from the premises.

2.78   Many licensees are not tenants because the owner of the property has the contractual right to enter the tenant's property to provide particular services, for example, room-cleaning or providing a change of linen. Clearly, the owner and his or her employees are not trespassing if they are only providing those services but if they carry out acts which are not within the contract, a trespass is committed. Such a contractual licensee also has an action against anyone who does not have a right to enter the premises.

Assault and battery: trespass to the person

2.79   The use of violence, or threats of violence, against a person are the torts of assault and battery. A battery is any intentional application of direct physical force on another person without lawful excuse. An assault is any act which puts another person in immediate and reasonable fear of a battery.[97] There must be some threatening act; threatening words alone are not usually enough,[98] although the victim may still have a cause of action under PHA 1997.

2.80   Assault and battery commonly go together but they are also actionable separately. Assault and battery are part of the law of trespass to the person. It is therefore not necessary to prove actual damage or harm in order to sustain an action. Where the claimant is seriously injured, he or she may claim general damages for pain, suffering and loss of amenity as well as special damages, for such losses as time off work.

Trespass to goods and conversion

2.81   A trespass to goods is a direct interference with another person's belongings. It frequently co-exists with conversion, in which a person entitled to the possession of goods is permanently deprived of that possession and the goods are converted to the use of someone else.

2.82   In harassment cases, the perpetrator often commits acts of vandalism to the complainant's property, for example, scratching the paintwork of a car. In unlawful eviction cases, the landlord commonly interferes with the occupier's belongings, either destroying

---

97 Although technically a separate tort, battery is often referred to as assault.
98 *Meade's Case* (1823) 1 Lew CC 184.

them or packing them up and placing them outside the premises. All these actions are instances of trespass to goods. If these belongings are retained this may amount to conversion. In either case, an action may be brought under the Torts (Interference with Goods) Act 1977 for the return of the goods, or their value, or damages.

2.83   If the tenant is in arrears of rent at the time of the eviction, the landlord often refuses to return the tenant's possessions until the rent is paid. A landlord of a residential occupier is not usually entitled to do this.[99] The landlord must sue for the arrears in court proceedings.

Deceit or fraudulent misrepresentation

2.84   Deceit consists of a representation of fact, whether made by words or by conduct, by a person who knows that it is false. Silence alone is not sufficient. The representation must be made with the intention that it be acted upon. It must have been acted upon and resulted in damage.

2.85   In *Mafo v Adams*[100] a landlord who had tricked his tenant into leaving his accommodation by falsely informing him that alternative accommodation was available at another address, was held liable for deceit.

Verbal threats

2.86   If verbal threats are sufficient to make their victim ill, they amount to an actionable tort.[101] The illness does not have to be physical but may be a recognisable psychiatric illness, although emotional distress falling short of illness is not sufficient. Someone merely suffering distress will, however, have a cause of action under PHA 1997 s3 or s3A.

---

99 Although there is a common law remedy known as distress, under which a landlord may enter premises, seize the tenant's possessions, sell them and recoup rent arrears from the proceeds, in the context of residential tenancies its application is extremely limited. Distress cannot be levied against an assured tenant (HA 1988 s19(1)) or a statutory tenant (RA 1977 s147(1)). Distress is also not available against a licensee.

100 [1970] 1 QB 548, CA.

101 *Khorasandjian v Bush* [1993] QB 727, (1993) 25 HLR 392, CA, citing *Wilkinson v Downton* [1897] 2 QB 57 and *Janvier v Sweeney* [1919] 2 KB 316.

Intimidation

2.87   Intimidation consists of any threat, by words or actions, which is intended to make someone do something that causes damage either to the intimidated person, or to some other person.[102] The threat must be intentional and must be a threat to do something unlawful (ie, a crime, breach of contract or a tort).[103] It must be a coercive threat, not mere persuasion, and it must be coupled with a demand. Thus, a landlord who threatens to harass or unlawfully evict a tenant for doing something that the tenant is entitled to do is intimidating the tenant. Similarly, intimidation occurs where the landlord threatens to evict someone else, eg, another occupier in a house in multiple occupation, if that person does not assist in harassing or evicting the occupier. The threat does not have to be carried out but it must be effective to make the person intimidated comply with the landlord's wishes.

2.88   The person entitled to sue for intimidation is the person who suffers the damage rather than the person intimidated, although that is often one and the same person.[104]

Breach of the Human Rights Act 1998

2.89   By article 8 of the European Convention on Human Rights, enacted in the Schedule to the HRA 1998:

(1) Everyone has the right to respect for his private and family life, his home and his correspondence.
(2) There shall be no interference by a public authority with the exercise of this right except such as is in accordance with the law and is necessary in a democratic society in the interests of national security, public safety or the economic well-being of the country, for the prevention of disorder or crime, for the protection of health or morals, or for the protection of the rights and freedoms of others.

2.90   Damages or an injunction may be awarded for a breach of article 8 in circumstances where it is just and appropriate to do so.[105]

---

102 *Allen v Flood* [1898] AC 1, HL.
103 *Rookes v Barnard* [1964] AC 1129, HL.
104 *Morgan v Fry* [1968] 2 QB 710, CA; *JT Stratford & Son Ltd v Lindley* [1965] AC 307, HL.
105 HRA 1998 s8(1) provides that a court may grant any remedy within its powers.

2.91   Only a public authority is bound by the Act.[106] Private bodies which exercise functions of a public nature – known as hybrid bodies[107] – are deemed to be public authorities unless the act in question is private.[108] Private companies who provide services that are regulated by statute, which would otherwise have been provided by a public authority, are likely to be public authorities, eg, a water company,[109] or a distributor – but not a supplier – of electricity.[110] Critically, a registered social landlord[111] has been held to qualify as a public authority in relation to its provision and management of social housing.[112] Plainly, a local housing authority is.

2.92   It follows that an unlawful act of harassment or eviction by such a body will additionally comprise a breach of article 8 and will be actionable as such. Indeed, while it is regrettably not difficult to think of other acts which would so obviously qualify as a breach of human rights, unlawful eviction and harassment plainly do. Anyone who is a victim of the breach may sue if his or her article 8 rights have been interfered with.[113] This may therefore benefit someone without a sufficient interest to claim for nuisance or trespass such as the family member of a tenant or a licensee without exclusive possession. The same loss cannot, however, give rise to two sets of damages so that, eg, a child is unlikely to be entitled to a separate award of damages under article 8 if his or her parents have been awarded damages in nuisance owing to an interference with the amenity of the family home.[114] Damages for nuisance amounting to breach of article 8 are likely to be less than those awarded for nuisance.[115]

106 HRA 1998 s6.
107 HRA 1998 s6(3)(b). Eg, termination of social housing in *R (Weaver) v London & Quadrant Housing Trust* [2009] EWCA Civ 587, [2010] 1 WLR 363, [2009] HLR 40.
108 HRA 1998 s6(3)(b), (5).
109 *Marcic v Thames Water Utilities Ltd* [2003] UKHL 66, [2004] 2 AC 42.
110 *James v London Electricity Plc* [2004] EWHC 3226 (QB).
111 Now, private registered provider of social housing, see Housing and Regeneration Act 2008 s80.
112 *R (Weaver) v London & Quadrant Housing Trust* [2009] EWCA Civ 587, [2010] 1 WLR 363, [2009] HLR 40.
113 *Dobson v Thames Water Utilities Ltd* [2009] EWCA Civ 28, [2010] HLR 9.
114 *Dobson v Thames Water Utilities Ltd* [2009] EWCA Civ 28, [2010] HLR 9.
115 *Dobson and others v Thames Water Utilities Ltd (No2)* [2011] EWHC 3253 (TCC).

Torts specific to unlawful eviction

2.93   In this section, the following torts are considered:

a) breach of HA 1988 s27; and
b) breach of PEA 1977 ss3 and 3A.

Breach of Housing Act 1988 s27

2.94   HA 1988 s27(1) and (2) creates a tort where a landlord[116] or any person acting on his or her behalf:

a) unlawfully deprives the residential occupier of any premises of his or her occupation of the whole or part of the premises; or

b) attempts unlawfully to deprive the residential occupier of any premises of his or her occupation of the whole or part of the premises; or

c) knowing or having cause to believe that the conduct is either likely to cause the residential occupier of any premises to give up his or her occupation of the premises or any part of them, or else to refrain from exercising any right or pursuing any remedy in respect of the premises or any part of them, does acts calculated to interfere with the peace or comfort of the residential occupier or members of his or her household or persistently withdraws or withholds services reasonably required for occupation of the premises, and, as a result, the residential occupier gives up his or her occupation of the premises as a residence.

2.95   This tort is modelled on the criminal offences of unlawful eviction and harassment created by PEA 1977 s1, which are discussed in detail in chapter 5. Reference should be made to chapter 5 for the definition of 'residential occupier' and the other elements which the claimant must prove.[117]

2.96   As the majority of tenants in the private sector are now assured shorthold tenants, the relevance of this tort has diminished somewhat as landlords can recover possession more easily than when most such tenants were fully protected. It still remains relevant, however, if the occupier is a secure, (fully) assured or Rent Act protected

---

116 Defined in HA 1988 s27(9) as the person who, but for the occupier's right to occupy, would be entitled to occupation of the premises and any superior landlord under whom that person derives title. This includes a purchaser let into possession prior to completion, who only occupies as a licensee: *Jones v Miah* (1992) 24 HLR 578, CA. It will not include a prospective purchaser who has no right of occupation: *Francis v Brown* (1997) 30 HLR 143, CA.

117 See below, paras 5.3–5.65.

or statutory tenant and may still be relevant exceptionally in cases where the occupier is an assured shorthold tenant and the landlord is unwilling to take court proceedings. Owing to the significant level of damages that may be awarded, it should always be considered.

Reinstatement

2.97   There is no liability under HA 1988 s27 if the occupier is reinstated (whether by agreement with the landlord or because of a court order) before proceedings are finally disposed of.[118] Proceedings are not finally disposed of until any appeal to the Court of Appeal has been determined or abandoned.[119]

2.98   Reinstatement was considered in *Tagro v Cafane*,[120] in which the landlord handed back the keys to the occupier, only for her to find that the lock did not work and that her room had been totally wrecked: unsurprisingly, this was held not to amount to reinstatement. In *Murray v Aslam*,[121] the tenant returned home to find the locks changed and her belongings in the street. She and her young child had to stand in the rain. Her possessions were damaged and her son fell ill. The police were called and they persuaded the landlord to allow her back in. Although the landlord did not harass her again, two weeks later she decided to leave. The landlord initially failed to defend the tenant's claim and judgment was entered against him. The Court of Appeal was only required to decide whether the landlord should be given the opportunity to defend the proceedings and so did not rule on whether there had been a reinstatement: Sir Thomas Bingham MR, however, thought that there was doubt about whether the tenant was entitled to rely on HA 1988 s27 because she had in fact been allowed back into the property; Sir Ralph Gibson, on the other hand, thought that a temporary return to the property might not be sufficient to amount to reinstatement, which is consistent with approach taken in *Mehta v Royal Bank of Scotland*.[122]

2.99   If reinstatement is offered before proceedings are commenced, the occupier is not obliged to accept the offer, although an unreasonable refusal to do so may reduce the level of damages.[123]

---

118 HA 1988 s27(6).
119 HA 1988 s27(6).
120 (1991) 23 HLR 250, CA.
121 (1994) 27 HLR 284, CA.
122 (1999) 32 HLR 45, QBD.
123 HA 1988 s27(7)(b); see *Tagro v Cafane* (1991) 23 HLR 250, CA, and chapter 3, paras 3.89–3.91.

No right to re-admission

2.100   HA 1988 s27 cannot be used to obtain an injunction re-admitting the occupier to the premises. Accordingly, where the occupier wishes to be re-admitted, one of the other causes of action referred to in this chapter needs to be relied on. If the occupier is then re-admitted, there will no longer be any cause of action under HA 1988 s27.

2.101   The most appropriate course for an occupier in this situation is to commence proceedings for breach of the covenant for quiet enjoyment and trespass to land as well as breach of HA 1988 s27. If the occupier is re-admitted, the claim under HA 1988 s27 can be withdrawn. Conversely, if the claim for the injunction fails (for example, because the property has been relet and the court is unwilling to dispossess the new occupier), the occupier can pursue the claim under HA 1988 s27.

Who can be sued?

2.102   Under HA 1988 s27(3), only the landlord is liable for damages. Where the acts in question have been committed by the landlord's agent, the landlord will be liable for them.[124]

2.103   The measure of damages in an action under HA 1988 s27 is defined in HA 1988 s28 and is discussed below in chapter 3.[125]

Defences

2.104   It is a defence to any action that the defendant believed and had reasonable cause to believe that the residential occupier had ceased to reside in the premises at the relevant time.

2.105   Where liability arises by virtue of the doing of acts, or the withdrawal or withholding of services, it is a defence that the defendant had reasonable grounds for the acts complained of.[126] These defences are also available under PEA 1977 and are discussed in chapter 5.[127]

---

124 *Sampson v Wilson* [1996] Ch 39, (1996) 29 HLR 18, CA.
125 See below, paras 3.69–3.95.
126 HA 1988 s27(8); see *Wandsworth LBC v Osei-Bonsu* [1999] 1 WLR 1011, (1999) 31 HLR 515, CA.
127 See below, paras 5.81–5.83 on reasonable belief that the claimant was not a residential occupier and paras 5.108–5.110 on reasonable grounds for withdrawing or withholding services.

Breach of Protection from Eviction Act 1977 s3

2.106 PEA 1977 s3(1) prevents an owner of residential property from recovering possession against certain occupiers of residential premises, after the end of the tenancy or licence, without a court order.[128]

2.107 The ambit of PEA 1977 s3 is limited because it does not apply to either 'statutorily protected tenancies'[129] or 'excluded' tenancies and licences.[130]

2.108 Breach of PEA 1977 s3 gives rise to the tort of breach of statutory duty.[131] The cause of action can be used for acts of harassment which fall short of actual eviction. A claim may be made for damages and/or an injunction.

Who can sue?

2.109 Tenants of any premises which have been 'let as a dwelling' may sue for breach of PEA 1977 s3 (unless the tenancy is an 'excluded tenancy', see below, paras 2.118–2.126).

2.110 By PEA 1977 s3(2B), the provisions of the section are extended to any 'premises occupied as a dwelling under a licence' (unless the licence is an excluded licence, see below, paras 2.118–2.126).

2.111 The requirement for a court order also extends to 'any person lawfully residing in the premises or part of them' at the moment when the tenancy or licence came to an end. Members of the occupier's family and household may therefore rely on PEA 1977 s3.[132]

2.112 There are two issues to consider:

a) whether the premises in question are let as 'a dwelling' (whether under a tenancy or a licence); and, if so

b) whether the provisions are disapplied because the letting is a statutorily protected tenancy or an excluded tenancy or licence.

---

128 The fact that the possession order is subsequently set aside does not render the eviction unlawful: *Brent LBC v Botu* (2001) 33 HLR 14, CA.

129 As defined in PEA 1977 s8, see below, paras 2.116–2.117.

130 As defined in PEA 1977 s3A, see below, paras 2.118–2.126.

131 *Warder v Cooper* [1970] 1 All ER 1112, CA.

132 The protection also applies to anyone lawfully living with a deceased statutory tenant under the Rent Act 1977 or Rent (Agriculture) Act 1976 when the owner's right to recover arises on the death of the statutory tenant: PEA 1977 s3(3).

Let as a dwelling

2.113   In *Uratemp Ventures Ltd v Collins*,[133] the House of Lords considered the meaning of the word 'dwelling' in the context of RA 1977.[134] The word was said not to be a term of art. It is the occupier's residence or home; the place where he or she lives and to which he or she returns and which forms the centre of his or her existence. A dwelling may consist of no more than one room. There is no requirement that any particular facilities be included. Accordingly, the absence of cooking facilities does not prevent premises from being the occupier's home; the occupier may live on take-away food or eat out in cafeterias. It is not even necessary for there to be a bed, although the room probably has to be big enough to sleep in.

2.114   In light of this decision, it might have been thought that earlier decisions on the application of PEA 1977 s3 would today be decided differently. In *Mohamed v Manek and Kensington & Chelsea RLBC*,[135] the Court of Appeal had held that interim accommodation provided by a local authority in a hotel while it made enquiries into the occupier's application for accommodation as a homeless person, was not 'occupied as a dwelling under a licence'.[136]

2.115   In *Desnousse v Newham LBC*,[137] however, the Court of Appeal upheld *Mohamed* and ruled that PEA 1977 s3(2B) did not apply even to self-contained accommodation provided to a homeless person under Part 7 of HA 1996 under a licence:[138] the accommodation in such circumstances was, it held, not 'let as a dwelling'.[139] The court left open, however, whether such accommodation provided under a tenancy might not be let as a dwelling. The court also rejected the argument that section 3 needed to be re-interpreted in order to

---

133 [2002] 1 AC 301, (2001) 33 HLR 4, HL.

134 Ie 'let as a separate dwelling' – the same phrase is used in HA 1985 and HA 1988.

135 (1995) 27 HLR 439, CA.

136 This ought also to have been cast into doubt by another subsequent decision of the House of Lords, in which it was held that such interim accommodation is the occupier's place of 'normal residence': *Mohammed v Hammersmith & Fulham LBC* [2002] 1 AC 547, (2002) HLR 7, HL.

137 [2006] EWCA Civ 547, [2006] QB 831, [2006] HLR 38. See also *Brouillet v Landless* (1995) 28 HLR 836, CA.

138 Unless continued on more than a transient basis – but as the occupier had been in the flat in question for six months in *Desnousse*, 'transience' would not seem to import a significant qualification.

139 See also *Rogerson v Wigan MBC* [2005] HLR 10, QBD.

conform with HRA 1998,[140] on the basis that any interference with article 8 was justified.[141]

Statutorily protected tenancies

2.116 PEA 1977 s3 does not apply where the tenancy is a statutorily protected tenancy. The following are statutorily protected tenants:[142]

a) protected tenants under RA 1977;[143]
b) assured tenants, assured shorthold tenants and assured agricultural occupants under HA 1988;
c) tenants of long leases of dwellings to which Landlord and Tenant Act (LTA) 1954 Part I applies;[144]
d) tenants holding over after the expiry of long leases;[145]
e) business tenants of premises to which LTA 1954 Part II applies;
f) protected occupants or statutory tenants as defined in the Rent (Agriculture) Act 1976;
g) tenants of agricultural holdings as defined in the Agricultural Holdings Act (AHA) 1986; and
h) farm business tenants within the meaning of the Agricultural Tenancies Act (ATA) 1995.

2.117 Statutorily protected tenants have their own rights not to be excluded from premises under the statutes which give them their own security of tenure and are therefore able to rely on other remedies to prevent unlawful eviction, for example, breach of the covenant for quiet enjoyment or trespass to land. PEA 1977 s3 is accordingly unnecessary, which is why they are excluded from it.

---

140 See above, para 2.115.
141 In light of subsequent domestic and European Court of Human Rights (ECtHR) law – including in particular *Hounslow LBC v Powell and other cases* [2011] UKSC 8, [2011] 2 AC 186, *Manchester CC v Pinnock* [2010] UKSC 45, [2011] 2 AC 104, *McCann v United Kingdom* (2008) 47 EHRR 913 and *Kay v United Kingdom* [2011] HLR 13 – to the effect that (in substance) an eviction by a public authority must be by court proceedings, in order to allow the proportionality of the eviction to be raised – this seems certain to be challenged and reconsidered.
142 PEA 1977 s8(1).
143 A statutory tenant under Rent Act 1977 is a former protected tenant and therefore a statutorily protected tenant for the purposes of PEA 1977.
144 A long lease is for 21 years or more.
145 On the expiry of a long lease, the tenant is entitled to hold over and, depending on when the tenancy commenced, may be entitled to a statutory tenancy under the Rent Act 1977 or an assured tenancy under HA 1988.

Excluded tenancies and licences

2.118   Section 3 does not apply if the tenancy or licence is 'excluded' and a landlord is therefore entitled to recover possession without a court order.[146] By PEA 1977 s3A, the following categories of tenancies or licences are excluded:

a) sharing with a resident landlord;
b) sharing with a member of a resident landlord's family;
c) temporary expedient to a trespasser;
d) holiday accommodation;
e) other than for money or money's worth;
f) accommodation provided to asylum-seekers or displaced persons; and
g) licence of a public sector hostel.

Sharing with a resident landlord

2.119   For the exclusion to apply, the following conditions must be met:

a) under the terms of the agreement, the occupier shares accommodation[147] with the landlord; and
b) immediately before the occupancy was granted and when it comes to an end, the landlord occupies, as his or her only or principal home, premises which includes the shared accommodation.

Sharing with a member of a resident landlord's family

2.120   For the exclusion to apply, the following conditions must be met:

a) under the terms of the agreement, the occupier shares accommodation[148] with a member of the landlord's family;[149]

---

146 But see *Morgan v Fry* [1968] 2 QB 710, CA and *JT Stratford & Son Ltd v Lindley* [1965] AC 307, HL: although the principal domestic cases have limited the point to eviction by public authorities, the ECtHR cases have not drawn this distinction and it is therefore open to argument that any person who is at risk of losing his or her home is entitled in principle to have the proportionality of the eviction determined by a court.

147 'Sharing' means having the use of the accommodation in common with another person; 'accommodation' is anything other than the common parts (ie, stairs, passageways, etc) or a storage area: PEA 1977 s3A(4) and (5).

148 PEA 1977 s3A(4) and (5).

149 'Family member' is a spouse, civil partner, cohabitant, parent, grandparent, child, grandchild, brother, sister, uncle, aunt, nephew or niece: PEA 1977 s3A(5), adopting the definition of family member in HA 1985 s113, as amended. Furthermore, relationships by marriage are treated as relationships by blood; relationships of half-blood are treated as relationships of whole blood; stepchildren are treated as children; and illegitimate children are treated as legitimate: HA 1985 s113.

b) immediately before the occupancy was granted and when it comes to an end, the member of the landlord's family occupies as his or her only or principal home premises which include the shared accommodation; and

c) immediately before the occupancy was granted and when it comes to an end, the landlord occupies as his or her only or principal home premises in the same building as the shared accommodation (unless the building is a purpose-built block of flats).

Temporary expedient to a trespasser

2.121 A tenancy or licence granted as a temporary expedient to an occupier who had entered the premises or any other premises as a trespasser,[150] for example, a squatter who later receives permission to stay in the premises, eg, for a short time until redevelopment or who is offered such a short-life property elsewhere.

Holiday accommodation

2.122 A tenancy or licence which confers the right to occupy the premises for a holiday only is excluded.[151]

Other than for money or money's worth

2.123 If the occupier is not obliged to pay for the accommodation, nor obliged to provide some other form of consideration for the right to occupy the property, for example, services in lieu of payment, the tenancy or licence is excluded.[152] Examples include family arrangements and weekend guests. A tenancy or licence was not for money's worth where the occupier was only required to pay for utilities, heating, water and food, ie, there was no payment or consideration for occupation of the land.[153] Conversely, an obligation to keep property repaired and insured, and to pay all relevant taxes, has been held to be a right to occupy for money's worth.[154]

Asylum-seekers or displaced persons

2.124 Tenancies or licences granted to asylum-seekers (and/or their dependants) under Immigration and Asylum Act (IAA) 1999 Part 6

---

150 PEA 1977 s3A(6).

151 PEA 1977 s3A(7)(a); if the agreement records that the letting is a holiday let but the reality is that this is not the case, the agreement is a sham and the letting is not excluded: see *R v Rent Officer for Camden LBC ex p Plant* (1980) 7 HLR 15, QBD and *Buchmann v May* (1978) 7 HLR 1, CA.

152 PEA 1977 s3A(7)(b).

153 *West Wiltshire DC v Snelgrove* (1998) 30 HLR 57, QBD.

154 *Polarpark Enterprises Inc v Allason* [2007] EWHC 1088 (Ch), [2008] 1 P&CR 4.

are excluded.[155] IAA 1999 established a system of support for asylum-seekers, provided by the secretary of state through the National Asylum Support Service (now the New Asylum Model). Support may include the provision of accommodation, which may be provided directly, or through arrangements with local authorities or others. Tenancies or licences granted to provide accommodation to displaced persons under the Displaced Persons (Temporary Protection) Regulations 2005 are also excluded.[156]

Licences to occupy a public sector hostel

2.125   A licence, but not a tenancy, will be excluded if it is a licence to occupy a hostel provided by a public sector landlord.[157] A hostel is:

> A building in which is provided, for persons generally or for a class or classes of persons:
> (a) residential accommodation otherwise than in separate and self-contained sets of premises, and
> (b) either board or facilities for the preparation of food adequate to the needs of those persons, or both.[158]

2.126   Accommodation is not separate and self-contained if the terms governing its occupation require the occupier to share facilities with someone with whom he or she has not chosen to share. Whether anyone is actually sharing the accommodation is irrelevant.[159]

---

155 PEA 1977 s3A(7A), added by IAA 1999 Sch 14 para 73 (with effect from 1 April 2000), as amended by Immigration, Asylum and Nationality Act 2006 s43(4).

156 PEA 1977 s3A(7C), added by Displaced Persons (Temporary Protection) Regulations 2005 SI No 1379 Sch 1 para 1 (with effect from 15 June 2005). This applies to any person granted temporary protection as a result of a decision of the Council of the European Union made pursuant to article 5 of the Temporary Protection Directive who are deemed for the purposes of provision of means of subsistence to have leave to enter or remain in the UK exceptionally, outside the Immigration Rules.

157 A local authority, a private registered provider of social housing or a registered social landlord or housing trust, the regulator of social housing, the secretary of state, a combined authority, a development corporation, an economic prosperity board, an urban development corporation, a Mayoral development corporation, a housing action trust, or any other person or body specified by the secretary of state: PEA 1977 s3A(8). To date, the secretary of state has specified the London Hostels Associations Ltd (Protection from Eviction (Excluded Licences) Order 1991 SI No 1943), the Shaftesbury Society (Protection from Eviction (Excluded Licences) (Shaftesbury Society) Order 1999 SI No 1758) and the Royal British Legion Industries Ltd (Protection from Eviction (Excluded Licences) (Royal British Legion Industries Ltd) (England) Order 2003 SI No 2436).

158 PEA 1977 s3A(8), adopting the definition of a hostel in HA 1985 s622.

159 *Rogerson v Wigan MBC* [2005] HLR 10, QBD.

CHAPTER 3

Remedies

Introduction

3.1   This chapter describes the remedies available to the victims of harassment and unlawful eviction:

   a) injunctions to prevent further harassment or to regain possession of the home; and
   b) damages, ie compensation for what they have suffered.

3.2   It describes the basis on which the court will grant an injunction and the different types of damages.

3.3   Finally, summaries of over 40 cases give examples of awards of damages (see below, para 3.100 onwards).

Relationship between injunctions and damages

3.4   The primary objective of a victim of harassment is to stop the perpetrator from continuing the behaviour complained of. A person who has been unlawfully evicted usually wants to be re-admitted to his or her home as soon as possible. The legal means to achieve each of these aims is to obtain an injunction.

3.5   Advisers do, however, need to keep the issue of damages firmly in mind from the outset of the proceedings, even though obtaining an emergency injunction may be of paramount importance.

3.6   There are three primary reasons for this:

   a) the amount of compensation can vary and depends on the particular cause of action chosen;
   b) the amount of compensation sought can affect the availability of public funding from the Legal Services Commission (see below, paras 4.31–4.40); and
   c) the occupier will continue to feel aggrieved if, although the harassment has ceased or re-admission to the property has been obtained, no or minimal compensation has been awarded for his or her distress and inconvenience and any incidental losses, for example, lost or damaged possessions.

Injunctions

3.7   An injunction is an order of the court requiring someone to do or refrain from doing something, for example, to cease acts of harassment or to re-admit an evicted occupier. There is no need to prove damage to get an injunction. For example, if a landlord has warned tenants that they will be thrown out of the premises if they do not leave by a certain date, an application can be made to prevent the landlord's actions.

3.8   An injunction is a discretionary remedy and the court has to be satisfied that damages alone are not an adequate remedy. This requirement is easily satisfied where the loss of a home is at stake, or where there has been a serious campaign of harassment.

Interim and final injunctions

3.9   Injunctions are either final or interim.

3.10   A final injunction is awarded at the end of a trial when the factual disputes between the parties have been resolved. The trial may not take place for some months after the commencement of proceedings and the prospect of a final injunction is of little assistance to the victim of an ongoing campaign of harassment or someone locked out of his or her home who is sleeping rough or staying with friends. In such circumstances, the victim may apply for an interim injunction, which may be granted at the commencement of proceedings, or exceptionally before proceedings have even been issued.[1]

3.11   In deciding whether to grant an interim injunction, the court does not attempt to resolve the dispute between the parties.

3.12   To obtain an interim injunction, the applicant must show that:

a) there is a serious dispute between the parties;

b) damages would not be an adequate remedy for the applicant; and

c) the balance of justice between the parties is in favour of granting the injunction and restoring or maintaining the status quo for the time being.[2]

---

1 Civil Procedure Rules (CPR) 25.2(1)(a).

2 The leading case is *American Cyanamid Co v Ethicon Ltd* [1975] AC 396, in which the House of Lords referred to maintaining the 'balance of convenience' pending the trial. In *Francome v Mirror Group Newspapers* [1984] 1 WLR 892, CA, Sir John Donaldson MR held that it was more appropriate to refer to the 'balance of justice'. In *Nottingham Building Society v Eurodynamics Systems* [1993] FSR 468, ChD, Chadwick J said that this involved considering what course would involve the least risk of injustice if after a trial it transpired that the granting of an interim order had been wrong.

3.13   If on the application for an interim injunction the defendant accepts the applicant's version of events – which is not unknown[3] – there is no serious issue between the parties and no issue of the balance of justice arises. The court should therefore grant the injunction restraining the harassment or re-admitting the occupier and give directions for how the rest of the case should proceed if damages are claimed.[4] Otherwise, the applicant does not have to show that the claim is a strong one to show that there is a serious dispute, merely that the facts asserted disclose that there is a cause of action recognised by the law, ie one of the grounds for proceedings described in chapter 2.

3.14   Most applications for interim injunctions therefore turn on the question of the balance of justice between the parties. In the majority of unlawful eviction and harassment cases, where an applicant is seeking an injunction which prevents his or her landlord from harassing or evicting him or her the balance of justice will be heavily in favour of maintaining the status quo, which means allowing the occupier peacefully to remain in the premises in question, enjoying all the normal facilities. Obtaining such an injunction should therefore present no problem.

3.15   The same is true of a mandatory injunction which requires a landlord to re-admit an evicted occupier to his or her home. While the court should not ordinarily grant an interim mandatory injunction unless it has a high degree of assurance that the applicant will succeed at trial, this does not apply where the refusal to make the order would carry a greater risk of injustice.[5] Thus, the balance is likely to favour the interests of a person who will be homeless against the interests of the landlord, who will in any event be able to continue to charge rent to the occupier pending the outcome of the trial.[6]

3.16   In harassment cases, there can be no injustice to the alleged perpetrator in being prevented from carrying out what are, in any event, unlawful acts.

3.17   The applicant is usually required to give an undertaking to pay damages to the person who is to be subject to the interim injunction,

3   The landlord may not have appreciated that the conduct was unlawful; or he or she may admit it anyway, claiming that he or she was 'provoked' (not uncommonly by reference to rent arrears).

4   *Love v Herrity* (1990) 23 HLR 217, CA.

5   *Nottingham Building Society v Eurodynamics Systems* [1993] FSR 468, Ch D.

6   In *Handley v Halsall* 1978 *LAG Bulletin* 189, CA, Waller LJ was extremely critical of a county court judge who had failed to exercise his discretion to issue an injunction in an unlawful eviction case.

to guard against a decision at trial that there had been no right to the injunction. This could create difficulties for applicants with limited funds but an interim injunction should not be withheld merely because a publicly-funded client cannot give a worthwhile undertaking[7] and in most unlawful eviction cases any undertaking should be no more than to pay the rent owed under the tenancy agreement. Advisers should nevertheless be aware of the need to explain this requirement to applicants before any application is made.

3.18   The most commonly encountered reason preventing the grant of an interim injunction in unlawful eviction cases is that the landlord has already re-let the property, on the basis that he or she cannot comply with an order to re-admit the occupier without unlawfully evicting someone else.

3.19   In *Love v Herrity*,[8] the Court of Appeal considered the appropriate procedure to follow in these circumstances. If the landlord admits the evicted occupier's right to occupy, the court should grant a declaration that the occupier is entitled to possession of the property and allow the parties to apply for further directions. These will depend on whether the evicted occupier wishes to be re-admitted to the property.

3.20   As between the landlord and the new occupier there is a valid agreement. Between the evicted occupier and the new occupier, however, it is the evicted occupier who has the right to possession. In *Love*, the Court of Appeal held that if the evicted occupier wishes to be re-admitted to the property, he or she may apply to the court for the new occupier to be joined as a party to the proceedings and claim possession against him or her.

3.21   The new occupier can have no defence to the evicted occupier's claim for possession. Assuming that the new occupier was unaware of the unlawful eviction, this may appear unjust. The new occupier would, however, be entitled to require the landlord to pay any costs associated with the legal proceedings against him or her and would also be able to claim damages against the landlord, for example, for breach of quiet enjoyment.

3.22   If the evicted occupier does not wish to be re-admitted to the property, he or she will be entitled to claim damages against the landlord, possibly including damages under Housing Act (HA) 1988 ss27 and 28,[9] and should seek directions for the assessment of those damages.

---

7 *Allen v Jambo Holdings Ltd* [1980] 1 WLR 1252, CA.
8 (1990) 23 HLR 217, CA.
9 See above, chapter 2, paras 2.94–2.105; below, paras 3.69–3.95.

Notice of application

3.23   An injunction is usually granted after hearing both sides but may be made 'without notice', ie, without the defendant even being informed of the application.[10]

3.24   The court only allows applications for injunctions without notice where there is a 'good reason'.[11] The written evidence in support of the application must set out those 'good reasons' for applying without notice.[12]

3.25   This requirement will be satisfied where the matter is so urgent that there is no time for notice, for example, where the victim of unlawful eviction is literally and immediately homeless. Another good reason for not giving notice about the application to a defendant is if the application is to prevent something being done, and the defendant is likely to retaliate on finding out about the application, ie, by carrying out the threatened action before the hearing, eg, where an unlawful eviction has been threatened for a particular date, suggesting that the landlord has a specific reason for it.

3.26   If the court grants an injunction without notice, it will usually order a further hearing within the following few days to allow the defendant the opportunity to have it set aside. (The procedure for obtaining injunctions is described in chapter 4.)

Damages

3.27   There are five different types of damages which can arise in harassment and unlawful eviction claims. The most common are *special* and *general* damages. In addition, there are *aggravated* damages and *exemplary* damages (only available in tort). If the facts justify it, a person may claim under all heads of damages in one action. In the case of certain torts which do not require the claimant to establish that loss has occurred,[13] it is also possible to be awarded *nominal* damages. In unlawful eviction cases, damages for breach of HA 1988 s27 may be awarded. These have their own particular basis of calculation under HA 1988 s28 (see below, paras 3.69–3.95).

---

10 CPR 25.3(1); prior to the introduction of the CPR, such injunctions were described as being 'ex parte' and are still commonly referred to as such.

11 CPR 25.3(1).

12 CPR 25.3(3).

13 Eg trespass to land.

3.28   Before addressing each of these different categories of damages, however, it is necessary to understand some of the basic principles on which damages are awarded. The principles are different in respect of claims for breach of contract and claims for torts.

Basic principles

Breach of contract

3.29   When two people enter into a contractual arrangement, they do so in order to put themselves in a better position than they were before it was made. Each wants something from the other; that is the basis of the exchange. In general, therefore, when there is a breach of contract the law will attempt to put the party who has suffered in the position he or she would have been in had the contract been properly fulfilled.[14]

Tort

3.30   An action for tort arises because one person has done to another something which the law considers ought not to have been done. The action is – and the damages are – therefore intended to restore the party who has suffered loss to the position he or she would have been in had the tort complained of not taken place.[15] In addition, however, the claimant in an action in tort may be able to recover other types of damages such as exemplary damages, for example, where the tort was committed deliberately.[16]

Mitigation of loss

3.31   Whether in contract or tort, a person who has suffered damage is under a duty to mitigate the loss if it is possible to do so, ie to reduce it. For example, it is common in unlawful eviction cases for the landlord to pack up the occupier's possessions and leave them outside the property. They may have suffered some damage by the time the occupier arrives home. If the occupier has somewhere to leave them, such as with a neighbour or friend, then he or she should do so in order to mitigate the loss. On the other hand, if the occupier has nowhere to leave them, he or she cannot be expected to stand guard over them or to carry them all around with him or her. In that case, the occupier

14 *Robinson v Harman* (1848) 1 Ex 850.
15 *Livingstone v Raywards Coal Co* (1880) 5 App Cas 25.
16 See below, paras 3.53–3.62.

cannot mitigate the damage and – if the possessions are lost or damaged – he or she will be entitled to full damages. It has been held in the county court that an evicted tenant does not fail to mitigate his or her loss if he or she chooses not to apply for an interim injunction requiring his or her landlord to re-admit him or her to the home.[17]

Causation and remoteness of damage

3.32   A person can only claim for loss that arises directly and naturally from the conduct complained of. For example, a tenant who is forced to take time off work after an unlawful eviction would not be able to claim for loss of earnings if he or she had already booked out to take a holiday that week anyway; the unlawful eviction would not have been the cause of him or her missing work. If the holiday was lost as a result, however, he or she would be likely to be able to recover its cost.

3.33   The line can be difficult to draw. By way of further example, where occupiers have been evicted and as a result have to walk the streets through the night during a thunderstorm, they may become ill. Under the duty to mitigate, they are obliged to seek such shelter as they can afford or find. Assuming that they have taken proper steps to try to mitigate the damage but were unable to do so, the landlord will be liable for illness and time off work that follows. (Loss of earnings will constitute special damage; suffering through illness will qualify as general damages, see below, paras 3.43–3.44.) If the illness was caused, however, not as a natural result of walking the streets but because of a car accident or an assault (by someone unconnected with the landlord and the circumstances of the eviction), the damage suffered will not be recoverable as it was not directly caused by the unlawful eviction.[18]

3.34   A claimant is not, however, necessarily entitled to recover all of his or her loss even if he or she can show that it has been caused directly by the unlawful eviction or harassment. The type of losses that will be recoverable will depend upon the damage that has been caused and the causes of action that are relied on.

3.35   Thus, the losses that a tenant may recover for breach of contract (eg breach of quiet enjoyment or derogation from grant)[19] are limited

---

17 *Garcia v Khan*, March 2005 *Legal Action* 21, Bow County Court.

18 Even this may be too absolute a proposition. If the eviction itself was late at night, and in a particularly dangerous area, might harm to a vulnerable person, eg, a single woman, not be considered the direct consequence in this day and age?

19 See above, paras 2.42–2.51.

to those that the landlord would have realised, when the tenancy was granted, were likely to result from breach of the tenancy agreement.[20] Thus, following an unlawful eviction, a tenant should be able to recover the expense of staying in bed and breakfast accommodation because the landlord ought to have realised that by evicting the tenant, he or she would be likely to incur the expense of staying in alternative accommodation.

3.36   In the case of some torts, a person will be able to claim all of his or her losses that have been caused by the harassment or unlawful eviction; in others, he or she will only be able to claim for losses that were reasonably foreseeable. In the torts of trespass to goods (where the taking of goods has been committed honestly),[21] possibly trespass to land[22] and nuisance,[23] a person will only be able to recover losses arising from damage that was reasonably foreseeable. Thus, where a landlord has unlawfully evicted a tenant, and accordingly trespassed on the tenant's land, the tenant would be able to recover damages for the shock, anxiety and inconvenience caused by the eviction because it would have been obvious that this would be the result of it. The tenant would, however, be unlikely to obtain damages for the loss of a lucrative business contract. In other torts, on the other hand, such as deceit,[24] assault or battery,[25] Protection from Harassment Act (PHA) 1997[26] and trespass to goods[27] (where the tort was committed intentionally),[28] the person would be able to claim damages for the loss of a lucrative business contract if it could be shown that it arose directly and naturally from the unlawful act.

3.37   In *Kuwait Airways Corp v Iraqi Airways Co*,[29] the House of Lords drew a distinction between someone who dishonestly converts another's goods and someone who does do so innocently. Both are liable in damages, but the person acting dishonestly (ie who knows the goods are not his or hers) is liable for all loss that flows directly

20 *Czarnikow v Koufos, The Heron II* [1969] 1 AC 350, HL.

21 *Kuwait Airways Corp v Iraqi Airways Co* [2002] UKHL 19, [2002] 2 AC 883.

22 The editors of *McGregor on damages* (18th edn, Sweet & Maxwell, 2011) at para 34-052, take the view that the principles that apply to trespass to goods are likely to apply equally to a trespass to land.

23 *Cambridge Water Co v Eastern Counties Leather plc* [1994] 2 AC 264, HL.

24 *Clark v Urquhat* [1930] AC 28, HL.

25 *Clerk & Lindsell on torts* (20th edn, Sweet & Maxwell, 2011) para 15-137.

26 *Jones v Ruth* [2011] EWCA Civ 804, [2012] 1 All ER 490.

27 *Kuwait Airways Corp v Iraqi Airways Co* [2002] UKHL 19, [2002] 2 AC 883.

28 [2002] UKHL 19, [2002] 2 AC 883.

29 [2002] UKHL 19, [2002] 2 AC 883.

and naturally from taking another's possessions, while the person who does so innocently (ie is unaware that the goods belong to some-one else) is only liable for the loss that was reasonably foreseeable.[30] It is arguable that this distinction should apply equally to other torts, which may be committed either honestly or otherwise; this is worth considering as, in many cases of unlawful eviction and harassment, the conduct is likely to be dishonest in this sense.

Types of damages

Special damages

3.38   Special damages are designed to compensate for any identifiable and quantified loss. The critical element is that the loss should be quan-tifiable in money terms. For example, the cost of alternative accom-modation or the cost of replacing lost possessions can be quantified. The loss of enjoyment resulting from being deprived of the use of a possession, however, cannot (but may be compensated within gen-eral damages, see below, paras 3.43–3.45).

3.39   There are two potential issues that the occupier must be able to address: the existence of the goods and their value. In unlawful evic-tion cases, the landlord will often argue that the items claimed were not in the premises when the eviction took place and/or that the value placed on them by the claimant is grossly inflated. Evidence from friends or neighbours may assist in establishing what the claimant owned. Proving the value of items can often be difficult, although in *Ayari v Jetha*,[31] the Court of Appeal refused to interfere with the award of £11,500 special damages, some of the value of which was proved with duplicate receipts.

3.40   Note that it is the market value of the item lost, as at the date it was taken, which is recoverable, not its purchase price, so that the damages awarded reflect any decrease since purchase. The cost of buying replacements will be a guide to value, but those figures will be reduced to reflect the actual value of the items or the element of 'betterment' which has crept in, even though the occupier might well not have wished to replace an item, or might have been unable to afford to do so (but this, too, may be compensated for by way of general damages). Conversely, however, if the item has increased in value since purchase, the occupier is still entitled to its true value. For example, if the occupier loses a watch which was a family heirloom,

---

30 [2002] UKHL 19, [2002] 2 AC 883 at [103]–[104].
31 (1991) 24 HLR 639.

the measure of damages will be the cost of buying a replacement. The fact that the occupier may not personally have paid for it is irrelevant.

3.41 Where an item lost was used by the occupier for the purposes of a trade, the loss of business resulting is also claimable[32] as would be the cost of hiring new tools at the market rate. The cost of emergency accommodation may be claimed as a quantifiable item and so also the additional cost of eating in restaurants or cafés over and above the cost of preparing one's own food. Note, however, that only the additional cost can be claimed, regardless of whether the claim is in contract or tort.

3.42 The court will only award reasonable, proper and necessary expenditure: the cost of relatively cheap bed and breakfast accommodation will be recoverable but the cost of staying in an expensive hotel will not. The court will, however, take into account the emergency nature of the situation. If an occupier returns home late at night to find that he or she has been evicted, and it is not possible to contact friends or relatives, it may very well be difficult for him or her to find cheap accommodation and the only option may be to stay somewhere expensive. The court may well allow the full cost of the first night, but if the occupier then makes no effort to find somewhere cheaper for the following nights, it will not allow the full cost of those later nights. As with all these issues, however, the key question is what is reasonable: just as a tenant evicted from cheap accommodation cannot expect to be accommodated while out of occupation in markedly superior property, so also would it not be reasonable to expect a tenant evicted from particularly high quality or costly accommodation, used to a particularly good standard, to go and stay in a run-down bed and breakfast just because it is cheaper.

General damages

3.43 General damages are unquantified damages. They include matters which would be claimed for as special damages were it not that the occupier cannot actually quantify the amount. For example, cutting off the gas may mean that all heating has to be by the more expensive means of electricity. Washing up may have to be done by the expensive process of boiling electric kettles. There would be a clear financial loss which would be substantial over a period of weeks, but

---

32 In *Bodley v Reynolds* (1846) 8 QB 779, a carpenter whose tools were taken obtained the value of the tools and a sum for lost work.

might be impossible to quantify unless the occupier happened to have exact figures for electricity consumption before and during the time the gas was shut off.

3.44   General damages can be claimed for, among other things, harm, discomfort, loss of enjoyment, pain and suffering, shock, physical injury and inconvenience. They are, therefore, particularly apt for cases of harassment and unlawful eviction. As a general rule, however, such damages are only recoverable in tort and not in contract, save where the purpose of the contract is to provide pleasure, relaxation, peace of mind or freedom from molestation.[33] As the purpose of the covenant for quiet enjoyment is not to provide pleasure, general damages for loss of enjoyment, discomfort and physical injury are not recoverable.[34] It is, therefore, important that, depending on the facts of each case, a tort is, if available, pleaded, ie trespass to land and goods, nuisance, deceit or breach of the statutory torts (PEA 1977 and PHA 1997),[35] as the level of damages otherwise available to the claimant will be reduced. From 1 April 2013, the proper level of general damages in, inter alia, nuisance and 'all other torts which cause suffering, inconvenience or distress to individuals' will increase by ten per cent.[36]

3.45   In unlawful eviction claims, general damages may be awarded for the pain and suffering of the unlawful eviction, any harassment leading up to the eviction and for the resulting loss of occupancy. Courts now commonly award a 'daily rate' to compensate the tenant for the time spent staying in accommodation inferior to that from which the tenant was evicted.[37] Where the tenant was fully assured or Rent Act protected an additional award should be sought to reflect the fact that they will not be able to obtain alternative accommodation with the same security of tenure.[38]

3.46   General damages overlap with HA 1988 s28 (see below), which are damages explicitly calculated with reference to the effect of the occupier's interest on the value of the premises. Where such statutory

---

33   *Watts v Morrow* [1991] 1 WLR 1421, (1991) 23 HLR 608, CA.

34   *Branchett v Beaney* (1992) 24 HLR 348, CA.

35   See above, paras 2.71–2.85 and paras 2.106–2.126.

36   *Simmons v Castle* [2012] EWCA Civ 1039; the decision follows the recommendations in *The final report on civil litigation costs* (commonly known as the 'Jackson Review').

37   See for example *Daramy v Streeks*, June 2007 *Legal Action* 37, Lambeth County Court.

38   See for example *Mafo v Adams* [1970] 1 QB 548 and *Grillo v Cant and Bassairi Ltd* March 1998 *Legal Action* 13, Central London CC.

damages are awarded, the occupier will not also be able to recover general damages for loss of occupancy.[39] As, however, assured short-hold tenants will not ordinarily be able to claim substantive damages under HA 1988,[40] general damages are more likely to produce a higher level of compensation for loss of occupancy. General damages should, in any event, always be sought in the alternative, to guard against a failure of the HA 1988 claim.

3.47 Where general damages are claimed for personal injury, the court should assess the quantum of damage with reference to the *Judicial Studies Board: Guidelines for the assessment of general damages in personal injury claims.*[41]

Aggravated damages

3.48 Aggravated damages are awarded to compensate the claimant for injury to his or her feelings of dignity and pride and for aggravation generally.[42] They cannot be awarded for breach of contract.[43] Awards for aggravated damages have been made, however, for the torts of assault, trespass to land and deceit.[44] Where available, therefore, advisers should ensure that the claim includes one of these causes of action.

3.49 Awards are commonly made in cases involving the use or threat of violence, or where the victim has been particularly demeaned, for example, in cases involving sexual or racial abuse. In unlawful eviction cases, aggravated damages are regularly awarded to reflect the suffering of a tenant who finds him or herself locked out on the street with his or her belongings packed up.

3.50 In *Drane v Evangelou*,[45] the tenant returned to his flat to find that entry to the building was barred by one of the landlord's associates. The door to his flat had been bolted on the inside and his belongings, some of which had been damaged, had been put in the back yard. The tenant and his partner were forced to store their belongings in a friend's garage and sleep on their friend's floor until they

---

39 HA 1988 s27(5); see discussion of this section below.
40 See below at para 3.73.
41 10th revised edition, Oxford University Press, 2010.
42 *Ramdath v Daley* (1993) 25 HLR 273, CA.
43 *Branchett v Beaney* (1992) 24 HLR 348, CA.
44 Aggravated damages are not available for all torts, eg, they cannot be awarded for negligence.
45 [1978] 1 WLR 455, CA.

were eventually re-admitted to the flat ten weeks later. The county court judge awarded the tenant £1,000 exemplary damages.

3.51   On appeal, the level of the award was upheld not only on the basis that exemplary damages were appropriate but also on the basis that even if £1,000 for exemplary damages had been high, the amount was justified given that the tenant was in any event entitled to aggravated damages.

3.52   Lawton LJ observed:[46]

> It seems to me that my task here is to look at the facts and to start by asking the question what sort of sum would it have been proper to award for aggravated damages in this case, which undoubtedly was one for aggravated damages. Counsel for the landlord at times seemed to be suggesting that this was a comparatively minor dispute between a landlord and a tenant. I emphatically dissociate myself from that. To deprive a man of a roof over his head is, in my judgment, one of the worst torts which can be committed. It causes stress, worry and anxiety ... I myself would not have regarded the sum awarded ... as excessive for aggravated damages.[47]

Exemplary damages

3.53   Exemplary damages are often confused with aggravated damages.[48] Aggravated damages are, however, compensatory; they reflect the victim's suffering. Exemplary damages are punitive and are awarded to punish the defendant and to deter him or her from similar behaviour in the future. Exemplary damages cannot be awarded for breach of contract.[49] Accordingly, where available, advisers should ensure that a claim in tort is included.

---

46 At 461E–G.

47 Goff LJ agreed that the level of the award could be justified if aggravated damages were taken into account.

48 The confusion between aggravated and exemplary damages is illustrated in a number of cases of unlawful eviction. In *Ramdath v Daley* (1993) 25 HLR 273, the Court of Appeal quashed an award of exemplary damages but was not prepared to substitute an award for aggravated damages as they have different purposes, and the recorder had already included a sum for aggravated damages in the award of general damages. Contrast *Nworkorie v Mason* (1993) 26 HLR 60, CA, in which an inappropriate award of exemplary damages was treated as aggravated damages. In *Francis v Brown* (1997) 30 HLR 143, CA, the trial judge made awards for both aggravated and exemplary damages, but it was clear from his judgment that he had confused the two.

49 *Addis v Gramophone Co Ltd* [1909] AC 488, HL; *Guppys (Bridport) Ltd v Brookling* (1984) 14 HLR 1, CA.

3.54   The leading case of *Rookes v Barnard*[50] sets out the principles on which they may be awarded. They may only be awarded in three circumstances:[51]

a) where they are expressly provided for by statute;
b) where there has been oppressive conduct by servants of the government; or
c) where the defendant's conduct has been calculated to make a profit which may well exceed the compensation available to the claimant.

3.55   It will readily be appreciated that harassment by someone other than the landlord would rarely fall into any of these categories. By contrast, exemplary damages are commonly awarded under the third category in cases of unlawful eviction or harassment by a landlord, on the basis that the landlord was intending to profit from his or her unlawful actions.

3.56   The need to establish the element of calculation on the part of the landlord would at first appear to make it necessary to establish that the landlord has profited financially from the eviction. In some cases, the profit may be self-evident, for example, where the landlord redevelops the flat to sell it on a long lease or the property is re-let at a higher rent. This will obviously be the case where the evicted tenant had a protected tenancy and paid a fair rent and – after the eviction – the landlord is then able to re-let the property at a market rent. The landlord may be forced to provide a copy of any agreement with a new occupier to show that a higher rent is now being obtained.[52]

3.57   In practice, however, it is not necessary to establish concrete financial advantages of this kind, albeit that the evicted tenant must prove that the motive of the landlord's actions was to profit in some way from his or her actions.[53] The category of damages is not confined to money-making in the strict sense but extends to cases in which the defendant is seeking to gain at the claimant's expense some coveted property, which either he or she could not obtain at all or could not obtain at a price greater than he or she wants to pay.[54] Obtaining

---

50 [1964] AC 1129, HL.
51 At 1226–1227.
52 This may be done through the process of disclosure under which the parties are obliged to allow each other the opportunity to see any documents which may be relevant to the issues between the parties: CPR Part 31.
53 *Mafo v Adams* [1970] 1 QB 548, CA.
54 *Cassell & Co Ltd v Broome* [1972] AC 1027, HL.

vacant possession without resorting to the difficulty and expense of possession proceedings falls within this category.[55]

3.58   In *Cassell & Co Ltd v Broome*,[56] Lord Hailsham commented on the application of exemplary damages to harassment and eviction:

> How ... about the late Mr Rachman, who is alleged to have used hired bullies to intimidate statutory tenants by violence or threats of violence into giving up vacant possession of their residences and so placing a valuable asset in the hands of the landlord? My answer must be that if this is not a cynical calculation of profit and cold-blooded disregard of a claimant's rights, I do not know what is.[57]

3.59   The tenant's conduct is irrelevant to whether exemplary damages should be awarded. The court is only concerned with the landlord's conduct.[58]

3.60   Likewise, the fact that the landlord may already have been fined for an offence under the PEA 1977 does not prevent an award being made.[59]

3.61   The correct approach is for the court to assess the general and special damages suffered by the claimant and any aggravated damages before going on to assess the amount of any exemplary damages.[60]

3.62   The level of award is not limited to any actual profit made by the landlord[61] but the amount must be kept within reason.[62] Awards of exemplary damages are usually in the region of £1,000 to £2,500. Relevant factors include the seriousness of the conduct complained of – for example, whether violence was used or threatened – and/or the extent to which the landlord may have disregarded warnings from the police, a tenancy relations officer or the claimant's solicitors. Where the landlord has deliberately disobeyed an order for readmission or has disobeyed other orders of the court relating to the conduct of the proceedings, a larger award is usually made.

---

55 *Drane v Evangelou* [1978] 1 WLR 455, CA.

56 [1972] AC 1027, HL.

57 At 1079.

58 *McMillan v Singh* (1985) 17 HLR 120, CA, in which the fact that the tenant was in arrears was held to be irrelevant.

59 *Ashgar v Ahmed* (1985) 17 HLR 25, CA; compare *Devonshire and Smith v Jenkins* (1978) 28 April, unreported, CA, in which the Court of Appeal decided that no exemplary damages should be awarded because of the size of the fine in that case.

60 *McMillan v Singh* (1985) 17 HLR 120, CA.

61 *McMillan v Singh* (1985) 17 HLR 120, CA.

62 In *Francis v Brown* (1997) 30 HLR 143, the Court of Appeal held that an award of £40,000 was manifestly excessive. In *Mehta v Royal Bank of Scotland* (1999) 32 HLR 45, QBD, an award of £7,500 was made.

Sufficient interest

3.63   Although it is not necessary to show that the defendant has profited in financial terms before an award can be made, it is necessary to show that the defendant had a sufficient interest in the matter to benefit.

3.64   This can be of significance in cases where both the landlord and his or her agent have been involved. In *Ramdath v Daley*,[63] the Court of Appeal upheld the award of exemplary damages against a landlord. The property was managed by the landlord's son, who had been authorised and encouraged to throw the claimant out of the flat. On this basis, it was found that an award of exemplary damages against the landlord was justified. A separate award of exemplary damages against the son was, however, quashed because it was not shown that he had a sufficient interest in the matter himself to benefit.

3.65   Arguably, however, exemplary damages should not have been awarded at all in that case, since, where a claim for exemplary damages is made against two or more defendants, only a single award should be made, reflecting as a matter of law the lowest figure for which any of the defendants could be held liable.[64]

3.66   Advisers need to consider this issue where a claim is proposed against both the landlord and an agent. The agent may not be profiting from the eviction and, as such, may have no sufficient interest to warrant an award of exemplary damages. By suing both landlord and agent, the occupier may therefore fail to obtain exemplary damages at all. It is perfectly proper for the occupier to sue only the landlord so that the right to exemplary damages is not lost.[65]

3.67   On the other hand, the agent may be holding on to the occupier's possessions, or have committed a serious assault on the occupier, so that the occupier's claim against the agent may be substantial. In such a case, the occupier can avoid the possibility of losing the right to exemplary damages against the landlord by commencing separate proceedings against the landlord and the agent and subsequently having the two claims heard together.[66]

---

63 (1993) 25 HLR 273, CA.

64 *Cassell & Co Ltd v Broome* [1972] AC 1027, HL; *Francis v Brown* (1997) 30 HLR 43, CA.

65 Suing only one of the two joint tortfeasors is a course of action specifically envisaged by Lord Hailsham in *Cassell & Co Ltd v Broome* [1972] AC 1027, HL at 1063H.

66 This course of action is also approved by Lord Hailsham in the passage in *Cassell & Co Ltd v Broome* [1972] AC 1027, HL, above para 3.58.

Nominal damages

3.68   Most causes of action require the claimant to show that he or she has suffered some form of loss. As noted in chapter 2, certain causes of action (most notably trespass to land) can be established without the need to prove any actual damage. The function of nominal damages is to recognise that a right has been infringed, even though no actual damage has occurred. Public funding is not available where only nominal damages are sought.

Damages for breach of Housing Act 1988 s27

3.69   Damages under HA 1988 can be sizeable and often the largest element of compensation for unlawful eviction; the benefit where the evicted tenant lacks long-term security of tenure is, however, limited.

Basis of assessment

3.70   The basis of assessment of damages under HA 1988 is the difference in value, as at the date when the residential occupier left the premises, between the value of the landlord's interest[67] with the occupier still enjoying the right to occupy and the value of the landlord's interest without such a right.[68]

3.71   The interest of the landlord to be valued is that of the whole building in which the premises are situated, together with the curtilage[69] of the building.[70] Accordingly, where the landlord owns the whole house but the tenancy is of only a flat in it, it is the difference in the value to the house not the flat which is to be assessed.

3.72   In reaching this valuation certain assumptions must be made:

a) the landlord is selling his or her interest on the open market to a willing buyer;[71]

---

67 It is only the interest of the landlord in default which is to be valued. Although a superior landlord can be in default, where it is an immediate landlord who is in default it is the value of the intermediate landlord's interest which is relevant: *Jones v Miah* (1992) 24 HLR 578, CA.

68 HA 1988 s28(1).

69 For instance, any garden or yard.

70 HA 1988 s28(2).

71 Where the landlord cannot sell, for example, because of a lease which prohibits assignment, the premises will still be treated as having a saleable value, although it will be assumed that the willing buyer would take a lease subject to the covenant: *Tagro v Cafane* (1991) 23 HLR 250, CA.

b) neither the occupier nor any member of his or her family[72] wishes to buy; and

c) it is unlawful to carry out any substantial development of the land in which the landlord's interest subsists or to demolish the whole or any part of any building on that land.

3.73 In determining the measure of damages, the legal status of the occupier is central. The greater the statutory protection from eviction, the greater the damages should be. If the occupier is a fully assured tenant, or a statutory tenant under the Rent Act (RA) 1977, there may be a significant difference in values with and without the tenant. By contrast, the presence of an assured shorthold tenant whose tenancy is at a market rent is unlikely to have any – or any real – effect on the value of the property.[73] Similarly, the eviction of a tenant who has only a few days of the tenancy remaining[74] or whose joint tenancy is precarious because the other joint tenant is likely to serve a notice to quit,[75] is unlikely to lead to any significant difference in value.

3.74 Before changes made by HA 1996, a landlord wishing to grant an assured shorthold tenancy had to comply with formal requirements. From 28 February 1997, these formalities are no longer required, and almost all new tenancies in the private sector are assured shorthold tenancies. This has greatly reduced the number of cases in which damages under HA 1988 s28 are likely to be available or, at any rate, substantial.

3.75 Where the tenancy was created before 28 February 1997, advisers should check whether the formal requirements were complied with, as what may appear from the tenancy agreement to be an assured shorthold tenancy may in law be a full assured tenancy. Even if the tenancy was created after 28 February 1997, there are circumstances

---

72 As defined by HA 1985 s113, see above, para 2.111.

73 See *Melville v Bruton* (1996) 29 HLR 319, CA, in which an award of £15,000 under HA 1988 s28 was quashed and substituted with an award of £500 in general damages. In that case, the valuers had failed to address the tenant's status in their reports.

74 *King v Jackson* (1997) 30 HLR 541, CA, in which the tenant was evicted a few days before the expiry of her notice to quit.

75 *Wandsworth LBC v Osei-Bonsu* [1999] 1 WLR 1011, 31 HLR 515, CA. In this case, the Court of Appeal accepted the authority's argument that a joint tenancy was clearly precarious because the claimant joint tenant's wife was anxious to serve a notice to quit at the relevant time so as to obtain new accommodation from the local authority. The Court of Appeal held that an appropriate award of damages would have been £2,000 (although held that it was bound by a concession made in the court below).

in which the tenancy may nonetheless be a fully assured tenancy, and an occupier should always check.[76]

3.76   Even where the occupier's rights of occupation may be limited, however, advisers should not necessarily rule out the possibility of a claim under HA 1988 ss27 and 28, for, in the particular circumstances, a valuer may still find that there is a significant difference in value, for example, if a particularly high price is available during a window of time too short for the landlord lawfully to evict and effect a sale, so that there has been a substantive increase by virtue of evicting without awaiting expiry of tenancy and/or court proceedings, which between them can be several months.[77] It is, however, the open market value which is in issue, not circumstances peculiar to the landlord, ie the circumstances giving rise to the qualification would have to be of a general order rather than peculiar to the landlord in question.

3.77   As it is the landlord's interest in the whole building which must be valued, not just the part of the building let to the occupier, the valuation must take into account the presence of any other residential occupiers in the building.[78]

3.78   This has the greatest effect in buildings let out as bedsitting-rooms. Where the remainder of the house remains let out at the time of the eviction, the eviction of one occupier may make little if any difference to the value of the property as a whole, because all the landlord can do with the vacancy is to re-let the room. As many unlawful eviction cases concern occupiers of bedsitting-rooms, this is also a substantial restriction on the effective application of HA 1988 ss27 and 28.

76 See below, appendix B.
77 See *Nwokorie v Mason* (1993) 26 HLR 60, CA, in which the Court of Appeal refused to interfere with an award of £4,500 under HA 1988 s28. The judge had preferred the valuation of the occupier's surveyor, even though the landlord's valuer had found that there would be no difference in value. The occupier had a very limited interest as the defendant was a resident landlord. The valuation took into account the 28 days' notice to quit required, and the time it would have taken for a possession action to come before the court. The case was decided before *Melville v Bruton* (1996) 29 HLR 319, CA, but in principle remains correct. Compare, too, the surprisingly high award given to a licensee in *Mehta v Royal Bank of Scotland* (2000) 32 HLR 45, QBD.
78 *Melville v Bruton* (1996) 29 HLR 319, CA.

Expert evidence

3.79 The level of HA 1988 s28 damages turns on expert evidence, although some of the reported cases illustrate how difficult it can be to reach a valuation in such cases.[79]

3.80 In providing the report, the expert's overriding duty is to assist the court; this duty overrides any obligation to the dispossessed occupier.[80] The valuer may have to provide a number of different valuations reflecting different versions of the facts put forward by the parties, for example, where the occupier claims to be an assured tenant but the landlord claims that only an assured shorthold tenancy was granted, or the tenancy was subject to the mandatory ground for possession available to a returning home owner.[81]

3.81 Expert reports must comply with CPR Part 35 and the practice direction made under it. The report must be addressed to the court[82] and must:[83]

a) give details of the expert's qualifications;
b) give details of any literature or other materials on which the expert has relied in making the report, for example, details of comparable properties or citations from textbooks;
c) where there is a range of opinion on the matters dealt with in the report, summarise that range and give reasons for the expert's own opinion;
d) contain a summary of the conclusions reached;
e) contain a statement that the expert understands his or her duty to the court and has complied with that duty; and
f) contain a statement setting out the substance of all material instructions, summarising the facts which are material to the opinions expressed in the report.

Reduction of damages

3.82 Damages under HA 1988 s28 may be reduced in two circumstances: first, on account of the conduct of the former residential occupier or someone living with him or her before the event which gave rise to the liability, eg before eviction, or, second, if the landlord offers

---

79 See, eg *Jones v Miah* (1992) 24 HLR 578, CA, *Nworkorie v Mason,* (1993) 26 HLR 60, CA, *Melville v Bruton* (1996) 29 HLR 319, CA.
80 CPR 35.3.
81 Under HA 1988 Sch 2 Ground 1.
82 CPR Part 35 PD 1.1.
83 CPR Part 35 PD 1.2.

reinstatement[84] and it would be (or, if he or she had obtained alternative accommodation before the offer was made, it would have been) unreasonable for the occupier to refuse to accept.[85]

3.83   A landlord who wishes to rely on HA 1988 s27(7) must plead the facts relied on in the defence.[86] Where a landlord neither does so nor makes submissions to that effect at trial, a court is not required to consider, of its own motion, whether damages should be reduced.[87]

Residential occupier's conduct

3.84   Mitigation of damages on account of the occupier's conduct before the act giving rise to the liability was considered in *Regalgrand v Dickerson*.[88] 'Conduct' means behaviour and is not limited to serious acts. The conduct complained of does not have to be a positive act; it may be a failure to do something. Accordingly, failure to pay rent may justify a reduction in damages, even where the landlord successfully counterclaims for the arrears.

3.85   It is for the court to decide in all the circumstances of the case whether or not it is reasonable to reduce the damages. If it decides that it is, it must go on to decide the extent of the reduction, although where there is a number of factors to be taken into account it does not have to apportion the amount deducted to each act or omission. In *Regalgrand*, the Court of Appeal upheld the judge's decision to reduce the award of damages from £12,000 to £1,500 because the tenants were in arrears of rent and had already decided to leave the property within a short time.

3.86   In *Wandsworth LBC v Osei-Bonsu*,[89] the claimant and his wife were joint tenants of a local authority house. The wife fled from the house with their children because of domestic violence. At the authority's suggestion, she served a notice to quit to determine the tenancy. That notice was invalid because it did not give 28 days' notice. Meanwhile, the claimant had been excluded from the house because his wife had obtained an ouster injunction. The authority treated the notice to quit as valid so that, when the claimant asked to be let back into

---

84   See above, paras 2.97–2.99, as to what is meant by reinstatement.
85   HA 1988 s27(7).
86   *Regalgrand v Dickerson* (1996) 29 HLR 620, CA; as to pleadings generally, see chapter 4.
87   *Kalas v Farmer* [2010] EWCA Civ 108, [2010] HLR 25.
88   (1996) 29 HLR 620, CA.
89   [1999] 1 WLR 1011, 31 HLR 515, CA.

the house once the ouster injunction had been discharged, it refused him re-admission.

3.87 In the county court, the claimant was awarded £30,000 under HA 1988 s28 (by way of a concession as to difference in values).[90] The Court of Appeal held that the husband's conduct was relevant to the level of damages. His violence towards his wife broke up the family and by way of the ouster injunction and the notice to quit led the authority to seek possession with a view to rehousing the wife and the children. The eviction was the culmination of an unbroken chain of events starting with the husband's conduct. The damages were reduced to £10,000.

3.88 The statutory limitation on conduct prior to the act giving rise to the liability means that subsequent conduct, however provocative, cannot affect the level of damages, save so far as it goes to the issue of reinstatement.

Reinstatement

3.89 As mitigation is only available if an offer for reinstatement is (or would have been) unreasonably refused,[91] HA 1988 s27(7)(b) necessarily accepts that sufficiently bad conduct by the landlord will justify (or would have justified) a decision not to return to the property, eg, where the tenant could not reasonably be expected to go back to the location of such events.

3.90 The reference to the possibility of mitigation of damages once the occupier has found alternative accommodation seems to have been directed to the occupier who has already taken (inferior) alternative accommodation (which he or she could give up in order to return) rather than opening up the possibility of an offer being made safe in the knowledge that the occupier has found somewhere else (suitable) so that he or she is unlikely to return.

3.91 Note that, in order to qualify, an offer must have been made before the occupier commences legal proceedings.[92]

---

90 See above, note 75.
91 See above, para 3.82.
92 Meaning action under HA 1988 s27, not any other action which may be taken in relation to the case: *Tagro v Cafane* (1991) 23 HLR 250, CA.

Relationship with common law damages

3.92   HA 1988 s27(4) and (5) makes clear that liability under HA 1988 s27 is in addition to any other liability which might arise. Damages may not, however, be awarded twice for the same loss.

3.93   Where an award is made under HA 1988 s28, the tenant is not entitled to any additional award for loss of occupation which may arise under another cause of action, for example, breach of contract, for the loss of the right of occupation.[93]

3.94   It is, however, only the damages relating to the loss of occupation which are set off in this way, ie, not any damages for conversion of goods or physical injury. Likewise, while general or aggravated damages attributable to the loss of right of occupation will be set off,[94] general damages for the landlord's acts of harassment prior to the eviction will not,[95] nor will aggravated damages unconnected with the right of occupation.[96]

3.95   Exemplary damages are not to be awarded in addition to statutory damages.[97]

Compensation in criminal proceedings

3.96   Where compensation in criminal proceedings is awarded (see chapter 5), the amount should be deducted from any damages subsequently awarded in civil proceedings.[98]

Interest

3.97   The court has power to award interest on any damages recovered by the claimant.[99] Interest is usually only awarded on special damages. It is not awarded on non-pecuniary losses, such as aggravated damages, exemplary damages or general damages,[100] unless they are general damages for pain, suffering and loss of amenity in a personal injury claim, in which case interest is fixed at two per cent per annum.[101]

---

93 HA 1988 s27(5).
94 *Nworkorie v Mason* (1993) 26 HLR 60, CA.
95 *Kaur v Gill* (1995) *Times* 15 June, CA.
96 *Francis v Brown* (1997) 30 HLR 143, CA.
97 *Nworkorie v Mason* and *Francis v Brown* (1997) 30 HLR 143, CA.
98 Powers of Criminal Courts (Sentencing) Act 2000 s134.
99 County Courts Act (CCA) 1984 s69; the rate of interest is currently 8 per annum but is within the discretion of the court.
100 *Saunders v Edwards* [1987] 1 WLR 1116, CA.
101 *Birkett v Hayes* [1982] 1 WLR 816, HL.

3.98   Interest cannot be awarded on damages under HA 1988 s28.[102]

3.99   The right to interest runs from the date on which the cause of action arises.[103]

Examples of damages awarded

3.100   The following cases illustrate the amount of general, aggravated and exemplary damages which the courts have awarded. It is important to stress that they are only illustrations, not in any sense 'precedents', because the facts will always vary from case to case. Advisers should note the date of each decision as older awards should be increased to reflect inflation.

3.101   Cases which solely concern the amount of statutory damages under HA 1988 s28 are not recorded as they turn on the principles set out above in paras 3.70–3.78 and expert evidence, so that the actual amount awarded in one case is irrelevant to another.

Cases in the Court of Appeal

Devonshire and Smith v Jenkins (1978) 28 April, unreported, CA

3.102   The claimant tenants were subjected to severe harassment by their landlord. The harassment included excessive and deliberate noise (from a record-player left on until 3 am), forcible entry, pressure to leave, abusive language and physical assault. The landlord breached an undertaking to the court to stop the harassment. In the magistrates' court, the landlord was convicted of 16 counts of harassment under the PEA 1977. He was fined £1,200. In the county court, the landlord was ordered to pay the first claimant: (a) £1,000 aggravated damages; and (b) £500 exemplary damages. He was also ordered to pay the second claimant: (a) £750 aggravated damages; and (b) £1,500 exemplary damages.

The landlord appealed to the Court of Appeal. The court held that this was a case in which exemplary damages could be awarded. Ormrod LJ observed that for five months the landlord had made the tenants' lives 'hell'. Nevertheless, the court held that when the fine was taken into account, the total amount which the landlord was required to pay was excessive. The court increased the awards of

102 *Jones v Miah* (1992) 24 HLR 578, CA.
103 CCA 1984 s69(1)(a).

aggravated damages to £1,250 for the first claimant and £1,000 for the second claimant but made no award for exemplary damages.

Guppys (Bridport) Ltd v Brookling (1983) 14 HLR 1, CA

3.103   The defendants were tenants of bedsitting-rooms in a house. They were elderly men who had lived in the house since the early 1970s. The claimant company bought the house knowing that it was occupied by approximately 16 people. The company intended to convert it into seven self-contained flats, which the present occupiers could not afford. The company served notices to quit. All bar three of the occupiers left. Possession proceedings were commenced against the defendants. During this period, building operations and works of reconstruction were started in the premises. The works caused serious disruption to the tenants. They brought proceedings which resulted in the company undertaking not to disconnect or discontinue the supply of electricity and water or the sanitary and washing facilities to the premises. Nonetheless, the sanitary and washing facilities were removed or discontinued by preventing access to them and the electricity supply was disconnected. For a period of six months, the company showed some restraint. Before the hearing of the action, however, while its undertaking to the court was still in force, it executed works in contravention of the undertaking. In view of the conditions in the property, in October 1981 the occupiers were forced out and were found alternative accommodation by the local authority, following which demolition work on their rooms was begun. In November 1981, the occupiers sought and obtained orders preventing further works on the building until after the action was heard. They also added counterclaims to their defences, including a claim for exemplary damages.

At the county court, the judge awarded general damages of £1,000, to include exemplary damages, in addition to agreed special damages. The company appealed. The Court of Appeal held that the award of £1,000 was not excessive given the company's obvious motive was to make profit and its breach of undertaking.

McMillan v Singh (1985) 17 HLR 120, CA

3.104   From 1979, the claimant was the tenant of a bedsitting-room. The rent for the room was £16 per week. The defendant landlord realised that he could re-let the room at £26 per week. He put the tenant's belongings out of the room. When the tenant returned to his room, he found that all his belongings had disappeared. He bought a camp bed and stayed in the room overnight. The next day, when he met the landlord, the landlord threatened him and threw the camp bed out of the house. At the trial of the action, the county court judge found that the landlord had taken advantage of the tenant's absence to obtain an increase of £10 per week rent. He was invited to make an award of exemplary damages, but declined to do so on the ground that the tenant had been in arrears from time to time, and it would be inequitable to award them.

The Court of Appeal allowed an appeal, holding that the arrears were irrelevant to an award of exemplary damages. The correct approach to the assessment of damages was to quantify (where appropriate) damage to property or person, any aggravated damages for damage to feelings, and only then exemplary damages. The Court of Appeal assessed damages: (a) £250 aggravated damages; and (b) £250 exemplary damages.

Millington v Duffy (1985) 17 HLR 232, CA

3.105 The claimant was the tenant of a bedsitting-room which he had rented for 15 years. In 1982, his rent was increased from £6.25 per week to £7.75 per week. At that time he was 66 years old. His landlord accused him of soiling the communal lavatory and demanded that he clean it. The tenant denied responsibility and was told to leave. The landlord spat at the tenant and entered the room and removed all his belongings. He re-let the room at £17.20 per week. The tenant had nowhere to take his belongings. For a few weeks he slept with a friend, after which he slept rough until accommodation was found for him by the local authority.

At trial, the tenant was awarded: (a) £119.50 special damages for lost possessions; and (b) £150 general damages for distress and inconvenience. The tenant appealed against the amount of general damages and against the refusal of an order for costs. The Court of Appeal held that the award of £150 for distress and inconvenience was so low as to be plainly wrong and a sum of £500 was substituted.

Ramdath v Daly (1993) 25 HLR 273, CA

3.106 The claimant was the tenant of the first defendant. The second defendant (the landlord's son) managed the premises. The son demanded a rent increase from £40 per week to £100 per week. The claimant refused to pay. On 14 August 1991, he returned home to find that the locks had been changed and that some of his possessions had been removed. Further incidents occurred during August with the son orally abusing the claimant. On 19 September, the claimant felt safe to return but found that many of his belongings had gone missing. At trial, the judge awarded against the landlord: (a) £2,000 general damages; (b) £510 special damages; and (c) £1,000 exemplary damages. The judge awarded against the son: (a) £1,250 general damages (including a sum of aggravated damages); (b) £2,674 special damages; and (c) £2,500 exemplary damages.

On appeal, the award of exemplary damages was upheld against the landlord but not against his son as there was insufficient evidence that the son was closely concerning himself with his father's interests and he had not sought to make any money out of his wrongdoing. The court refused to hold that the award should stand alternatively as aggravated damages as these had already been encompassed in the award of general damages. The Court of Appeal found that neither award of general damages was excessive.

Francis v Brown (1997) 30 HLR 143, CA

3.107   The claimant was a tenant. The first defendant was her landlord and the second defendant was the landlord's daughter. The defendants unlawfully evicted the claimant who brought proceedings for damages against them. The first defendant wanted vacant possession to sell it to the daughter. The judge awarded £40,000 damages against the second defendant under HA 1988 s28. He also awarded £40,000 against the first defendant, expressed to be for aggravated damages. The judge indicated that if he had not awarded HA 1988 s28 damages against the second defendant, he would have awarded the same sum against her in aggravated damages. The judge also awarded £1,500 special damages and £1,000 expressed to be for exemplary damages against both defendants. The second defendant appealed to the Court of Appeal.

At the hearing, it was conceded that the judge had confused aggravated damages with exemplary damages, and that the award for aggravated damages should be treated as for exemplary damages and vice versa. The award for HA 1988 s28 damages against the second defendant was set aside because she had no rights in the property. Nor, as the second defendant had no intention to profit from the eviction, could an award for exemplary damages be made against her. As an award for exemplary damages against joint tortfeasors should be the lowest for which any of the defendants could be liable, nor could any award be made for exemplary damages against the first defendant. In any event, even if an award of exemplary damages had been appropriate, £40,000 was clearly excessive.

King v Jackson (1997) 30 HLR 541, CA

3.108 The claimant was the assured shorthold tenant of a flat let to her by the defendant landlord. The tenant gave the landlord four weeks' notice to quit and promised to move out. The landlord arranged for another tenant to move in and unlawfully evicted the tenant six days before the day on which she had promised to leave. The tenant was awarded £11,000 under HA 1988 s28. The judge held that if statutory damages were not appropriate, he would have made an award of £1,500 general damages. The landlord appealed to the Court of Appeal.

The appeal was allowed. The claimant was not entitled to significant statutory damages as she had only had a very limited right to remain in the property at the date of the eviction, with only six days of her tenancy remaining. An award for £1,500 general damages was substituted.

Cases in the High Court

Islam v Yap & Others [2009] EWHC 3606

3.109 The claimant was the non-secure tenant of Redbridge LBC. Redbridge let the property from a company who let the property from the defendant freeholder. Redbridge served the tenant with a notice to quit, but did not issue a claim for possession. The defendant decided to sell the property. His agent found a willing buyer and a sale price was agreed on condition that the property was obtained with vacant possession. The defendant's agent asked the tenant to leave the property. She agreed to leave provided she could find alternative accommodation. During the next few weeks, however, the tenant was unable to do so. The defendant's agent telephoned the tenant to tell her that the locks would be changed the following day, to forget about calling the police and that he would squat in the property until she left. His tone was threatening. The defendant's agent then contacted the defendant to tell him that he was going to change the locks. The defendant did not discourage him. The following day, the agent attended the property and changed the locks. He sat in the property for a few hours before the tenant agreed to leave. The tenant had nowhere else to go and was forced to leave her possessions in the property.

The tenant was awarded: (a) £36 per day general damages from the date of her eviction to the order of the court assessed as being the rental rate that was chargeable during that time from the defendant;

(b) £3,000 aggravated damages from the defendant's agent; and (c) £5,000 exemplary damages against the defendant.

Unlawful eviction and harassment county court cases[104] since 1998[105]

Grillo v Cant and Bassairi Ltd March 1998 *Legal Action* 13, Central London County Court, HHJ Butter

3.110   The claimant was the assured tenant of a room in a house. The second defendant was a company which bought the property. The first defendant was the company secretary. The first defendant evicted the tenant and left her belongings in black bin liners on the communal stairs. The tenant spent two nights sleeping on the communal staircase to look after her belongings. She then spent two weeks sleeping on a friend's sofa. She then obtained the tenancy of another property under an assured shorthold tenancy. The first defendant was found guilty of offences under the PEA 1977 and fined £250.

In the county court, the tenant was awarded: (a) £6,000 for loss of the assured tenancy; (b) £2,000 for the manner of the eviction; (c) £1,000 exemplary damages; and (d) £45 special damages.

Pillai v Amendra October 2000 *Legal Action* 24, Central London County Court, HHJ Green QC

3.111   The claimant was the assured shorthold tenant of a one-bedroomed flat. The rent was £300 per month. The tenant refused to move out for two weeks to allow the landlord temporarily to re-instate a previous tenant in order to defeat an investigation by a housing benefit fraud team. The tenant returned from holiday to find that the locks had been changed and that his possessions were in the front garden. He was re-admitted with the assistance of the police. In addition, his car windscreen was smashed and a threatening note left for him. He was then locked out again and his goods were once more put in the garden. He obtained an injunction against the landlord but it was not complied with. He went to stay with a friend for six months in cramped accommodation before finding another flat. As a result, he spent a lot of time off work which was a contributory factor in his employer's decision to sack him from his job as an accountant. The landlord denied the claimant's case, failed to comply with orders for

---

104 The court and the judge are identified where known.
105 See previous editions for earlier cases.

disclosure, failed to provide a witness statement and gave a mislead-ing address for service. The landlord did not give evidence at trial but did cross-examine the tenant.

The tenant was awarded: (a) £6,000 general damages; (b) £10,000 aggravated and exemplary damages for trespass to land; (c) £3,000 aggravated damages for trespass to goods; and (d) £17,000 special damages for loss of possessions and incidental expenditure. Costs were awarded against the landlord on an indemnity basis. The judge expressed the view that it was 'a bad case, but not at the very top end' because there was no actual violence and the tenant was not a vulner-able person.

Dimoutsikou v Penrose October 2000 *Legal Action* 24, Leeds County Court, DJ Bellamy

3.112 The claimant was an assured shorthold tenant. On 19 July 1998, she went to Greece for a three-week holiday. While she was away, the defendant landlord changed the locks. The tenant was not in arrears of rent and had left a post-dated cheque for the rent for the time she was away. On 10 August, the tenant was told about the eviction by a friend. Her solicitors advised the defendant that his conduct was unlawful. At that point, the property had not been re-let. The defend-ant refused to re-admit her.

The tenant was awarded: (a) £4,750 general damages (calculated at the rate of £125 for each day that she was homeless); (b) £1,750 to acknowledge that the alternative accommodation she eventually found was less agreeable and more expensive; (c) £1,500 aggravated damages; (d) £1,500 exemplary damages; (e) £338.40 special dam-ages; and (f) £100 for the return of her deposit.

Biga v Martin June 2001 *Legal Action* 25, Ilford County Court, HHJ Platt

3.113 The claimant was an assured shorthold tenant of a room. The ten-ant asked the defendant landlord for a tenancy agreement so that he could apply for housing benefit. The defendant refused and asked the tenant to leave. The tenant's solicitors wrote to the defendant and warned him that he required a court order before evicting the tenant. The defendant ignored this letter, changed the locks and placed the tenant's belongings in a corridor outside of his room. The tenant obtained an injunction and was re-admitted to the property. Shortly after the tenant returned, however, the defendant attended the prop-erty with a sledge-hammer and three other men. The defendant broke in through a window and assaulted the tenant. The tenant suffered no significant physical injury but was subsequently diagnosed as suffering from post-traumatic stress disorder. He left the property and spent three nights in a night shelter before being provided with bed and breakfast accommodation by the local authority.

The tenant was awarded: (a) £10,000 general and aggravated damages to include the tenant's personal injury; (b) £900 special damages; and (c) £2,500 exemplary damages.

Ahmed v Bains September 2001 *Legal Action* 25, Brentford County Court, HHJ Edwards

3.114 The claimant was the assured shorthold tenant of a bedroom. He shared the use of a living room, bathroom and kitchen with other tenants. Some months after he was granted the tenancy by the defendant, the defendant moved into the living room. The tenant complained about this, but was threatened with violence by the defendant. On the day that a notice seeking possession expired, the defendant assaulted the tenant as he left the property and stole his keys from him. The defendant then disposed of the tenant's property and re-let the property on the same day. The tenant was forced to stay with friends for two months.

The tenant was awarded: (a) £1,695 special damages for the loss of possessions; (b) £1,000 general damages for the acts of harassment prior to the eviction; (c) £7,800 general damages for the unlawful eviction and the time spent with friends assessed at £100 per day; (d) £1,500 aggravated damages; and (e) £1,500 exemplary damages as the defendant plainly knew that the eviction was unlawful and had arranged to re-let the whole of the premises from the date of the eviction.

Porbeni v Chaabdiss September 2001 *Housing law casebook* (5th edn, LAG), Willesden County Court, HHJ Bevington

3.115 The claimant was a Rent Act protected tenant. He was the victim of a campaign of harassment spanning seven years which included both actual and threatened violence, threats to kill, racial abuse, regular trespass and the commencement of possession proceedings on a blatantly false basis.

The tenant was awarded for the harassment: (a) £17,750 general damages assessed at £2,500 per annum; (b) aggravated damages of £1,000; and (c) £12,500 exemplary damages.

Nation v Collie and others February 2003 Legal Action 37, Shrewsbury County Court

3.116 The claimant was an assured shorthold tenant of a room. The second defendant (the first defendant's ex-husband) was the tenant's landlord. A dispute arose between the tenant and the defendants over a telephone bill. While the tenant was out for the day, the defendants changed the locks to the property. On her return, the tenant found the property unlocked and the burglar alarm was activated as she walked into the house. The first defendant came to the property and asked the tenant to leave. The second defendant arrived shortly after, called the police and asked the tenant to leave. The tenant spent one night at a bed and breakfast, five nights at a friend's house and eight nights in a caravan before finding alternative accommodation.

The tenant was awarded: (a) £2,500 general and aggravated damages for the unlawful eviction and (b) £265 special damages.

Stephenson v Southwark LBC March 2003 Legal Action 29, Edmonton County Court

3.117 The claimant was the son of a deceased local authority tenant. On the death of his father, he succeeded to the secure tenancy. He notified the local authority of this fact but, while on holiday, the local authority, without a court order, forced its way into the property to carry out gas maintenance. The local authority then placed grilles over the doors and windows and refused the tenant entry on his return on the (incorrect) basis that he had not succeeded to the tenancy. The tenant's possessions were disposed of. For the first six months the tenant stayed with friends, his girlfriend and her parents and then for six months with his mother.

The tenant was awarded: (a) £5,300 general damages for trespass to land and breach of quiet enjoyment and (b) £7,500 special damages for the loss of his possessions.

Sam-Yorke v Ali Jawad March 2003 Legal Action 30, Wandsworth County Court

3.118 The claimant was the assured tenant of a flat. The defendant landlord asked the tenant to leave and visited the flat while the tenant's wife and child were there. He refused to leave and the tenant called the police. Before the police arrived, the defendant slapped the tenant on the face, which caused bruising to the left side of his head, and kicked him.

The tenant was awarded £900 general damages for the assault and breach of quiet enjoyment.

Youziel v Andrews March 2003 *Legal Action* 29, Lambeth County Court, DJ Jacey

3.119 The claimant was the assured shorthold tenant of a one-bedroom flat. The defendant managed the property for the tenant's landlord. Rent arrears quickly began to accrue as the tenant was an asylum-seeker and as such was not entitled to housing benefit. Over a period of six weeks, the defendant subjected the tenant to a campaign of harassment. The defendant threatened the tenant on ten separate occasions and on one occasion threatened the tenant with his life. The tenant was also assaulted by the defendant and two other men. The tenant sustained an injury to his knee for which the defendant was prosecuted. The harassment caused the tenant further stress and anxiety and resulted in him losing 12 pounds in weight. Six months later he vacated the premises voluntarily.

The tenant was awarded: (a) £13,000 general damages for the assault; (b) £2,700 general damages for the other acts of harassment; and (c) £4,300 aggravated damages.

Dorival v Simmons August 2003 *Legal Action* 30, Lambeth County Court, HHJ Cox

3.120 The claimant was the assured shorthold tenant of a room. She complained to the defendant landlord about disrepair in the property. The defendant responded by assaulting and abusing the tenant and then turning off the electricity and water supply. The tenant complained to the local authority and a tenancy relations officer spoke to the defendant. Four days later, the water and electricity supply were restored but the tenant continued to have difficulties with the electricity supply. The defendant then threatened to evict the tenant. A tenancy relations officer warned the defendant, under caution, that an eviction without an order of the court would be both unlawful and illegal. The tenant subsequently became pregnant and, four months into her pregnancy, was unable to enter the property as the front door had been locked from the inside while she was out. The defendant refused to re-admit the tenant despite a tenancy relations officer attending the property. The local authority provided the tenant with bed and breakfast accommodation for the following six months. Six days after the eviction the defendant allowed the tenant to collect her belongings.

The tenant was awarded: (a) £1,500 general damages for the disconnection of the water and electricity supply; (b) £750 general damages for the assault; (c) £2,000 general damages for the nature of the eviction; (d) £1,000 general damages for the time spent in bed and breakfast accommodation for a period of three months; (e) £2,000 aggravated damages; and (f) £1,000 exemplary damages.

Garcia v Khan March 2005 *Legal Action* 21, Bow County Court, HHJ Hornby

3.121 The claimant was the assured shorthold tenant of a flat and lived there with his wife. He complained to his landlord that there was disrepair. His landlord did nothing and then, without the knowledge of the tenant, sold the property to the defendant. Shortly after purchasing the property, the defendant attended the property and told the tenant's wife that she had to leave so that repairs could be carried out. The tenant agreed that he would vacate the property during the day and return at night to sleep there, while his wife, who was then six months pregnant, would stay with her family. The following evening, the defendant's husband bolted the front door from the inside and refused the tenant access. Two days later, the tenant's wife was also refused access. The following day, the tenant entered the property to find that some of their belongings had been removed and that the defendant was sleeping on his bed. The police were called and the defendant told them that she was the owner. The tenant and his wife were required to leave and subsequently did not return to the property. The following week, the local authority contacted the defendant. She first accused the tenant of committing housing benefit fraud and then claimed that she had bought the property with vacant possession. She refused to reinstate the tenant or his wife. Two weeks after the eviction, the local authority confirmed that they would grant the tenant and his wife a secure tenancy. Before it was granted, however, the tenant had to stay with relatives, sleeping on floors, for a further five weeks.

The tenant was awarded: (a) general damages of £5,500 assessed at £100 per night for the time spent away from the property; (b) £2,000 aggravated damages; and (c) £2,500 exemplary damages. The court rejected the defendant's argument that the award should be reduced because the tenant had failed to mitigate his loss by failing to apply for an interim injunction.

Cooper v Sharma October 2005 *Legal Action* 15, Brentford County Court, HHJ Marcus Edwards

3.122   The claimant was the assured shorthold tenant of a one-bedroom flat in which she lived with her son. The defendant landlord interfered with her post and disconnected the gas, electricity and hot water supply. Eight days later, the tenant obtained an injunction requiring the defendant to reconnect them. The defendant delayed for two weeks before complying with the injunction. The defendant then issued a claim for possession, but did not serve the tenant. He obtained a possession order in her absence and 12 days later forcibly evicted her from the property. He threw the tenant's belongings onto the pavement outside. The tenant and her son were forced to sleep on a friend's floor. Six days later, the tenant successfully set aside the possession order and obtained an injunction requiring the defendant to re-admit her to the property. The defendant refused to do so and the tenant remained on her friend's floor until she was provided with bed and breakfast accommodation by the local authority. In all, she spent 19 days on her friend's floor and 70 days in bed and breakfast accommodation.

The defendant appealed against the award of damages made by a district judge. HHJ Marcus Edwards, allowing the appeal in part, awarded the tenant: (a) £2,300 general damages for the period she was without gas, electricity or hot water assessed at £100 per day; (b) £400 general damages for the interference with her post; (c) £3,800 general damages for the period she slept on her friend's floor assessed at £200 per day; (d) £500 general damages for the 70 days spent in bed and breakfast accommodation; (e) £4,000 aggravated damages; and (f) £2,500 exemplary damages.

Bamberger v Swaby December 2005 *Legal Action* 19, Lambeth County Court, HHJ Welchman

3.123   The claimant was an assured shorthold tenant. She lived at the property with her two sons. She owed the defendant arrears of rent. The defendant told her that he would go to any lengths necessary to remove her from the property. The defendant served notice to quit, rather than a notice under HA 1988 s21, and served it one night just after midnight. At the same time, he cut the electricity supply by removing the fuses. This forced the tenant to leave the property for eight days and resulted in her having to throw away food that was in her freezer. An injunction was obtained which required the defendant to restore the electricity. The electricity was restored and the tenant returned to the property. Shortly after the tenant returned, the defendant attended the property for an inspection. During the inspection, he was abusive, offensive and unnecessarily intrusive to the tenant. This unsettled the tenant and caused her to leave the property.

The tenant was awarded: (a) £2,400 general damages assessed at £300 per day for the eight days she was away from the property; (b) £600 general damages for the anxiety surrounding her departure from the property; (c) £50 special damages for the contents of the freezer and additional catering costs; (d) £1,000 aggravated damages; and (e) £2,000 exemplary damages.

Daley and others v Mahmood [2006] 1 P&CR DG10, August 2005, Central London County Court, HHJ Medawar QC

3.124   There were four claimants. They lived in a shared house. Three of the claimants had Rent Act protected tenancies of their rooms and the fourth had acquired the freehold interest of his room by adverse possession. The defendant decided to purchase the property. Before he did so, he had attended the property and verbally abused the occupiers and threatened that he would unlawfully evict them. Shortly after purchasing the property, the defendant gained entry to the property by smashing a window. He gave the fourth claimant one week's notice to quit and threatened him. The stress caused the fourth claimant to collapse and he was taken to hospital. The first claimant was required to move rooms. A week later, the defendant returned with a skip and began removing the first and fourth claimants' belongings and disconnected the gas and electricity supply. He then demolished the internal walls of the ground floor. The following day, the claimants left the property. The first and fourth claimants were housed by the local authority in bed and breakfast accommodation. The second and third claimants lived on a campsite. The eviction had a serious impact on all of the claimants and reduced their employment prospects. At trial, HHJ Medawar QC found that: 'there had been a deliberate campaign of intimidation, harassment and threats designed to make the occupiers leave the property. The actions were wrongful and, at times, criminal. This is one of the most serious cases of harassment followed by unlawful eviction.'

Each claimant was awarded: (a) £10,000 general damages for the unlawful eviction; (b) £2,500 aggravated damages for the eviction; (c) £1,500 aggravated damages for the harassment leading up to the eviction; and (d) £7,500 exemplary damages. The first and fourth claimants were also awarded £5,000 general damages for the harassment prior to the eviction; the second and third claimants were awarded £3,500 because they were less vulnerable. The fourth claimant also received £1,250 general damages for the assault and £16,000 general damages for exacerbation of pre-existing depressive illness and alcoholism, which had resulted in brain damage.

Poku-Awuah v Lenton February 2006 *Legal Action* 28, Lambeth County Court, DJ Jacey

3.125   The claimant was an assured shorthold tenant of a room. Late one night, the defendant attended the property with four men and two women. After the tenant opened the door, the defendant and her companions entered the property and began packing away all of her belongings. They then forcibly removed her from the property and changed the locks. The tenant spent the night in her car. The following day, she stayed with her daughter and then spent 15 nights in an hotel.

The tenant was awarded: (a) £5,100 general damages assessed at £300 per day; (b) £390 special damages (which included hotel costs); (c) £1,000 aggravated damages; and (d) £2,000 exemplary damages.

Hadden v Nicholson November 2006 *Legal Action* 32, Carlisle County Court

3.126   The claimant was an assured shorthold tenant of a flat. The defendant landlord notified him that urgent electrical repairs needed to be carried out at the flat and that he would have to live in alternative accommodation while they were carried out. The tenant agreed to leave. On arrival at the proposed alternative accommodation, the tenant was not given entry to the property by the defendant's agent because he was unable to pay £40 rent in advance. The tenant returned to his flat only to find that the locks had been changed. He was forced to spend a night on the streets and then four nights in a shelter until the tenant obtained an injunction against the defendant, which ordered that he be re-admitted to his flat or provided with alternative accommodation. At trial, no evidence was adduced that the repairs had been needed.

The tenant was awarded: (a) £1,000 in general damages for the night on the streets and four nights in the shelter; (b) £350 aggravated damages for the night the tenant slept on the streets; and (c) £1,000 exemplary damages as the defendant had profited by evicting him.

Diallo v Brosnan January 2007 Legal Action 21, Willesden County Court, DJ Morris

3.127 The claimant was an assured shorthold tenant of a room. His land-lord was the assured shorthold tenant of the defendant. The defend-ant attended the property and discovered that the tenant's landlord was no longer living at the property. The tenant and the defendant entered into a new oral tenancy agreement. The tenant paid rent to the defendant for several months, but ceased paying rent after the defendant refused to provide him with a written tenancy agreement which meant that he was unable to obtain housing benefit. Three weeks after the tenant stopped paying rent, he returned to the prop-erty to find that the locks had been changed. He broke back in. The following morning, the defendant attended the property with another man and threatened the tenant with a knife before forcibly evicting him. The tenant spent three nights at his partner's flat and one night sleeping in a car. The tenant was subsequently re-admitted to the property after an injunction was obtained.

The tenant was awarded: (a) £1,000 general damages; and (b) £1,000 'exemplary' (aggravated) damages for the use of a knife dur-ing the eviction.

Daramy v Streeks June 2007 Legal Action 37, Lambeth County Court, HHJ Crawford Lindsay

3.128 The claimant was an assured shorthold tenant. He lost his job and was unable to pay his rent. After he had accrued two months of arrears, the defendant landlord began to harass him for the rent and assaulted his wife. The defendant obtained a possession order, but evicted the tenant without a warrant and sold his belongings to recover the rent he was owed.

The tenant was awarded: (a) £1,500 general damages for the harassment; (b) £2,500 general damages for the eviction and the time spent out of the property; and (c) £1,250 aggravated damages.

Naveed v Raja July 2007 Legal Action 32, Willesden County Court, HHJ Copley

3.129 The claimant was an assured shorthold tenant. After he was injured in a car accident, he was unable to work and therefore had no means of paying his rent. The tenant asked the defendant landlord for a writ-ten tenancy argument so that he could apply for housing benefit. The defendant refused and served him with a HA 1988 s21 notice. On the day the notice expired, the defendant's father attended the property with three other men, assaulted the tenant and forcibly evicted him. They then took all of his property. The tenant was forced to spend three nights in a car before he was re-admitted to the property after he obtained an injunction. His belongings were never returned. Three weeks later, three men, one of whom had attended on the day of the eviction, came to the property and assaulted the tenant again, this time with wooden sticks. The tenant suffered injuries to his head, body and legs. His injuries required that he remain in hospital overnight. After being released from hospital, the tenant was too scared to return to the property.

The tenant was awarded: (a) £10,000 general damages for the assaults and time spent out of the property; (b) £2,000 special damages for his lost possessions; and (c) £15,000 aggravated and exemplary damages.

Evans v Copping January 2008 *Legal Action* 30, Ashford County Court, DDJ Cagney

3.130   The claimant was an assured shorthold tenant of a flat. One day she returned home to find that the locks had been changed. She applied for an injunction to require the defendant landlord to re-admit her, but was unsuccessful after the defendant lied and told the court that he had already re-let the flat. The tenant was forced to stay with friends for the three months between the eviction and the date of trial.

The tenant was awarded: (a) £2,500 general damages for the time spent away from the flat; (b) £500 aggravated damages; and (c) £1,500 exemplary damages.

Arabhalvaei v Rezaeipoor January 2008 *Legal Action* 36, Central London County Court, DJ Taylor

3.131   The defendant was the assured shorthold tenant of a one-bedroom flat. He lived at the flat with his wife. The flat suffered from disrepair. The claimant landlord harassed the tenant for a period of nearly eight years, despite being warned by a tenancy relations officer about his conduct. The harassment comprised verbal abuse, disconnecting the water supply, nuisance telephone calls, locks to the property being filled with glue and the smashing of a window. The tenant felt uncomfortable leaving his wife alone in the property and took time off work which meant he lost his job. In 2004, the claimant brought a claim for possession on the basis of rent arrears. The tenant counter-claimed for, amongst other things, harassment.

The tenant was awarded in respect of the harassment: (a) £46,500 general damages assessed at £6,000 per annum; (b) £67,500 for losing his job; (c) £5,000 aggravated damages; and (d) £5,000 exemplary damages.

Addison v Croft June 2008 *Legal Action* 31, HHJ Appleton

3.132 The claimant was an assured shorthold tenant. The defendant landlord decided to sell property. One day, he entered the property without warning and demanded that the tenant leave. Two weeks later, the defendant returned this time with other men. They forcibly evicted the tenant. The tenant spent 20 nights sleeping in his van and staying with friends before he was re-admitted to the property following an injunction.

The tenant was awarded: (a) £3,000 general damage for the eviction; (b) £1,000 aggravated damages; and (c) £1,000 exemplary damages.

Evans v Ozkan and Hussein April 2009 *Legal Action* 20, Bromley County Court, HHJ Hallan

3.133 The claimant was the assured shorthold tenant of a room. Before entering into his tenancy agreement, he told his landlord, the first defendant, that his rent would be paid by housing benefit. The tenant fell into arrears after delays in the processing of his application for the benefit. A month into the tenancy, the first defendant attended the property and demanded that the tenant pay £1,000. The tenant told the first defendant that he did not have £1,000 to give him and the defendant left. At a later date, the tenant returned home to find the first defendant and two other men throwing his belongings on the pavement. The first defendant verbally abused the tenant. The police attended, but it was the tenant who was arrested. On his release that evening, the tenant found some of his belongings lying on the pavement; they had been crushed or smashed and some smelt of urine. The lilo he had been using as a mattress was full of holes and deflated. Some of his other belongings were missing. The tenant spent the night in his car away from the property, but returned the following day when he found that the locks had been changed. Both defendants, who had been waiting at the property, followed the tenant to the local pub where they threatened him with baseball bats and demanded £1,000. The tenant applied to his local authority as homeless and was eventually re-housed. He did, however, spend 63 nights in total without a home, which caused his health to deteriorate and he had suicidal thoughts.

The tenant was awarded: (a) £15,750 general damages assessed at £250 per day for the period that he was homeless; (b) £5,000 special damages for his lost possessions; (c) £1,000 aggravated damages; and (d) £2,000 exemplary damages.

Khan v Iqbal May 2009 *Legal Action* 25, Bury County Court, HHJ Tetlow

3.134   The claimant was the assured shorthold tenant of a property in which she lived with two children aged 15 and 12. After she accrued arrears of rent, the defendant landlord attended the property and demanded that she pay rent. He verbally abused the tenant, disconnected the central heating and electricity supply and also cut the telephone line to the property. At a later date, one of the defendant's sons entered the property without permission and began removing the tenant's belongings. The police were called; they provided the tenant with the telephone number of a women's refuge and said she should return to collect her belongings later. Instead she applied to the local authority for homeless assistance and they provided her and her children with bed and breakfast accommodation immediately. The tenant subsequently returned to the property to find that the locks had been changed and that most of her belongings were either missing or damaged.

The tenant was awarded: (a) £10,200 general damages for 102 nights spent in bed and breakfast accommodation assessed at £100 per night; (b) £2,000 in respect of the harassment prior to the eviction; (c) £2,338.32 special damages; (d) £2,000 aggravated damages; and (e) £3,000 exemplary damages.

Abbas v Iqbal June 2009 *Housing law casebook* (5th edn, LAG) Bow County Court, HHJ Redgrave

3.135   The claimant was the assured shorthold tenant of a room. He had shared access to a kitchen and bathroom. He was an elderly man in poor health. In April 2008, the defendant served written notice (which did not comply with HA 1988 s21) on the tenant that he was required to leave the property within two weeks as he required vacant possession to convert the property into separate flats. The tenant did not leave. In May 2008, contractors started work at the property and disconnected the gas and water supply. The tenant was unable to cook his own meals, wash or take his medication. The tenant obtained an injunction ordering the defendant to reinstate the gas and water supply but this order was not complied with and within a week the property was uninhabitable. The tenant was forced to leave and slept in his friend's business premises for three nights before the local authority accommodated him. The tenant's belongings and his furniture were subsequently disposed of by the defendant.

The tenant was awarded, in respect of the unlawful eviction: (a) £750 general damages assessed at £250 per day for the three nights he had to spend in his friend's business premises; (b) £1,950 general damages assessed at £150 per day for the 13 days in which he had to endure the buildings works and been without gas or water; (c) £1,000 general damages as compensation for being forced to leave the property before the end of his tenancy agreement; (d) £10,000 aggravated damages; (e) £7,500 exemplary damages; and (f) £5,494 special damages for his lost possessions.

Salah v Munro July 2009 Legal Action 31, Willesden County Court, HHJ Copley

3.136   The claimant was the assured shorthold tenant of a room. The defendant landlord discovered that the tenant was in receipt of housing benefit and told the tenant that he did not accept tenants who claimed housing benefit and that, if she did not leave, he would forcibly evict her from her room. Shortly afterwards, the tenant returned home one day to find that the locks had been changed and her belongings left in black bags on the driveway. Some of her belongings were missing. She was forced to spend one night in hospital (following an asthma attack), two nights in bed and breakfast accommodation and eight nights on the sofa of a friend before she was re-admitted to the property after she obtained an injunction. She subsequently found out that some of her furniture had been removed and the defendant continued to harass her, which harassment included alleging that she was a prostitute. When the fixed term expired, the defendant disabled the electricity and gas supply. The tenant was forced to stay with a friend for a further 32 nights until, under the threat of a committal application, the defendant restored the electricity and gas supply.

The tenant was awarded: (a) £8,600 general damages for the 43 nights she was away from the property assessed at £200 per night on the basis that the usual range was between £100 to £300 per night; (b) £1,000 special damages; (c) £2,000 aggravated damages; and (d) £2,000 exemplary damages.

Ogle v Bundhoo September 2009 *Legal Action* 33, Mayor's and City of London County Court, HHJ Birtles

3.137   The claimant was the assured shorthold tenant of a room. He fell into arrears and the defendant landlord wrote to him stating that his tenancy had ceased. The tenant telephoned the defendant and said that he would clear the arrears. The defendant said that he wanted him to leave the property. That day, the tenant left the premises to attend the job centre. On his return home, he found that the lock to his room had been changed. The tenant contacted the defendant and asked to be re-admitted. The defendant refused. The tenant sought the advice of the Citizens Advice Bureau who contacted the defendant but he refused to speak to them. The tenant then spent seven nights sleeping rough on the streets and 13 nights in bed and breakfast accommodation before he was re-admitted to the premises after he obtained an interim injunction.

The tenant was awarded: (a) £2,171 general damages for the 13 nights spent in bed and breakfast accommodation assessed at £167 per night; (b) £2,338 general damages for the seven nights that he was street homeless assessed at £334 per night; (c) £1,054 special damages (which included the cost of the bed and breakfast accommodation); (d) £2,300 aggravated damages; and (e) £1,400 exemplary damages.

Anslow v Hayes October 2009 *Housing law casebook* (5th edn, LAG) Manchester County Court, Recorder Yip

3.138   The claimant was the assured shorthold tenant of a room. He failed to pay the rent and, a couple of months after the tenancy had started, the defendant threatened to evict him. One day, the tenant returned home to find that he could not gain access to the property. He contacted the defendant and asked to be admitted. This request was refused. A tenancy relations officer of the local authority contacted the defendant on the tenant's behalf and asked that the tenant be re-admitted. This request was also refused, although the defendant said that the tenant could attend the property to collect his belongings. When the tenant arrived at the property, he found some of his belongings already packed up and only his girlfriend was given access to the property to collect his belongings. He later discovered that some of his belongings had been disposed of. The tenant was forced to spend 73 days in cramped conditions with his girlfriend before he found accommodation of his own.

The tenant was awarded: (a) £7,000 general damages for the 73 days he had spent in cramped accommodation; (b) £2,000 aggravated damages; and (c) £1,000 exemplary damages (being the sum the defendant may have incurred had he evicted the tenant lawfully).

Aricioglu v Kaan October 2009 Housing law casebook (5th edn, LAG) Clerkenwell and Shoreditch County Court, HHJ Mitchell

3.139 The claimant was the assured shorthold tenant of a room. Shortly after moving in, he lost his job and told the defendant landlord that he was unable to pay the rent. The defendant told the tenant he would not accept housing benefit and gave him a week to find work. The defendant was subsequently warned by a tenancy relations officer not to evict the tenant without a court order. Despite this, the tenant was harassed on a daily basis for the next eight days before he was forcibly evicted. During the eviction, he was kicked and pushed down the stairs. He suffered a bruise to the head and a cut on his shoulder. His belongings were then packed and brought down to him. The police declined to intervene because the tenant did not have a tenancy agreement. The tenant was provided with bed and breakfast accommodation by a councillor over the weekend and slept on a sofa on the Monday night. A friend then agreed to accommodate him for a short period. The tenant applied for an injunction granting him re-entry to the room, but decided to withdraw the application after the defendant and a friend threatened him following a court hearing. Twenty-three days after his eviction, the tenant secured alternative accommodation.

The tenant was awarded: (a) £2,875 general damages for 23 days before he found alternative accommodation, assessed at £125 per night; (b) £1,000 general damages for the harassment before the eviction; (c) £1,000 general damages for the assault, and trespass to goods and land; (d) £2,500 aggravated damages; and (e) £2,000 exemplary damages.

Hunt v Hussain October 2009 Legal Action 25, Epsom County Court, HHJ Reid QC

3.140 The claimant was the assured shorthold tenant of a room. He lost his job three months after the tenancy began. When he applied for housing benefit, the defendant landlord told him that he had to leave. An officer of the local authority wrote to the defendant and warned her that she could not evict the tenant without a court order. Despite this warning, the defendant changed the locks while the tenant was away from the property. The tenant was street homeless for 76 days before he was able to find alternative accommodation. During that period, he occasionally stayed with friends but mostly slept in either a broken down car or on the street in his sleeping bag. Both his physical and mental health deteriorated. Four years after the eviction, a psychiatrist gave evidence that the tenant suffered from severe depression, agoraphobia and paranoid ideation, all of which had been exacerbated by the time he had spent living on the streets. The defendant was prosecuted by the local authority, fined £300 and ordered to pay costs of £250.

In the county court proceedings, the tenant was awarded: (a) £8,125 general damages assessed at £125 per day for a period of 65 days (rather than 76 days as the defendant could lawfully have determined the tenancy after 65 days); (b) £100 special damages; and (c) £45,000 general damages for the psychiatric harm.

Ordera v Iqbal January 2010 *Legal Action* 33, Luton County Court, HHJ Kay QC

3.141   The claimant was the assured shorthold tenant of a room in a property with shared facilities. She lived there with her 11-year-old daughter. Throughout the duration of the tenancy, the defendant landlord would often enter the property unannounced and without warning. Then, in January 2008, the defendant served her with an invalid notice of seeking possession. The tenant sought and obtained alternative accommodation. In February 2008, the tenant packed away her belongings and told the defendant that she was leaving to collect her keys for her new accommodation. She was not, however, provided with the keys because she was unable to give her new landlord all of the deposit. The tenant returned to the room. Later that night, the defendant and another man attended the property, removed the tenant's belongings and dragged both the tenant and her daughter from the property. The tenant was forced to spend the night in emergency accommodation and then spent three nights with her sister before she moved into her new accommodation. When the tenant returned to collect her belongings, she found that they had been left in the back garden and they had been damaged by rain.

At trial the court accepted that the tenant had not surrendered her tenancy and that she had been unlawfully evicted. The tenant was awarded: (a) £500 general damages for breach of quiet enjoyment and trespass for the two weeks prior to eviction; (b) £1,000 for the assault and method of eviction; (c) £1,500 aggravated damages; and (d) £1,000 exemplary damages.

Fakhari v Newman June 2010 *Legal Action* 35, Woolwich County Court, DJ Lee

3.142   The claimant landlord granted the defendant tenant an assured shorthold tenancy for a fixed term of one year. Seven months into the tenancy the claimant repeatedly told the tenant, in the form of telephone calls and continuous text messages, that he did not want him to remain as a tenant. The claimant also threatened the tenant and told him that it was no longer safe for him to remain in the property and on occasions attended the property without appointment. The claimant told the police, untruthfully, that the tenant intended to blow up the property. The claimant issued a claim for possession on the basis of rent arrears. The tenant counterclaimed.

The tenant was awarded, in respect of the harassment: (a) £2,000 general damages; and (b) £2,000 exemplary damages.

Keddey v Hughes June 2010 *Legal Action* 36, Sheffield County Court, Recorder Khan

3.143   The claimant was an assured shorthold tenant. In October 2008, the defendant landlord decided to let the property to other tenants. He did not, however, determine the tenancy and the tenant refused to leave. The defendant physically assaulted the tenant before returning later in the day with three other men. The tenant was assaulted again and forcibly removed from the property. The locks, however, were not changed and the tenant returned to the property later that day. The local authority warned the defendant not to evict the tenant without a court order. Later that month, the tenant returned home to find the defendant in the property packing the tenant's belongings into bin liners. Some of his possessions were damaged. At this point the tenant opted to leave the property. He applied to the local authority for homeless assistance and was provided with bed and breakfast accommodation for four weeks before he was granted a non-secure tenancy under HA 1996.

The tenant was awarded: (a) £4,620 general damages assessed at a rate of £165 per night for the 28 days he spent in bed and breakfast accommodation; (b) £1,500 general damages for the assault, harassment and trespass to his property; (c) £1,000 aggravated damages; and (d) £2,000 exemplary damages.

Walsh v Shuangyan June 2010 *Legal Action* 35, Manchester
County Court, DJ Richmond

3.144   The claimant was the assured shorthold tenant of a room in a house
of multiple occupation. He shared the house with six other tenants.
The defendant landlord disconnected the boiler and electricity supply,
which caused the other tenants to leave the property. After the tenant
declined to leave, the defendant subjected him to harassment and
threats. On one occasion, he was physically assaulted by the defendant's father and on another was forced to barricade his room after the
defendant and her father stayed the night at the property. Eventually,
the tenant returned home one evening to find that the locks had been
changed. Some of his possessions had been put in bin bags outside
the property but the majority remained inside his room. A tenancy
relations officer contacted the defendant and told her that she must
re-admit the tenant; she refused to do so. The tenant subsequently
obtained an injunction requiring the defendant to re-admit him to the
property but the defendant still refused to do so which resulted in her
being committed to prison for 28 days. The tenant was forced to stay
with various friends and families for 30 days (sleeping on their sofas)
until he obtained alternative accommodation. During this period, he
developed a bad back and was forced to miss work on occasions.

The tenant was awarded: (a) £6,000 general damages assessed at
£200 per night for the 30 days spent sleeping on sofas; (b) £2,000 for
the harassment before the eviction; (c) £5,570 special damages; (d)
£4,000 aggravated damages; and (e) £1,500 exemplary damages.

Schuchard v Fu June 2010 *Legal Action* 36, Brentford County
Court, DJ Plaskow

3.145   The claimant was the assured shorthold tenant of a room in a house
of multiple occupation. The defendant landlord wrote to each tenant
of the property and asked that they give up possession as she intended
to re-develop the property. She did not serve a HA 1988 s21 notice on
the tenant. When the tenant did not leave, the defendant sent him
a letter which demanded that he leave the following day because he
owed arrears of rent. The following day, when the tenant was away
from the property, the defendant changed the locks to the front door.
That evening, the tenant returned and was unable to gain access. All
of his belongings remained in his room. The following day, a tenancy
relations officer contacted the defendant and asked that she re-admit
the tenant, but she refused to do so. The tenant then instructed solicitors who wrote to the defendant and demanded that she re-admit the

tenant to the property which she refused to do. The local authority initially refused to accommodate the tenant and he was street homeless for 120 days. He was subsequently accommodated by the local authority for 77 days before they decided that they did not owe him a duty under National Assistance Act 1948 s21. The tenant was forced to spend the next 35 days, until trial, sleeping on a friend's floor.

The tenant was awarded: (a) £24,000 general and aggravated damages assessed at £200 per night for the 120 days when the tenant was street homeless; (b) £2,000 general damages for the remaining 77 days he was accommodated by the local authority; (c) £4,375 general damages and aggravated damages for the period he slept on his friend's floor assessed at £125 per night; and (d) £1,750 exemplary damages.

Naughton v Whittle & Chief Constable of Greater Manchester Police July 2010 Legal Action 29, Manchester County Court, HHJ Morgan

3.146   The claimant was an assured shorthold tenant. The first defendant was the tenant's landlord. He told the tenant that he wanted him to leave the property. When the tenant refused to do so, the first defendant's brother threatened the tenant and the first defendant assaulted the tenant's girlfriend. The first defendant then changed the locks. The police were called but arrested the tenant for a breach of the peace. The tenant was away from the property for 28 days.

The second defendant agreed, in an out of court settlement, to pay the tenant £2,500 for the wrongful arrest and trespass to land. At trial, the first defendant was ordered to pay the tenant: (a) £7,700 general damages assessed at £275 per day; and (b) £1,500 aggravated damages.

Shyngle v Simmons July 2010 Legal Action 29, Slough County Court

3.147   The claimant was an assured shorthold tenant. The tenant withheld rent from the defendant landlord because of a dispute over payment of the utility bills. One day, he returned home to find that the locks had been tampered with and that he was unable to gain access. The tenant obtained an injunction which required that the defendant re-admit the tenant to the property. The injunction, however, could not be enforced because the defendant's mortgage lender had taken possession of the property in the interim.

The tenant was awarded: (a) £5,075 general damages for 29 nights assessed at £175 per night; and (b) £1,000 aggravated damages.

Boyle v Musso March 2011 *Legal Action* 27, Bristol County Court, DJ Watson

3.148   The claimant was an assured shorthold tenant. The tenant withheld rent following a flood to the property. The defendant landlord and another man attended the property and assaulted the tenant. The tenant was punched and stamped on when he fell to the floor. The tenant was forced to leave the property without his belongings. He spent 22 nights with friends, in bed and breakfast accommodation and hostels before he found alternative accommodation. The defendant was subsequently convicted of assault occasioning actual bodily harm.

The tenant was awarded: (a) £4,000 general damages for the 22 nights in below standard accommodation; (b) £15,000 general damages for the assault; (c) £750 special damages for the loss of his belongings; and (d) £2,000 exemplary damages.

Deelah v Rehman March 2011 *Housing law casebook* (5th edn, LAG) Clerkenwell & Shoreditch County Court, DJ Millard

3.149   The claimant was the assured shorthold tenant of a room and had shared access to a kitchen and bathroom. He lived in the room with his wife and two sons aged nine and 16. In June 2010, the defendant landlord, accompanied by a friend, asked the tenant to leave and threatened to change the locks if his family did not do so. The tenant refused to leave and, during the row, the defendant twisted his arm. A month later, the tenant's wife returned home to find that the locks had been changed. The defendant threatened to kill the tenant's son with a crowbar after he had climbed over a fence to try and gain access. As the family were ineligible for assistance under HA 1996 Part 7, they were forced to sleep in a friend's living room for four nights until the tenant obtained an injunction and secured re-entry to the property. During that period the children missed school. The defendant continued to harass the tenant and his family after they were re-admitted.

The tenant was awarded: (a) £1,000 general damages for the four days he spent away from the property assessed at £250 per night; (b) £1,500 general damages for the harassment before and after the eviction; (c) £1,500 aggravated damages; and (d) £2,500 exemplary damages.

Dada v Adeyeye March 2012 *Legal Action* 23, Central London County Court, HHJ Gerald

3.150 The claimant was an assured shorthold tenant of a room in a shared house. The defendant landlord began to harass him when he fell behind with his rent after losing his job. The defendant's adult son and an unknown man threatened to kill the tenant. The tenant's solicitors warned the defendant not to harass or unlawfully evict the tenant, despite which the defendant changed the locks. The tenant was street homeless for 13 nights and spent 53 weeks in temporary accommodation provided by the local authority. He became depressed.

The tenant was awarded: (a) £1,500 general damages for the harassment and trespass; (b) £2,600 for the 13 nights he was street homeless; (c) £10,000 for the period spent in temporary accommodation; (d) £2,000 exemplary damages; and (e) £570 special damages.

Aiyedogbon v Best Move Estate Agent Ltd June 2012 *Legal Action* 35, Clerkenwell and Shoreditch County Court, DJ Cooper

3.151 The claimant was the assured shorthold tenant of a flat. The defendant landlords alleged that the tenant was in arrears of rent and threatened to change the locks. The tenant warned them not to do so and said that he would be away for a short period of time. In his absence, the defendants did change the locks. The tenant obtained an injunction and was readmitted. He discovered that some of his property was damaged and missing, his front door had been broken and could not be locked and he had to stay in a hotel for 20 nights until he could get it repaired.

The tenant was awarded: (a) £3,800 general damages for the 20 nights spent in hotel accommodation assessed at £190 per night; (b) £1,340 general damages for the distress caused by the unlawful eviction; (c) £1,800 aggravated damages; (d) £1,500 exemplary damages; and (e) £1,603 special damages for the cost of the hotel accommodation and his lost belongings.

Henson v Blackwood and Blackwood August 2012 *Legal Action* 26, Mayor's and City of London Court, HHJ Birtles

3.152 The claimant was the assured shorthold tenant of a flat. The defendant landlords served her with a s21 notice. The day before the notice expired, one of the defendants (Mr Blackwood) attended the flat. He told the tenant that she had to leave the following day and became aggressive. The following day, the tenant returned to the flat to find that the supply of gas, electricity and water had been disconnected. Some of her possessions were also missing. She decided to spend the night at a friend's flat. The following day, she found that the locks to her flat had been changed and went back to her friend's flat. Two days later, the tenant's solicitors wrote to the defendants and warned them that they had unlawfully evicted her. The defendants did not reply and the tenant issued a claim for an injunction to re-admit her to the flat and for the utilities to be re-connected. The injunction was granted. The defendants initially refused to re-admit the tenant to the flat as they contended that the flat had been re-let. They had not, however, re-let the flat and, four days after she had been evicted, the tenant was re-admitted. On returning, she found that her property had been put in bin bags in the communal hallway and her food had been disposed of. She also received a telephone call from Mr Blackwood who told her that as she had involved other people he would be sending 'more people' round. Accordingly, the tenant decided to stay with her mother for a week. On returning to the flat, she continued to receive nuisance telephone calls and was forced to change her telephone number. One evening, Mr Blackwood's brother let himself into the property and attempted to assault the tenant while she was in her underclothes; on another occasion, she found her lock had been glued. She eventually chose to leave the flat voluntarily.

The tenant was awarded: (a) £2,000 general damages for the harassment prior to the eviction; (b) £1,000 general damages for the eviction and three nights spent with her friend; (c) £2,000 general damages for the harassment after the eviction; (d) £2,000 aggravated damages; and (e) £2,000 exemplary damages.

Hussain v Mir September 2012 *Legal Action* 20, Clerkenwell and Shoreditch County Court, DJ Stary

3.153   The claimant was the assured shorthold tenant of a room. He shared the house with six other tenants. The defendant landlord told the claimant and the other tenants that they had to move out immediately because his letting agent had failed to give him the rent they had paid. Some of the tenants left the following day. The claimant remained in occupation with two of the other tenants. Subsequently, the defendant, accompanied by his letting agent, changed the locks. When the claimant tried to regain access, the defendant pushed him away. Although the claimant called the police three times, the letting agent pushed him to the floor and kicked him in the back and chest.

The claimant suffered soft tissue injuries to his neck and back and a grazed elbow. He was taken to hospital. After leaving hospital, the claimant spent one night staying with one of the other tenants in the house and 29 nights on a friend's floor. He was subsequently provided with hostel accommodation where he remained for five months. Six weeks after the eviction, the defendant marketed the property for a tenancy of the whole building.

The tenant was awarded: (a) £1,000 general damages for the assault; (b) £11,360 general damages assessed at £300 per night for the 29 days spent on a friend's floor and £190 per night restricted to 14 nights he spent in the hostel, because he was under an obligation to mitigate his losses; (c) £2,000 aggravated damages; and (d) £1,800 exemplary damages.

Oyzen v Bell-Gam September 2012 *Legal Action* 21, Croydon County Court, DJ Major

3.154 The claimant was the assured shorthold tenant of a flat. He could not access the part of the building where the payment meters for gas and electricity were and, accordingly, was without both for the first two days of his letting. The defendant then put money into the meters but, after the tenant connected his washing machine, it sparked and the fire brigade disconnected the electricity supply the next day. The following day, on discovering this, the defendant shouted at the tenant, accused him of wrecking the flat and told him to leave immediately. The tenant was subsequently street homeless for seven weeks and spent three weeks staying in a hostel.

The tenant was awarded: (a) £14,000 general damages assessed at a daily rate of £200 for 70 days; (b) £2,000 aggravated damages; and (c) £1,500 exemplary damages.

Starting county court proceedings

continued

Application notice for interim injunction

Draft order

Witness statement

Introduction

4.1 This chapter describes the steps necessary to start civil proceedings in the county court. In particular, the chapter concentrates on how to get the most immediate remedy that is likely to be needed in cases of harassment or unlawful eviction, ie a 'without notice interim injunction'. Examples are offered of the documents required to apply for a without notice interim injunction in an unlawful eviction claim (see below from para 4.61).

4.2 Civil proceedings are governed by the rules set out in the Civil Procedure Rules (CPR). The CPR is a 'procedural code with the overriding objective of enabling the court to deal with cases justly'.[1] As far as possible, advisers should ensure that they always comply with the rules. Minor deviations, however, are permitted; nor does failure to comply with the CPR invalidate any step in proceedings (unless the court so orders) and the court has power to remedy any defect.[2]

4.3 There are two ways of commencing proceedings: under CPR Part 7 or CPR Part 8. Part 8 is not appropriate where there is a dispute of fact between the parties.[3] Accordingly, claims involving harassment or unlawful eviction are usually commenced under CPR Part 7. The person who brings a claim is called a 'claimant' and the person against whom the claim is brought is the 'defendant'.

Injunctions – an overview

4.4 The primary concern of a victim of harassment is to ensure that the harassment ceases. An evicted occupier usually wants to get back into his or her home as soon as possible.

4.5 As already noted, this can be achieved by an interim injunction (see chapter 3). Such an application can be made without notice to the defendant, where the circumstances are urgent or where alerting the defendant to the application would defeat its aim, for example where there is a risk of reprisals if papers are served and there is no injunction in place to protect the victim.[4] Both circuit judges and district judges have the jurisdiction to make such an order.[5]

---

1 CPR 1.1(1).
2 CPR 3.10.
3 CPR 8.1(2).
4 CPR 25.3(3).
5 CPR 2.4.

4.6   Given that the claimant is without a home, the courts are usually prepared to hear an application in an unlawful eviction case without notice. In more general harassment cases, the courts may be prepared to hear the application without notice if the situation is sufficiently urgent, for example, where violence is likely to occur in the near future.

4.7   The most common reason for refusing to hear an application without notice is that the claimant has delayed before making the application. The claimant's witness statement filed in support of the application should explain any reason for any delay, for example, inability to obtain advice over a weekend, illness or particular vulnerability. In cases where the claimant is, or will be, street homeless, the court is likely to hear the matter unless there has been significant delay in making the application. If the judge refuses to grant the injunction, the application will be adjourned to allow notice to be given to the defendant rather than dismissed. In cases where it is beneficial or necessary to return the matter to court as soon as possible, the court can be asked to abridge time for service so that the usual three days' notice[6] is not required.[7]

4.8   Usually, proceedings should be commenced before the application for an interim injunction is made. The court does, however, have the power to hear the application beforehand,[8] ie, where there is insufficient time, but if this happens, the court will usually require the proceedings to be properly commenced the following day.[9]

4.9   If the judge makes an order without notice, the court must fix a date for a further hearing at which the defendant can be present.[10] This second hearing is called the 'return date' and is usually held a few days after the without notice hearing.

4.10   Whether the injunction ought to continue until the trial is not decided by resolving the factual disputes between the parties. It is, rather, a question of where the balance of justice between the parties lies.[11] If the order is continued, the court usually orders that it remain in force until the trial or further order.

4.11   After an injunction has been granted, it is necessary to serve the order on the defendant; the order will have no effect until served.

---

6   CPR.23.7(1)(b).
7   CPR 23.7(4).
8   CPR 25.2(1)(a).
9   CPR Part 25 PD 25A 5.1(4), (5).
10 CPR Part 25 PD 25 5.1(3).
11 See *American Cyanamid Co v Ethicon Ltd* [1975] AC 396, HL; *Francome v Mirror Group Newspapers* [1984] 1 WLR 892, CA and chapter 3.

This is best done by the use of a professional process server. If more than one person is subject to the injunction, they must each be served with their own separate copies. A certificate of service should be completed by the person who served the order in order to prove that the defendant has been served. Without this evidence, a court will be unable to commit the defendant for contempt of court or – in the event that the defendant fails to attend court for the return date – make a final order.

4.12 The order should be served together with all documents which supported the application. If the landlord is evading service, so that it proves impossible to serve the order, it is possible to apply to the judge for an order allowing service by a substituted method[12] or dispensing with service.[13] An application to dispense with service can itself be made without notice.[14]

Undertakings

4.13 At the return date, it will be unnecessary to have a full hearing if the defendant is willing to submit to the terms of the injunction. In this case, the appropriate course is for the defendant to give an 'undertaking' in the same terms as those sought under the injunction. A court cannot make someone give an undertaking but if the defendant does not do so, there will have to be a hearing into the merits of the application, even if the defendant does not oppose it.

4.14 By giving an undertaking, the defendant does not make any admission as to the truth of any events which are alleged to have taken place. The defendant is giving a solemn promise to do, or restrain from doing, certain acts in the future. In a harassment case which does not involve unlawful eviction, the defendant should usually give such undertakings, as he or she is only promising not to do acts which are in any event unlawful. Advisers dealing with unrepresented defendants may find it useful to emphasise this, as many people feel that by giving an undertaking they are making some form of admission.

4.15 An undertaking should be made on the appropriate court form[15] and should set out precisely what the defendant is promising to do or not to do.

---

12 CPR 6.15.
13 CPR 6.9(1).
14 CPR 6.9(2).
15 N117; this is readily available from the court office.

Committal proceedings

4.16   A person who disobeys an order which has been served, or who has breached an undertaking, may be committed to prison for contempt of court, ie for refusing to obey a court order. The committal procedure[16] must be followed carefully, as the court is reluctant to waive any irregularity where a person's liberty is at stake.

4.17   Before applying to commit the defendant, advisers must check that the court has endorsed the order with a penal notice (a formal warning to the recipient of the order that if it is not obeyed imprisonment may result). A failure to include the correct penal order will not, however, necessarily prevent the court from committing the defendant to prison, provided it is otherwise made clear that the defendant is at risk of being sent to prison if he or she breaches the order.[17] The terms of the order should be carefully scrutinised to ensure that the act which the landlord has done, or failed to do, is in fact in breach of the terms of the order. (This will be straightforward enough if what is required is re-admission.)

4.18   If the order drawn up by the court inaccurately records the order, an application may be made to cure the defect under what is known as 'the slip rule'.[18] The amended order must, however, then be served personally on the person who is subject to the injunction, giving him or her an opportunity to comply before any question of committal recurs.

4.19   An application to commit is made by an application notice.[19] The notice must identify what parts of the injunction have been broken, give details of the way in which the breaches have happened and generally set out sufficient information to show all the allegations being made against the person sought to be committed.[20]

4.20   The application must be supported by an affidavit[21] from the claimant setting out the facts relied on. Two other affidavits are necessary: one to show that the original order was served, the other to show that the defendant was served with the notice to commit and the affidavit in support.

4.21   If the defendant is not legally represented at the committal hearing, the judge should warn him or her about the seriousness of the

16   Set out in CPR Sch 2 CCR Ord 29 r1.
17   *Jolly v Hull* [2000] 2 FLR 69, CA.
18   CPR 40.12; the application can be made without notice.
19   CPR Sch 2 CCR 29 r1(4); form N244.
20   CPR Sch 2 CCR 29 r1(4A).
21   A witness statement sworn on oath or affirmed.

proceedings and an adjournment may be allowed for legal advice to be taken. Many judges prefer to adjourn the committal application to the trial of the action. On the hearing of the committal application, the standard of proof is higher than for other civil proceedings, ie, the allegations have to be proved beyond reasonable doubt rather than on the balance of probability.

4.22   In exceptional circumstances, an application for committal can be made without notice to the defendant. Such a course should be adopted only where no alternative is open to protect the claimant's position and to uphold the order of the court.[22]

4.23   The court takes a very serious view of any breach of an order, unless there is a good reason for non-compliance. This is particularly so where the order is to re-admit the occupier, as the consequences for someone who has been unlawfully evicted are serious.

4.24   In *Saxby v McKinley*,[23] a landlord unlawfully evicted his tenants. He ignored a warning from their solicitor that he was not allowed to do this and then deliberately evaded service of an order of a without notice interim injunction to re-admit the tenants. Bearing in mind the consequences to the tenants of being kept out of the property and the cynical disregard for the court displayed by the landlord, the Court of Appeal upheld the imposition of an immediate, 28-day custodial sentence as fully justified.

Starting civil proceedings

4.25   Against this background, the steps necessary to launch civil proceedings are now considered in more detail, as follows:

a) taking a statement;
b) applying for public funding;
c) warning the court;
d) drafting forms;
e) starting proceedings in the court;
f) getting an interim order;
g) serving the order; and
h) after service.

22 *Wright v Jess* [1987] 1 WLR 1076, CA.
23 (1996) 29 HLR 569, CA.

Taking a statement

4.26 When a client comes to the office, it is necessary to take a statement which identifies the causes of action which may be available (chapter 2) and the remedies to which the client may be entitled (chapter 3).

4.27 In unlawful eviction cases, it is necessary to identify:

a) the premises – the address; room, flat or house; whether facilities were shared with others; who else lived there;

b) the status of the occupier – tenancy or licence; assured, assured shorthold or protected tenancy;

c) details of the tenancy or licence – when it began, whether there is a written agreement, the amount of the rent, whether it is weekly, monthly or fixed-term, whether notice has been given;

d) the landlord's name (and the names of any other persons involved);

e) what has been done, by whom, to whom and when;

f) the effect on the occupier – distress, personal injury, no cooking facilities, no heating, nowhere to sleep, how many people affected (such as family, flatmates); property damaged or taken;

g) evidence of occupation – rent book, tenancy agreement, letters from the housing benefit department, bills in the occupier's name, etc (which, if available, should be copied and exhibited to the witness statement).

4.28 In harassment cases, it is necessary to identify:

a) the premises – the address; room, flat or house; whether facilities were shared with others; who else lived there;

b) the status of the occupier (whether or not the claim is between landlord and tenant) – this is particularly relevant if the tort relied on requires the claimant to have possession of land, for example, nuisance;

c) the defendant's name (and the names of any other persons involved);

d) what has been done, by whom, to whom and when;

e) the effect on the occupier – for example, distress, personal injury, property damaged or taken.

4.29 At this stage, it may be sensible to try to contact the defendant, personally or by telephone, or to contact the tenancy relations officer. This is to make sure that the dispute has not arisen through misunderstanding, for example, because the landlord thought that the tenant had left the property, or because the landlord was wholly unaware of the occupier's rights. If public funding is being sought, advisers are usually required to make contact with the landlord, managing agent or defendant.[24]

4.30 If the landlord has made it clear that he or she has no intention of allowing the tenant back in, his or her reactions can be set out in a witness statement to show that an injunction is justified. Any telephone conversations should be confirmed by letter, which should include the suggestion that the defendant seek independent advice.

Public funding

4.31 It is not possible to deal with public funding in detail,[25] but some general points may be made.

4.32 Presently, legal representation[26] under the Community Legal Service scheme may be available for litigants in harassment and unlawful eviction cases, subject to financial eligibility and the merits of the case. On 1 May 2012, the Legal Aid, Sentencing and Punishment of Offenders Act (LASPO) 2012 was passed. Generally, the Act, when brought into force, will reduce the availability of legal aid. Legal representation, however, will remain available for harassment and unlawful eviction cases, albeit that funding will not be available in harassment cases unless an injunction is sought against the perpetrator.[27] The Act has abolished the Legal Services Commission and the Lord Chancellor will assume responsibility for the provision of public funding.

4.33 Until the Legal Services Commission is abolished, however, the guidance set out below remains in force.

4.34 The Legal Services Commission has made guidance available as to when public funding is available in unlawful eviction claims and claims against a landlord for harassment.[28]

4.35 Legal representation will be refused if the conduct complained of is not recent and is unlikely to be repeated, or where other steps would be more appropriate.[29]

---

24 See below, para 4.39.
25 See *Legal Services Commission manual* for full details.
26 The expression in the scheme used to denote work provided by a solicitor under a public funding certificate.
27 LASPO 2012 Sch 1 paras 27(6) and 31(1)(a).
28 *Funding code,* para.19.9.
29 The examples given include referral to the tenancy relations officer followed by a prosecution by the local authority.

4.36   Legal representation is likely to be granted, however, where the complainant can show that he or she has a claim under one of the causes of action set out in chapter 2 and that he or she has at least moderate prospects of obtaining one or more of the following remedies:

a) re-admission to the premises;
b) recovery of any personal possessions;
c) damages; or
d) an injunction.

4.37   If only re-admission is sought, legal representation may be refused if the nature and length of the tenancy are such that the order would only last for a short period of time.

4.38   If criminal proceedings are being taken in the magistrates' court, for example, under PEA 1977 or PHA 1997, legal representation will be refused unless some separate benefit from civil proceedings can be shown, although it will not uncommonly be possible to do this.[30]

4.39   Before legal representation is granted, some contact must be made with the defendant with a view to resolving matters without the need for proceedings. No contact is required, however, if the matter is urgent, such as cases where the claimant is homeless, or the situation is so serious that contact would be inappropriate, for example, if to do so would only increase the likelihood of violence.

4.40   Where the primary remedy sought is an injunction or re-admission to the property, legal representation may be refused unless the matter has first been reported to the tenancy relations officer although – again – this may not be so if the urgency of the situation justifies the omission to do so.

Warning the court

4.41   If a without notice application for an interim injunction is to be made, the county court must be warned in advance to ensure that there is a judge available to hear the application. This is particularly important if it is likely that it will not be possible to arrive at court before 4.00 pm. District judges, as well as circuit judges, can grant injunctions, however, so that, as long as the court has been forewarned, it should always be possible for a judge to be made available.

---

30 The remedies available in civil proceedings are far wider than those in criminal proceedings. The criminal courts cannot order re-admission to the premises and their powers to award compensation are more restricted.

Drafting documents

4.42　To commence proceedings, the following documents are required:

　　　a) claim form (form N1); and
　　　b) particulars of claim.

4.43　If an application for an interim injunction is also to be made, the following additional documents are required:

　　　a) application notice (form N16A);
　　　b) witness statement; and
　　　c) draft order (form N16).

4.44　Three copies of all the documents are required, one for each side and one for the court. Guidance on drafting these documents and examples of some of them appear at the end of this chapter from para 4.61 onwards.

Starting the proceedings at the court

4.45　In unlawful eviction and harassment cases there is no restriction on which county court may be used. Obviously, however, the claimant will, for convenience, wish to use his or her local court.

4.46　　At the court office, an issue fee must be paid.[31] The claim is then allotted a claim number. This is stamped on all the documents referred to above and is used in all future documents. The first two letters will indicate the county court, for example, WT is Wandsworth County Court, LB is Lambeth County Court. If it is late in the day and not possible to issue the claim, the court has the power to hear the application but will insist on the proceedings being issued on the following day.[32]

Obtaining a 'without notice' order

4.47　The actual hearing is usually very brief and in private. The judge reads the documents (usually before the hearing). As the documents should show an entitlement to the injunction, the only issues which usually arise are delay, the precise wording of the order and the return date. The judge may also ask the occupier some questions either informally or on oath.

31　Fees vary depending on the size of the claim and are subject to frequent change.
32　CPR Part 25 PD 25A 5.1(4), (5).

4.48   If an order is granted by the judge, it will remain in force until the return date, which will be specified by the judge. If an order is not made, the judge will fix a return date for the injunction to be heard with the other side present.

Serving the order

4.49   For it to be effective, an order must be served on the landlord or other person subject to the injunction. Where there is more than one defendant, the order must be served on each of them. It is necessary to obtain enough copies of the order so that one can be served on each defendant and one retained for further reference by the applicant.

4.50   In urgent cases, the court office usually types the order at once, or within a matter of hours. Although service can be effected by the court (on payment of an additional fee), this is unlikely to be of assistance in an urgent case because it may take several days before it happens. Accordingly, a process server should be used. Advisers should warn the process server in advance of the hearing.

After service

4.51   Unless there is to be an application for committal, the next stage is the hearing on the return date. At this, the other side is given an opportunity to be heard and to argue that the injunction should not be continued until trial. If the defendant is unwilling to give an undertaking, the application will be heard and determined according to the principles considered in chapter 3.[33]

4.52   At the return date, the judge will issue directions, ie, the timetable for the procedure to be adopted before the trial. It is not possible in this book to describe county court procedure in detail. The order will, however, usually provide for the following steps:

a) allocation of the claim to a track;[34]

b) the defendant to file a defence (an answer to the particulars of claim);

c) both parties to provide disclosure of their documents by list;[35]

---

33 See above, paras 3.11–3.22

34 See above, paras 2.3–2.10.

35 Disclosure is the process by which the parties provide each other with all documentation relevant to the case. This does not include communications between adviser and client. It is initially done by a list of the documents and then an opportunity is given to look at the documents on the list and obtain copies.

d) the parties to exchange witness statements of the facts to be relied on at trial;

e) the parties to exchange (or agree) expert evidence on which they intend to rely (eg in a case involving damages under Housing Act (HA) 1988 s28, or general damages for loss of right of occupation);[36]

f) a date to be fixed for the trial, or that the parties file 'listing questionnaires' by a certain date (documents which show whether the parties have complied with the directions and dates on which the trial should not be held because witnesses are unavailable).

4.53 Alternatively, the judge may simply order that the defendant file a defence. Once this is done, the court sends out 'allocation questionnaires', which the parties must complete and return to the court. The district judge then reads the questionnaires and decides to which track the claim should be allocated and makes directions at that stage, or he or she may order that there is a case management conference at which the directions can be made.

4.54 The directions order should contain specific dates by which each of these steps must be completed. Advisers should note the importance of ensuring that both parties comply with the directions. If it is clear that the claimant needs extra time, an application should be made to the court to extend time for compliance with the order.[37] Conversely, if the defendant fails to comply with a direction, it is possible to apply to the court for 'an unless order', ie, an order that unless the defendant complies within a specified time, he or she will not be allowed to defend the action at all.[38]

4.55 If the defendant fails to comply with the order, an application can be made to debar him or her from defending the action. The matter can then be set down for an assessment of damages. The defendant will not be able to dispute liability although he or she can still challenge the amount of the compensation sought.

The forms used

4.56 No example is provided of a claim form (form N1) because it is a simple document, the completion of which is straightforward. The parties' names need to be inserted. Information is also set out which

---

36 See above, paras 3.79–3.80.
37 The court has the power to extend time under CPR 3.1(2).
38 The power to attach conditions to an order is set in CPR 3.1(3).

assists the court in allocation of the claim. Brief details of the claim are required, for example, 'claim for damages and an injunction in a case of unlawful eviction and harassment of a residential tenant'.

4.57   There is space for an estimate of the value of the claim. This need not be completed if the claim is for unlawful eviction or harassment by a landlord.[39]

4.58   Form N1 also includes space for the particulars of claim to be set out but the space provided is small and it is far more usual to insert the words 'see particulars of claim attached' and to set out the particulars of claim in a separate document.

Statement of truth

4.59   The claim form, particulars of claim, witness statement and application notice must all contain a statement of truth. If the document is signed by the claimant, the standard form is 'I believe that the facts stated in this [insert the type of document] are true'. A solicitor may sign the statement of truth on the claimant's behalf, in which case the statement commences 'The claimant believes ...'.

4.60   If a person without an honest belief in its truth makes a false statement in a document verified with a statement of truth, proceedings may be brought for contempt of court.[40] While this is rare, it serves to emphasise the importance of ensuring that the claimant fully understands what has been written on his or her behalf in all the documents, in particular, the witness statement and the particulars of claim. First, there is a duty not to mislead the court. Second, inconsistencies between the documents and the claimant's subsequent evidence provide ammunition for cross-examination at trial which may seriously undermine the witness's credibility.

Example documents

4.61   The following documents are examples of documents required. They are not intended to lay down detailed or exhaustive rules on drafting. In particular, they are not reproductions of the court forms, which must always be used where applicable. (There is no court form for particulars of claim or witness statements.) All that has been omitted, however, are marginal notes to assist completion of the forms and certain formal parts, which are completed by the court clerk.

39 See above, para 2.6.
40 CPR 32.14.

4.62   Examples are offered of:

a) particulars of claim;
b) application notice;
c) draft order; and
d) witness statement.

4.63   There are three sets of particulars of claim. The first is for an unlaw-ful eviction claim against an assured shorthold tenant; the second, for an unlawful eviction claim against a secure tenant. The third is for a claim in harassment. The other example documents all relate to the first unlawful eviction claim but it will readily be observed how other documents can be adapted to other situations.

PARTICULARS OF CLAIM (1)
UNLAWFUL EVICTION OF ASSURED SHORTHOLD TENANT

<u>IN THE ANYTOWN COUNTY COURT</u>

<u>Claim No (see note 1)</u>

B E T W E E N:

(1) JANE FIELDS
(2) JOHN JONES

Claimants

-and-

WARDEN DRANE

Defendant

PARTICULARS OF CLAIM

1   At all material times the claimants have been the joint assured shorthold tenants of the premises known as 16A Maxwell Square, Anytown AT16 1AB ('the flat'). The defendant is their landlord. (see note 2)

2   The premises are a self-contained one-bedroomed flat situated in the basement of a terraced house. The defendant is the freehold owner of the house.

3   The said assured shorthold tenancy commenced on 19 January 2011 and was for a fixed term of 12 months at a monthly rent of £700. On its expiry, it became a statutory monthly periodic tenancy. It is evidenced by a written tenancy agreement. As a term of the agreement, the claimants paid a deposit of £700 to the defendant. (see note 3)

4   It is an implied term of the tenancy that the defendant would allow the claimants quiet enjoyment of the flat. (see note 4)

5   By reason of the matters hereinafter set out, the defendant has been in breach of the said term and has trespassed to the claimants' flat, property and persons, and has pursued a course of conduct which he knew amounted to harassment of the claimants in breach of s1 of the Protection from Harassment Act 1997.

PARTICULARS (see note 5)

(i)   On 25 January 2012, during a telephone conversation, the defendant told the first claimant that the claimants had to leave the flat. When the first claimant told the defendant that the claimants were legally entitled to remain in the premises until evicted by court order, the defendant became angry and swore at the first claimant. He told the first claimant that he was coming round to 'sort the matter out'.

(ii) At about 8 pm on the same day, the defendant attended the flat. The first claimant explained to the defendant that the claimants were in financial difficulties but that they hoped to pay the rent arrears soon. The defendant became extremely angry and swore at the first claimant. He threatened the first claimant and said that he 'knew people'. The defendant refused to leave the premises when asked to do so.

(iii) On 28 January 2012, the defendant telephoned the first claimant in response to a letter from the claimants' solicitors informing him of the claimants' rights. He told her that the claimants had to leave 'or else'.

(iv) On approximately ten occasions between 28 January 2012 and 15 March 2012, the defendant telephoned the claimants. Some of the telephone calls were made in the early hours of the morning when the claimants were asleep. On the first occasion, the defendant said 'As you sow so shall you reap'. On the subsequent occasions, the defendant did not say anything but put the telephone down without speaking. The defendant was identifiable because his number was displayed on the claimants' phone. The claimants felt threatened by the telephone calls.

(v) On 20 March 2012, the defendant in the company of two other men entered the flat by breaking down the front door. They packed the claimants' belongings into black bin liners. One of the men punched the second defendant in the face. The claimants were in fear of a further assault and left the flat.

(vi) On their return to the flat, the claimants were unable to secure entry because the locks had been changed. The claimants found that their possessions had been placed outside the flat. Some items were missing.

6 By reason of the matters aforesaid the claimants have suffered loss, damage, distress, discomfort and inconvenience.

PARTICULARS OF GENERAL DAMAGES (see note 6)

(a) The claimants were obliged to sleep on a friend's floor for the night of 20 to 21 March 2012.

(b) The claimants were distressed and frightened by the defendant's conduct. The second claimant had to attend hospital because of the blow to his face. His face was severely bruised and he was prescribed pain-killers.

PARTICULARS OF SPECIAL DAMAGES (see note 7)

The following items have not been returned to the claimants:
(a) flat-screen television £500
(b) laptop computer £400
(c) various items of jewellery £380

7 The claimants claim to be entitled to exemplary and/or aggravated damages. (see note 8)

PARTICULARS

(i) The defendant was warned of the illegality of his actions by a letter from the claimants' solicitors dated 28 January 2012. Despite the warning, and in cynical disregard of the claimants' legal rights, the defendant acted in a way calculated to obtain vacant possession without incurring the cost of bringing a claim for possession in the courts. In the circumstances, the defendant has sought to profit from his own unlawful acts and the claimant is entitled to exemplary damages.

(ii) The manner of the eviction was very distressing and demeaning to the claimants. In the circumstances, the claimants claim aggravated damages.

8   Further or in the alternative, the defendant has failed to protect the claimants' deposit and/or in the event that the deposit has been protected has failed to provide the claimants with the prescribed information and the claimant accordingly seeks the return of the deposit and the sum of £2,100.

9   The claimants claim to be entitled to interest on such damages as the court may award in respect of their claim pursuant to s69 of the County Courts Act 1984, at such rate and for such period as the court thinks fit. (see note 10)

AND the claimants claim: (see note 11)

(1) An injunction requiring the defendant forthwith to re-admit the claimants to the flat and restraining the defendant by himself, his servants or agents, or otherwise from further interfering with the claimants' quiet enjoyment of the flat or further trespassing on the claimants' premises, persons or goods, or in any way harassing the claimants;

(2) An order for the delivery up of their property or special damages in the sum of £1,280.

(3) An order that the defendant return the claimants' deposits of £700 and pay the sum of £2,100.

(4) Damages including general, special, aggravated and exemplary damages;

(5) Interest;

(6) Costs.

The claimants believe that the facts set out in these particulars of claim are true. (see note 12)

Signed ....

Dated: 22 March 2012

....

Leo and Nevil
242–4 Nashville Road, Anytown AT5 6UN
Solicitors for the Claimant
who will accept service at this address

PARTICULARS OF CLAIM (2)
UNLAWFUL EVICTION OF SECURE TENANT

IN THE ANYTOWN COUNTY COURT

Claim No (see note 1)

B E T W E E N:

JOHN SMITH

Claimant

-and-

ANYTOWN DISTRICT COUNCIL

Defendant

PARTICULARS OF CLAIM

1   At all material times the claimant has been the secure weekly periodic tenant of a one-bedroom flat situated at 16c Grove Park, Anytown AT7 4XY ('the flat'). The defendant is his landlord. (see note 2)

2   The said secure tenancy commenced on 13 May 1995.

3   On 7 July 2011, the claimant's mother became seriously ill.

4   On 12 July 2011, the claimant left the flat and went to stay with his mother in Newtown so as to care for her. The claimant did not tell the defendant that he was staying with his mother. At all material times, the claimant intended to return to the flat.

5   On 6 January 2012, the claimant's mother died.

6   It is an implied term of the tenancy that the defendant would allow the claimant quiet enjoyment of the flat. (see note 4)

7   By reason of the matters hereinafter set out, the defendant has been in breach of the term for quiet enjoyment and has trespassed to the claimant's flat and property.

PARTICULARS (see note 5)

(i)   On 2 April 2012, the claimant, after his mother had died on 6 January 2012 and he had settled her affairs and her landlord had indicated an intention to recover possession of her property, returned to the flat. On his return he discovered that the locks had been changed and he could not gain entry to the flat.

(ii) At 4pm that day, the claimant telephoned the defendant and spoke to Mr Jones, the housing officer responsible for the flat. Mr Jones told the claimant that, on 2 February 2012, the defendant had recovered possession of the flat because the claimant was presumed to have abandoned it. All of the claimant's belongings had been stored for 14 days before being disposed after the claimant had failed to contact the defendant for their return.

(iii) Mr Jones said that the defendant would not provide the claimant with alternative accommodation as he had abandoned his property and, as the claimant did not have a priority need, nor would he be provided with temporary accommodation under Part 7 of the Housing Act 1996.

8   By reason of the matters aforesaid the claimants have suffered loss, damage, distress, discomfort and inconvenience.

PARTICULARS OF GENERAL DAMAGES (see note 6)

(i)   On 2 April 2012, the claimant was forced to stay in bed and breakfast accommodation.

(ii)   From 3 April 2012, until the date of the claim, he has been forced to sleep on a friend's sofa.

PARTICULARS OF SPECIAL DAMAGES (see note 7)

(i)   The cost of bed and breakfast accommodation on 2 April 2012: £55.

(ii)   The following items, which were disposed of by the defendant:
   (a) Bed: £400.
   (b) Sofa: £500.
   (c) Table: £100.
   (d) 4 Chairs: £100.
   (e) Television: £300.
   (f) DVD player: £100.
   (g) Digital radio: £100.
   (h) Hi-fi system: £200.
   (i) Kitchen utensils: £50.
   (j) Linen: £50.

9   The claimant is entitled to aggravated and exemplary damages. (see note 8)

PARTICULARS

(i)   The defendant has obtained possession of the flat in a way calculated to obtain vacant possession without incurring the cost of bringing a claim for possession in the courts. In the circumstances, the defendant has sought to profit from its own unlawful act and the claimant is entitled to exemplary damages.

(ii)   The defendant's actions have caused the claimant stress, anxiety and worry.

10   Further or in the alternative, by reason of the matters set out in paragraph 7 herein the defendant has unlawfully deprived the claimant of his occupation of the premises in breach of section 27 of the Housing Act 1988. In the event that the claimant is not reinstated to the flat, the claimant will claim damages to be assessed in accordance with s28 of the Housing Act 1988. (see note 9)

11 The claimant claims to be entitled to interest on such damages as the court may award in respect of his claim pursuant to section 69 of the County Courts Act 1984, at such rate and for such period as the court thinks fit. (see note 10)

AND the claimant claims:

(1) An injunction requiring the defendant to re-admit the claimant to the flat forthwith.

(2) An order for the delivery up of his property or special damages in the sum of £1,900.

(3) General, aggravated, special or exemplary damages.

(4) Interest.

(5) Costs.

The claimants believe that the facts set out in these particulars of claim are true. (see note 12)

Signed ....

Dated: 18 April 2012

....

Leo and Nevil
242–4 Nashville Road, Anytown AT5 6UN
Solicitors for the Claimant
who will accept service at this address

PARTICULARS OF CLAIM (3)
HARASSMENT BY LANDLORD

IN THE ANYTOWN COUNTY COURT

Claim No (see note 1)

B E T W E E N:

MEG M SWADDLEY

Claimant

-and-

BEN CARACHEC

Defendant

PARTICULARS OF CLAIM

---

1   At all material times, the claimant has been the sole assured shorthold tenant of a flat known as 74 Finton Court, Anytown AT5 0DX ('the flat'). The defendant is her landlord. (see note 2)

2   The premises are a self-contained one-bedroom flat situated on the top floor of a terraced house, which includes a car parking space at the front of the building. The defendant is the freehold owner of the house and lives in the ground-floor flat.

3   The assured shorthold tenancy commenced on 21 May 2010 and was for a fixed term of 12 months at a monthly rent of £800. On its expiry, it became a statutory monthly periodic tenancy. It is evidenced by a written tenancy agreement. As a term of the agreement, the claimant paid a deposit of £800 to the defendant. (see note 3)

4   By reason of the matters hereinafter set out, the defendant has, in breach of s1 of the Protection from Harassment Act 1997, pursued a course of conduct which he knew amounted to harassment of the claimant. (see note 4)

PARTICULARS OF HARASSMENT (see note 5)

(i)   On 14 February 2012, the claimant returned home from work to find the defendant filling her parking space with car parts. When the claimant pointed out that the parking space was hers to use under the terms of the tenancy agreement, the defendant became abusive and threatened to hit her with a spanner.

(ii)   On 15 February 2012, the claimant removed the car parts from the parking space and was able to park her car in it. Later that day, she found that the bonnet of her car had been badly scratched. The claimant believes that it was the defendant who scratched the car.

(iii) On 17 February 2012, the claimant took her car to the garage to be resprayed. Later that day, the defendant put the car parts back in the parking space. Despite numerous requests to remove them, the defendant has refused to remove the car parts which remain in the parking space as of today's date.

(iv) On 18 February 2012, the claimant found notes which had been posted through her letter box stating 'Watch yourself'. The claimant believes that the defendant posted the notes.

(v) On 19 February 2012, the claimant asked the defendant whether he had posted the notes. The defendant replied 'What if I have?'. The defendant then became abusive and threatened the claimant.

(vi) On at least seven occasions during the following week, the claimant was woken in the early hours of the morning by telephone calls from the defendant.

(vii) On the evenings of 20, 22, 23 and 24 February 2012, the defendant stood outside the claimant's flat in the communal area, staring through the window of the front door for several hours at a time.

(viii) On 25 February 2012, the defendant once again stood outside the claimant's flat. The claimant went out to confront the defendant. The defendant was abusive and pushed the claimant in the chest.

5 Additionally or alternatively, by reason of the matters set out at paragraph 4, above, the defendant has assaulted and/or intimidated and/or trespassed to the goods of the claimant.

6 By reason of the matters aforesaid, the claimant has suffered loss, damage, distress, discomfort and inconvenience.

PARTICULARS OF GENERAL DAMAGES (see note 6)

(a) The claimant has been distressed and frightened by the defendant's conduct. She tries to stay away from her home because she is frightened of meeting the defendant.

(b) As result of the defendant's blocking of the claimant's parking space, the claimant has had to park her vehicle two streets away from her flat. The claimant drives to and from work every weekday.

PARTICULARS OF SPECIAL DAMAGES (see note 7)

(c) Cost of respraying bonnet of the car: £300

7 The claimant claims aggravated damages. The claimant has been very distressed by the defendant's conduct, in particular, the assault. The claimant no longer feels safe in her own home. (see note 8)

8 The claimant is entitled to interest on such damages as the court may award in respect of her claim pursuant to section 69 of the County Courts Act 1984, at such rate and for such period as the court thinks fit. (see note 10)

AND the claimant claims: (see note 11)

(1) An injunction restraining the defendant by himself, his servants or agents, or otherwise from trespassing on the claimant's premises, persons or goods, or in any way harassing or abusing the claimant.
(2) An injunction requiring the defendant forthwith to remove any items which he has placed in the claimant's parking space and restraining the defendant from in any way interfering with the claimant's right to park her car in the parking space.
(3) Damages including aggravated damages.
(4) Interest.
(5) Costs.

I believe that the facts set out in these particulars of claim are true. (see note 12)

Signed ....

Dated: 27 February 2012

....

Leo and Nevil
242–4 Nashville Road, Anytown AT5 6UN
Solicitors for the Claimant
who will accept service at this address

Notes to particulars of claim

Note 1 – Heading to form

Fill in the name of the appropriate county court. Leave the case number blank until one is provided by the court. There may be more than one claimant or defendant (see chapter 3), in which case the names should all be set out on separate lines and the parties identified by putting a number in brackets before them showing who is the first claimant, second claimant, first defendant, second defendant and so on. It may not be possible to identify a defendant, for example, an agent, except by one name. It is perfectly permissible to identify someone by a forename or surname alone and gender if that is all that is known.

Note 2 – Introductory paragraphs

The purpose of the introductory paragraphs is to set out the relationship between the parties, which forms the basis of the causes of action (see chapter 2). In unlawful eviction cases, this involves identifying the basis of the agreement under which the claimant occupies the premises and the claimant's status, for example, assured tenant, assured shorthold tenant, secure tenant or licensee (see appendix B).

In some cases, this may not be straightforward and may have to be set out in separate paragraphs. If there is likely to be a dispute between the parties, for example, assured tenant versus assured shorthold tenant or tenant of resident landlord, assert the claimant's best case.

If the claimant only occupied a single room, or a flat in a house, do not give just the address of the house but identify clearly the subject matter of the agreement, for example, first floor flat, flat 2, middle room on the second floor, attic room or back room.

In some harassment cases, the status of the parties and their relationship is irrelevant. There may be no contractual relationship between the parties and torts such as assault or harassment under PHA 1997 do not depend on the status of the parties. Information about any relationship between the parties may, however, assist in explaining how the acts complained of arose. In certain torts, for example, nuisance, the status of the claimant is significant and must be included (see above, paras 2.66–2.68 and 2.77–2.78).

Note 3 – Pleading the whole claim

Remember that the particulars of claim form the basis of the whole action. These details may not be necessary for the immediate hearing but will be relevant later.

Note 4 – Causes of action

In this and the first part of the next paragraph, the 'causes of action' are introduced (see chapter 2). There may be several causes of action. State them all, for example, breach of the covenant for quiet enjoyment, trespass to goods, property and person, nuisance.

Note 5 – Particulars

Using particulars makes the claim more easily understood. Here, set out in a sequence of numbered sub-paragraphs the actual events which constitute the breach. It is helpful to use different numerals to those already in use for the principal paragraphs. The sequence of events should be set out logically and in chronological order from the first act complained of to the point at which all remedies short of turning for help to the civil courts have been attempted.

Lawyers differ about the need for detail. The document is intended to assist the court not to confuse it. Brevity is therefore important and reduces the risk of annoying the court. It also reduces the possibility of including inaccuracies which may subsequently be exposed when the claimant gives evidence, thereby undermining his or her credibility. On the other hand, graphic details make a strong impression both on the judge and the other side, revealing the strength of the claimant's case from the outset and creating a picture in the judge's mind, which the other side may well find hard to shift. A balance must be struck between the desirable aim of imposing a vivid picture upon the court from the outset and the danger associated with lengthy papers. On any approach, however, the key or critical details cannot be omitted, even if the claim is made in haste, and their omission may also undermine the claim at a later date.

Much of the detail, for example, the actual words spoken as opposed to the substance of what they mean, should appear in the witness statement rather than these particulars. It is appropriate to use the actual words if they are central to the case, for example, to make clear the threatening nature of the defendant's actions, or to establish a claim for exemplary or aggravated damages (see chapter 3).

Note 6 – Particulars of general damages

Set out any distress, inconvenience or injury suffered (see above, paras 3.43–3.44). If the injunction is not granted, the inconvenience suffered will increase. The particulars of claim may subsequently be amended to plead any further losses.

Note 7 – Particulars of special damages

Here, set out the particulars of special damages, which must be pleaded, listing each item and value or cost as in the example. The basis for an award of special damages depends on whether the possessions have been either lost or damaged beyond repair, or are capable of repair. If they have been lost, the measure of damages is the value of the possessions, taking into account their condition at the time. If the possessions can be repaired, the measure of damages is the cost of repair. In a case of emergency, occupiers will often not be able to give precise details of special damages, in which case the particulars of claim should say: 'a schedule of special damages will be served in due course'. See generally above, paras 3.36–3.42. Alternatively, where numerous items have been damaged or removed, it will be appropriate to attach a schedule of special damages to the particulars of claim rather than plead each item in the body of the pleading. In such circumstances, the claimant should indicate that they are claiming special damages for the losses set out in attached schedule of special damages.

Note 8 – Exemplary and aggravated damages

If exemplary and/or aggravated damages are to be sought (see above, paras 3.48–3.67), a specific claim must be made and the facts on which the claim is based must be stated: CPR 16.4(1)(c).

Note 9 – Housing Act 1988 s27

A claimant is entitled to damages under HA 1988 ss27 and 28 only where he or she has been permanently deprived of occupation (see above, paras 2.94–2.99). For this reason, the cause of action is pleaded in the alternative to cover the eventuality that an injunction may be refused or proves, in practical terms, to be unenforceable.

If the occupier is reinstated into the premises, the claim under HA 1988 ss27 and 28 will have to be abandoned. If the claim proceeds for damages only, then both types of damages can be claimed, although there could only be one award under the head of damages for loss of home (see above, paras 3.92–3.95).

Note 10 – Interest

The claim for interest must be pleaded: CPR 16.4(2)(a). The form of words used here is that usually adopted. Interest is only available on special damages, not general damages (unless they are damages for personal injury) nor damages in respect of HA 1988 ss27 and 28 (see above, paras 3.97–3.99).

Note 11 – The prayer

This part of the particulars of claim is called 'the prayer'. It contains all the elements of the relief or remedy the occupier is seeking from the court.

Note 12 – Statement of truth

The particulars of claim must contain a statement of truth: CPR Part 16 PD 3.4. If the document is signed by the claimant, the standard form is 'I believe that the facts stated in these particulars of claim are true'. A solicitor may sign the statement of truth on the claimant's behalf, in which case the statement of truth is 'The claimant believes that the facts stated in these particulars of claim are true'.

APPLICATION NOTICE FOR INTERIM INJUNCTION
(see note 1)

IN THE ANYTOWN COUNTY COURT

Claim No

B E T W E E N:

(1) JANE FIELDS
(2) JOHN JONES

Claimants

-and-

WARDEN DRANE

Defendant

By an application in pending proceedings X (see note 2)

Under Statutory provision

This application raises issues under the Human Rights Act 1998 Yes/No (see note 3)

The Claimants Jane Fields and John Jones

apply to the court for an injunction order in the following terms:

That the Defendant Warden Drane

be forbidden (whether by himself or by instructing or encouraging any other person (see note 4)

    (1)   assaulting or threatening or otherwise harassing the first and/or second claimants,

    (2)   interfering with the claimants' quiet enjoyment of 16A Maxwell Square, London AT16 1AB ('the premises').

And that the Defendant:

    (3)   forthwith re-admit the first and second claimants to the premises;

    (4)   forthwith provide the first and second claimants with keys to the premises.

And that:

    (5)   this order remain in force until further order;

    (6)   costs reserved.

The grounds of this application are set out in the written evidence of Jane Fields

signed on 22 March 2012

This written evidence is served with this application

This application is to be served upon Warden Drane

This application is filed by

Leo and Nevil Solicitors
the solicitors for the Claimant
whose address for service is
242–4 Nashville Road,
Anytown AT5 9UN

Signed Leo and Nevil   Dated 22nd March 2012

Notes to application notice

Note 1 – Prescribed form

This application is based on the county court prescribed form N16A (application for injunction). Marginal notes and certain formal parts are omitted for convenience. The prescribed form must be used.

Note 2 – Basis of application

The form requires the claimant to state whether the injunction is sought in proceedings which have been commenced or under a specific statutory provision.

Note 3 – Human rights

Unlawful eviction is a breach of a person's right to respect for the home under article 8 of the European Convention on Human Rights. This is only likely to be the case where the eviction is by a social landlord who qualifies as a public authority.[41]

Note 4 – Terms of the injunction

Set out clearly the terms of both the prohibitory part of the order sought (ie, restraining the defendant from specified actions), and the mandatory part of the order (ie, telling the defendant what he or she must do). The terms should specify a time within which the defendant is to comply with the order. Here, as in most unlawful evictions, the order is to be carried out forthwith. Costs of a without notice application are usually reserved to the return date to allow the defendant to make representations.

41 See above, para 2.91.

DRAFT ORDER
(see note 1)

IN THE ANYTOWN COUNTY COURT

Claim No

BETWEEN

(1) JANE FIELDS
(2) JOHN JONES

Claimants

-and-

WARDEN DRANE

Defendant

If you do not obey this order you will be guilty of contempt of court and you may be sent to prison. (see note 2)

On 22 March 2012 the court considered an application by the claimants for an injunction

The Court ordered that Warden Drane (see note 3)
is forbidden whether by himself or by instructing or encouraging any other person from
    (1) assaulting or threatening or otherwise harassing the first and/or second claimants,
    (2) interfering with the claimants' quiet enjoyment of 16A Maxwell Square, London AT16 1AB ('the premises').

This order shall remain in force until the 27 March 2012 at 10 o'clock unless before then it is revoked by a further order of the court.

And it is ordered that Warden Drane shall: (see note 4)
    (3) re-admit the first and second claimants to 16A Maxwell Square, London SE16,
    (4) provide the first and second claimants with keys to 16A Maxwell Square

on or before forthwith on service of this order.

It is further ordered that costs are reserved.

Notice of further hearing

The court will reconsider the application and whether the order should continue at a further hearing at the Anytown County Court, Belmont Road, Anytown AT12 5BW on the 27 March 2012 at 10 o'clock.

If you do not attend at the time shown the court may make an injunction order in your absence.

You are entitled to apply to the court to re-consider the order before that day.

The claimants gave an undertaking promising to pay any damages ordered by the court if it later decides that the defendant has suffered loss or damages as a result of this order. (see note 5)

Notes to draft order

Note 1 – Prescribed form

This draft order is based on the county court prescribed form N16 (interim injunctions) although marginal notes and certain formal parts are omitted for convenience. An applicant for an interim injunction should provide the court with a draft order.

Note 2 – Penal notice

This part of the order is known as the penal notice. It is included to warn the defendant(s) of the possible consequences of disobeying the order. A defendant cannot be committed for contempt of an order unless he know about the possibility (above, para 4.17); the normal means of ensuring this, and the best evidence of it, is to include a penal notice in the order and, therefore, it should be included in the draft order. An order can be addressed to more than one person (or one or more people and/or one or more companies or corporate bodies) but each must be served with a copy. If the defendant is a corporate body, the order can be addressed to either the company or to a suitable individual in the company: *R v Wandsworth County Court ex p Munn* (1994) 26 HLR 697, QBD.

Note 3 – Restraining injunction

This is the prohibitory part of the order, ie, restraining the defendant from specified actions.

Note 4 – Mandatory injunction

This is the mandatory part of the order, ie, telling the defendant what he or she must do. The order should specify a time within which the defendant is to comply with the order. Here, as in most unlawful evictions, the order is to be carried out forthwith. Any order for an injunction must set out clearly what the defendant must or must not do: CPR Part 25 PD 25A 5.3.

Note 5 – Undertaking

The court has a discretion whether or not to require this undertaking from a claimant: CPR Part 25 PD 25A 5.1(1). The promise by the claimant is that he or she will pay damages if it emerges on further consideration that the injunction should not have been granted and the defendant has suffered loss in consequence. Where a claimant is publicly funded, such an undertaking may be disproportionately onerous and if necessary it should be submitted that the claimant's financial position ought not to affect the position in regard to what is the essential justice of the case: *Allen v Jambo Holdings Ltd* [1980] 1 WLR 1252, CA. Alternatively, if the claimant has been unlawfully evicted and the court insists that such an undertaking be given, it can be argued that the undertaking should go no further than to require the claimant to pay the defendant a sum equivalent to the rent.

WITNESS STATEMENT

Witness statement on behalf of the claimants
Witness: J Fields
First Statement
Exhibits: JF1, JF2
Date: 22 March 2012
(see note 1)

IN THE ANYTOWN COUNTY COURT

Claim No

B E T W E E N

(1) JANE FIELDS
(2) JOHN JONES

Claimants

-and-

WARDEN DRANE

Defendant

WITNESS STATEMENT OF JANE FIELDS

(see note 2)

I JANE FIELDS, unemployed, of 16A Maxwell Square, London AT16 1AB, say as follows: (see note 3)

1. I am the first claimant and make this statement in support of the application for an interim injunction to enable us to move back into our home. I believe that the facts stated in this witness statement are true. (see note 4)

2. I and my partner, the second claimant, have been the joint tenants of the above property since 19 January 2011. The property is a self-contained, one-bedroom, basement flat. We responded to an advertisement in a local newspaper and met the defendant, who is our landlord. We agreed to take the flat for a fixed term of 12 months and to move in the following Wednesday. This was 19th January 2011. The rent was agreed to be £700 per month, payable in advance. We were provided with a written tenancy agreement. I refer to a true copy of the tenancy agreement marked 'JF1'. We also provided the defendant with a deposit of £700. I have been advised by my solicitor that the defendant should have protected this deposit within a statutory scheme. As far as I am aware the defendant has not done this. If he has, however, he has not provided us with the prescribed information to indicate that he has.

3. At the start of the tenancy we were able to pay the rent with no difficulties. In November 2011, however, I lost my job. The second claimant is

a builder who works on short-term contracts. In January 2012, he had serious cash-flow problems and it was difficult for us to pay the rent. (see note 5)

4. During the last week of January 2012, the defendant telephoned and told us that we would have to be out of the property as our tenancy had expired and we were no longer paying the rent. I was very disappointed and thought that we could not be made to leave straightaway.

5. I spoke to a former work colleague and from our conversation it appeared that we were now periodic assured shorthold tenants and that the defendant would have to serve a s.21, Housing Act 1988 notice and then get a court order if he wanted us to leave. On 25 January 2012, I telephoned the defendant to tell him that we would not be leaving and that it was our legal right to stay in the flat. He became extremely angry and shouted and swore at me. He told me he was coming round to sort the matter out.

6. The defendant came round to the flat that evening at about 8 pm. The second claimant was out and I was alone and nervous about letting him in. When he arrived, he was perfectly polite and apologised for sounding so angry over the telephone. I let him in and he started to talk about how he really needed the rent because he had a few debts to pay. I explained to him that we were also having financial difficulties but that we hoped to pay the arrears soon. He then suddenly flew into a rage and started swearing. He said that that was not good enough and that he 'knew people'. During the course of his shouting and swearing, he repeated this phrase a number of times in a threatening manner. I asked him to leave. He replied that he would leave when he wanted to as it was his flat. I became very nervous, but eventually he left and slammed the door behind him.

7. We were worried about what our rights were, so we decided to check the legal position. I went to a solicitor who told us that we were assured shorthold tenants and that the defendant needed a court order to evict us. She said that she would write a letter to the defendant informing him of our rights. I refer to the true copy of the letter dated 26 January 2012 marked 'JF2'.

8. On 28 January 2012, the defendant telephoned me. He was in a rage and told me in no uncertain terms what my solicitor could do with her letters. He said that he did not care what the law was, he needed the rent and he already had a tenant lined up who would be able to pay in a proper manner. I was very frightened by the call.

9. After that occasion, we received a number of very strange telephone calls, sometimes very late at night. On the first occasion, someone who I am sure was the defendant, because his number appeared on my phone, said 'As you sow, so shall you reap'. The caller then just put the telephone down. On the other occasions, the caller did not say anything, there was just silence. I am sure that these calls were made by the defendant because his number appeared on my phone on each occasion. These calls happened about every three days during February and the first two week

of March. They were very inconvenient because they often woke us up in the early hours of the morning, but we also found them very disturbing.

10. On 14 March 2012, a man came round to the flat. He looked through the windows and generally looked over the outside. I went out and asked him what he was doing. He was perfectly friendly and said that he hoped that I did not mind but he was moving in soon. From our conversation, it became clear that the defendant had told him we were going on 20 March 2012. (see note 6)

11. We were really worried about what might happen on 20 March and both stayed in. At about midday, the defendant came round to the flat. Two men were with him. He banged on the door and demanded to be let in. We shouted through the door and asked him to go away. He said that we 'should not be stupid' and told us we had to be out. The two men with him then broke down the front door. The defendant told us to get out and the two men started to pile our belongings into black bin liners. By this stage, I was in tears. The second claimant tried to stop the two men. One of them punched him in the face. We were very scared and went to the local police station.

12. About an hour later, we returned with a police officer but found that the locks to the front door of the flat had been changed and we could not get in. The police officer told us to see our solicitor. When we saw our solicitor later that afternoon, she tried to telephone the defendant but could not get any reply. Most of our belongings were piled outside the door but it now appears that our television set, our laptop computer and my jewellery are missing.

13. The second claimant's face was hurting very badly and was swelling up alarmingly so we decided to go to the hospital. The hospital treated the bruise which was now very apparent and prescribed some strong pain-killers. We had to wait a long time at the hospital and by the time we had got the prescription it was too late to see our solicitor.

14. Our application for an injunction is being made without giving notice to the defendant because we spent last night on a friend's floor and have nowhere to sleep tonight. If we are not re-admitted to the flat we will be street homeless. (see note 7)

15. I therefore ask that the court order grant an order requiring Mr Drane to re-admit us to the flat as soon as possible. Given the circumstances of the eviction, I would also ask that the court grant the orders we seek restraining the defendant from further unlawful conduct.

Signed: *Jane Field*

Dated: 22 March 2012

Notes to witness statement

Note 1

The top right-hand corner of the witness statement must set out five matters (CPR Part 32 PD 17.2): (a) the party on whose behalf the witness statement is made; (b) the initials and surname of the witness; (c) the number of the statement in relation to the witness, ie whether the first, second, third, etc; (d) identifying initials and number of each exhibit referred to; and (e) the date the statement was made.

Note 2

The same remarks on the title apply as under the particulars of claim. A statement may be made by a party or by a witness. Although it is unusual and often impractical, given time constraints, to put in more than one statement on an application for a without notice interim injunction, there is no limit on the number of statements.

Note 3

The witness statement must include the words: 'I believe that the facts stated in this witness statement are true'. This does not mean that the witness has to have had direct experience of everything in the statement. It is perfectly acceptable to include evidence which the witness has heard from other sources, although this should be made clear in the statement, for example, 'I was told by X that ...'.

Note 4

Here, set out the evidence in a sequence of logical statements, in numbered paragraphs, using a new paragraph for each new matter: CPR Part 32 PD 19.1–2. If the witness is the claimant or other occupier then it is best to set out the details of occupation in the early part of the statement.

If the claimant has a written agreement or any other evidence of the arrangement, for example, a rent book or housing benefit statements, this should be produced as an exhibit to the witness statement, as in the example. The number of the exhibit includes the initials of the person making the witness statement. Each new exhibit is likewise known by the initials of the person making the witness statement and its number, ie, a new number in sequence for each new exhibit. Other relevant exhibits may include letters from the landlord telling the occupier to get out, notes found on doors, notices to quit and so on. Any document can be produced. Each reference to an exhibit should be in bold type: CPR Part 32 PD 19.1(7).

The comments made in relation to the particulars of claim on how much detail to include apply here with the same reservations and qualifications. Some people draft extremely lengthy particulars of claim for their clients and short witness statements swearing that the details in the particulars of claim are true. Others draft extremely short particulars of claim and fill out the whole of the detail in the witness statement. There is no single correct method. A balance must be sought so as not to put off the judge or provide too much room for inconsistency but on the other hand to show that there is a strong case and make an impact on the court.

Note 5

When applying for an interim injunction, it is important always to include any facts which may militate against the claimant's case, for example, rent arrears or any occasions when the occupier behaved in such a way as to give the landlord reason for complaint. This applies in particular to without notice applications where the court is asked to take the claimant's case on trust. In any event, it is tactically better to anticipate the defendant's case than to have to respond to allegations at a later date.

Note 6

The conversation with the stranger is hearsay evidence but such evidence may be included (see note 2). Note that this information supports any claim for exemplary damages.

Note 7

Applications for without notice injunctions will only be considered if there is a good reason for not giving notice: CPR 25.3(1). The urgency of the situation or the danger to the occupier will justify an order being made in the absence of the defendant. The statement should therefore include a factual explanation of these matters. In the absence of such an explanation, the court will adjourn the application to allow notice to be given to the defendant.

PART II

Criminal proceedings

CHAPTER 5

Unlawful eviction and harassment – Protection from Eviction Act 1977

Introduction

5.1   The aim of the Protection from Eviction Act (PEA) 1977 is to protect a broad range of occupants, known as 'residential occupiers', from being harassed or unlawfully evicted. To achieve this, it creates three criminal offences: unlawful eviction and two offences of harassment. The full text of the PEA 1977 is set out in appendix C.

5.2   The essential distinction between the two harassment offences is that one can only be committed by a landlord or an agent, whereas the other can be committed by anyone but requires specific intent to be proved.

Residential occupiers

5.3   The starting-point is the definition of residential occupier. A residential occupier is:

> ... a person occupying ... premises as a residence, whether under a contract or by virtue of any enactment or rule of law giving him the right to remain in occupation or restricting the right of any other person to recover possession of the premises.[1]

5.4   There are two issues:

a) whether the premises in question are occupied 'as a residence'; and, if so,

b) whether the person has a sufficient right of occupation.

Occupation as a residence

5.5   Residence is not defined by the PEA 1977, but has been held to have the same meaning as in the Rent Act (RA) 1977.[2] The phrase 'occupying the premises as a residence' is almost identical to that used in RA 1977 when defining a statutory tenancy[3] or when defining who is a resident landlord.[4]

5.6   Whether an occupier is resident is a question of fact and degree. An occupier must have a home at the premises and there must be:

---

1 PEA 1977 s1(1).
2 *Schon v Camden LBC* (1986) 18 HLR 341, QBD.
3 RA 1977 s2(1) refers to the tenant 'occupying the dwelling house as his residence'.
4 RA 1977 s12.

> A substantial degree of regular personal occupation ... of an essentially personal nature.[5]

5.7 There is no need for constant occupation; residence is preserved if there is both some evidence of occupation and an intention to return.[6] Even if there is no intention to return, residence will also be preserved by the tenant's spouse residing in the premises.[7] It is possible to have more than one residence.[8]

5.8 In *Uratemp Ventures Ltd v Collins*,[9] it was held that a hotel room without cooking facilities could be let as a 'dwelling'; the term was said[10] to mean more than mere 'residence', the term used in PEA 1977 s1.[11] It follows that there is no requirement for cooking facilities before someone can be said to be occupying as a residence.

Right of occupation

5.9 If the person is resident, the second question is whether he or she occupies:

> ... under a contract, or by virtue of any enactment or rule of law, giving him the right to remain in occupation or restricting the right of any other person to recover possession.[12]

5.10 It is necessary to apply this criterion to the various types of occupation arrangement that may have been made.[13]

---

5 *Herbert v Byrne* [1964] 1 WLR 519, CA.
6 *Brown v Brash* [1948] 2 KB 247, CA.
7 *Old Gate Estates Ltd v Alexander* [1950] 1 KB 311, CA; *Wabe v Taylor* [1952] 2 QB 735, CA.
8 *Hampstead Way Investments Ltd v Lewis-Weare* [1985] 1 WLR 164, HL.
9 [2002] 1 AC 301, (2001) 33 HLR 85, HL.
10 At [30].
11 In any event, PEA 1977 s3(2B) requires proceedings – and thus brings into PEA 1977 s1 – in relation to 'premises occupied as a dwelling under a licence, other than an excluded licence': see para 2.106 onwards, above. 'Residential occupiers' within PEA 1977 s1 are, primarily, those who enjoy forms of statutory protection, which apply where there is a letting 'as a separate dwelling-house' (the term under consideration in *Uratemp*). In context, it is hard to think that anything that qualified within *Uratemp* as a home would not qualify as residential occupation under PEA 1977.
12 PEA 1977 s1(1).
13 See appendix B for more details of classification of occupation.

Freeholders

5.11   Freeholders are residential occupiers because they occupy under a rule of law.

Tenants

5.12   Tenants occupy under contract until the tenancy comes to an end; the majority of them will also be able to stay on by statute until a court orders them to leave.

Long leaseholders

5.13   A tenant under a long lease[14] is a residential occupier while the contractual tenancy continues. When it comes to an end, whether by the landlord exercising a right of re-entry or forfeiture[15] or on the expiry of the term, the former leaseholder has a statutory right to remain and thus continues to be a residential occupier until the expiry of a possession order.

Assured tenants

5.14   A landlord cannot bring an assured tenancy to an end except by obtaining and executing a court order.[16] An assured tenant is, thus, a residential occupier (by contract) until he or she is evicted by a court order.

Protected and statutory tenants

5.15   A protected tenant has a right to remain until the contractual tenancy is brought to an end (for example, by notice to quit) and is, thus, a residential occupier. Thereafter and so long as he or she occupies the premises as a residence, the tenant is a statutory tenant, with the statutory right to remain unless and until an order for possession is obtained and executed.[17] A statutory tenant is, therefore, a residential occupier (by RA 1977) until he or she is evicted by a court order.

---

14 A tenancy for a fixed term in excess of 21 years at a low rent: Landlord and Tenant Act (LTA) 1954 s2. For tenancies commencing on or after 1 April 1990, see Local Government and Housing Act (LGHA) 1989 s186 and Sch 10 para 1.

15 Which cannot be exercised other than by court proceedings: PEA 1977 s2.

16 Housing Act (HA) 1988 s5(1); *Knowsley Housing Trust v White* [2008] UKHL 70, [2009] 1 AC 636, [2009] HLR 17. In the case of a fixed-term tenancy, a 'statutory periodic tenancy' arises automatically on expiry: HA 1988 s5(2). Note, however, that statutory protection does not apply where the tenancy is brought to an end by the tenant or by surrender.

17 RA 1977 ss2, 98 and 100.

Secure and flexible tenants

5.16 A landlord cannot bring a secure or flexible tenancy to an end except by obtaining and executing a court order.[18] Such a secure tenant is, thus, a residential occupier (by contract) until he or she is evicted by a court order.

Introductory tenants

5.17 A landlord cannot bring an introductory tenancy to an end except by obtaining and executing a possession order.[19] An introductory tenant is also a residential occupier (by contract) until he or she is evicted by a court order.

Demoted tenants

5.18 A landlord cannot bring a demoted tenancy to an end except by obtaining and executing a possession order.[20] A demoted tenant is likewise a residential occupier (by contract) until he or she is evicted by a court order.

Assured agricultural occupiers

5.19 A landlord cannot bring an assured agricultural occupancy to an end except by obtaining and executing a court order.[21] An assured agricultural occupier is a residential occupier (by contract) until he or she is evicted by a court order.

Rent (Agriculture) Act 1976 protected occupiers and statutory tenants

5.20 A protected occupier has a right to remain until the contractual tenancy or licence is brought to an end (for example, by notice to quit) and is, thus, a residential occupier. Thereafter, if a statutory tenancy arises,[22] he or she remains a residential occupier until an order for possession is executed.[23]

---

18 HA 1985 s82(1A). In the case of a fixed-term tenancy, a periodic tenancy arises automatically on expiry: HA 1985 s86(1).

19 HA 1996 s127(1).

20 HA 1996 s143D(1).

21 HA 1988 ss5(1), 24 and 25. In the case of a fixed-term tenancy, a 'statutory periodic tenancy' arises automatically on expiry: HA 1988 s5(2). Note, however, that statutory protection does not apply where the tenancy is brought to an end by the tenant or by surrender.

22 It arises automatically on termination of the protected occupancy: Rent (Agriculture) Act (R(A)A) 1976 s4, provided the landlord is not excepted, eg a local authority (see s5).

23 RA 1977 ss2, 98 and 100.

Assured shorthold tenants

5.21   A landlord cannot bring an assured shorthold tenancy to an end except by obtaining and executing a possession order.[24] An assured shorthold tenant is a residential occupier by contract until he or she is evicted by a court order.

Protected shorthold tenants

5.22   As a protected shorthold tenancy is a particular type of protected tenancy, the same provisions apply. Accordingly, a protected shorthold tenant remains a residential occupier until he or she is evicted by a court order.

Restricted contract tenants[25]

5.23   A restricted contract tenant is a residential occupier until he or she is evicted by a court bailiff because there is a statutory right to remain.[26]

Unprotected tenants[27]

5.24   An unprotected tenant is a residential occupier until a possession order is obtained and executed because there is a statutory right to remain under the PEA 1977.[28]

Excluded tenants

5.25   An excluded tenant, whose tenancy began before 15 January 1989, is a residential occupier until a possession order is obtained and executed because there is a statutory right to remain under the PEA 1977.[29]

5.26   An excluded tenant whose tenancy was granted on or after 15 January 1989, however, is only a residential occupier up to the termination of the right to occupy (ie expiry of a notice to quit, by effluxion

---

24 HA 1988 ss5(1) and 21(1).

25 Particular care should be taken as restricted contracts are now very unusual. In most cases they have been 'converted' into a different type of occupancy, often an excluded tenancy (see appendix B).

26 PEA 1977 s3(1).

27 This term is used throughout this book to refer to any tenancy which is not protected by LTA 1954, R(A)A 1976, RA 1977, HA 1985, HA 1988 and LGHA 1989 nor is an excluded tenancy.

28 PEA 1977 s3(1); *Haniff v Robinson* [1993] QB 419, (1994) 26 HLR 386, CA.

29 PEA 1977 s3(1) and (2C)(a). Also included are tenancies which started on or after 15 January 1989 pursuant to a contract made before that date: PEA 1977 s3(2C)(b).

of time, by forfeiture or by surrender), as there is thereafter no statutory protection, nor even a requirement that a court order be sought before he or she is evicted.[30]

Licensees

5.27   As a general rule, all licensees occupying premises as a dwelling are residential occupiers by contract until the termination of the licence; thereafter, those who are not excluded licensees will remain residential occupiers until a possession order is obtained and executed.[31]

Non-excluded licensees

5.28   Licensees of premises (occupied as a dwelling), who are not excluded licensees, cannot be evicted without a court order.[32] Accordingly, a non-excluded licensee remains a residential occupier until a possession order is obtained and executed.

Excluded licensees

5.29   Excluded licensees, whenever their licences were granted, are residential occupiers only up to the end of the right to occupy.[33] Thereafter, they are trespassers.

Restricted contract licensees[34]

5.30   A restricted contract licensee, whose licence was entered into before 28 November 1980[35] is a residential occupier only until termination of the contract;[36] thereafter, he or she is a trespasser.

---

30   They are specifically excluded from PEA 1977 s3(1).
31   PEA 1977 s3(1).
32   PEA 1977 s3(1) and (2B). See above, paras 2.109–2.115, as to the ambit of this provision.
33   PEA 1977 s3(1) and (2B). A contractual licence will end in accordance with its terms. Accordingly, a licence for a fixed term cannot be determined during the term by giving one month's notice to quit: *R v H* [2008] EWCA Crim 483. Even a bare licence requires reasonable notice (which will depend on all the circumstances) before it comes to an end.
34   Particular care should be taken as restricted contracts are now very unusual. In most cases they have been 'converted' into a different type of occupancy, often an excluded licence (see appendix B).
35   When the HA 1980 came into force.
36   Including any periods during which the operation of a notice to quit is deferred by a rent tribunal.

5.31   If the licence was created on or after 28 November 1980, the restricted contract licensee is a residential occupier until possession order is obtained and executed.[37]

Trespassers

5.32   Trespassers have neither contractual rights nor rights under the principal Acts providing statutory security of tenure to occupiers of residential accommodation.[38] Owners of property with an immediate right to possession are restricted by law in the way they secure entry to premises and may not use or threaten violence to enter residential premises[39] unless they are occupied by a displaced residential occupier or a protected intending occupier[40] (see chapter 7). Once section 144 of the Legal Aid, Sentencing and Punishment of Offenders Act (LASPO) 2012, is brought into force, a trespasser who lives in a residential building and who entered it as a trespasser may be removed by a police officer[41] as he or she is committing a criminal offence.[42]

5.33   In general, a trespasser can only be regarded as a residential occupier if the restriction on entry imposed by the Criminal Law Act (CLA) 1977 s6(1) is interpreted as restricting the right to recover possession.

5.34   This presents difficulties. There is no case-law[43] on the issue, but mere trespassers are unlikely to be regarded as residential occupiers. Given that CLA 1977 s6(1) has effect only if the trespasser is present at the time of entry to the premises, it would lead, for instance, to the anomalous position of a trespasser being a residential occupier only when he or she was physically on the premises. Furthermore, CLA 1977 s6(1) neither gives a trespasser a right to remain in occupation

---

37   PEA 1977 s3(2A) specifically includes such licences.

38   LTA 1954, R(A)A 1976, RA 1977, PEA 1977, HA 1985, HA 1988 and LGHA 1989.

39   CLA 1977 s6.

40   CLA 1977 s6(1A). A protected intending occupier is a person with a freehold interest or a leasehold interest with not less than two years to run, who requires the premises for his or her own occupation as a residence: CLA 1977 s12A.

41   Police and Criminal Evidence Act (PACE) 1984 s17(1)(c)(vi).

42   LASPO 2012 s144(1).

43   It is worth noting that, although the point was not argued in *R v Phekoo* [1981] 1 WLR 1117, CA, the court accepted that trespassers were not residential occupiers and held that a genuine belief that an occupier was a trespasser was a defence to a charge of harassment; nor was the point taken in *West Wiltshire DC v Snelgrove* (1997) 30 HLR 57, QBD, when the basis of the defence in *Phekoo* was considered by the court.

nor does it restrict the right of the owner to recover possession.[44] It merely makes violent entry unlawful and only then if the occupier opposes the entry.

5.35   In limited circumstances, however, a trespasser can be a residential occupier, ie, where he or she:

a) is entitled to remain by virtue of PEA 1977 s3(1); or

b) can claim title by adverse possession.

Protection from Eviction Act 1977 s3(1)

5.36   Where premises were formerly let under a tenancy which was neither statutorily protected nor excluded,[45] and a person was lawfully residing there when the tenancy under which they were let came to an end,[46] that person is a residential occupier until the possession order is executed, despite the fact that – as a matter of law – he or she became a trespasser when the tenancy came to an end.[47]

Adverse possession

5.37   Where a trespasser is in possession of a property and intends to exclude everyone else from it (including the true owner of the land), he or she is said to be in 'adverse possession'. The trespasser must demonstrate this intention by unequivocal acts so that if the owner visited the land, it would be clear to him or her that the trespasser intends to exclude him or her from the property.[48]

5.38   In the context of residential accommodation, these conditions are satisfied if the trespasser changes the locks to the property and lives in it as his or her home.[49]

5.39   An adverse possessor has his or her own possessory interest in the property from the moment he or she takes adverse possession.[50] This interest, however, is not binding on the owner of the property until the trespasser has been in continuous adverse possession for

---

44 The test under PEA 1977 s1(1).

45 It also applies if the premises were let under a non-excluded licence rather than a tenancy: PEA 1977 s3(2B).

46 Note, this occurs when the contractual tenancy is determined (ie, by notice to quit, etc). At common law, if the tenant remains he or she becomes a trespasser, but is, nevertheless, entitled to do so by virtue of PEA 1977 s3(1) until the landlord obtains a court order; PEA 1977 s3(2) extends this right to any person lawfully residing with the tenant.

47 PEA 1977 s3(1) and (2).

48 *Pye v Graham* [2002] UKHL 30, [2002] 3 WLR 221.

49 *Lambeth LBC v Blackburn* (2001) 33 HLR 74, CA.

50 *Rosenberg v Cook* (1881) 8 QBD 162.

a specified period of time, which is generally 12 years.[51] Prior to the expiry of this period, in respect of the owner, the adverse possessor is a mere trespasser and not a residential occupier.[52]

5.40   After the specified period of adverse possession has expired, the trespasser becomes a residential occupier, although the reasons for this vary depending on:

a) whether the land is unregistered or registered; and
b) if the land is registered, whether the period of adverse possession expired before or after 13 October 2003.

Unregistered land

5.41   If the land is unregistered, once the trespasser has been in adverse possession for 12 years, the owner's title is automatically extinguished and the trespasser becomes the owner of the property by virtue of his or her own possessory title.[53] At this point, he or she is therefore a residential occupier because he or she occupies the property under a rule of law.

Registered land

5.42   As a result of the Land Registration Act (LRA) 2002, the question in relation to registered land depends on whether the trespasser has been in adverse possession for 12 years prior to 13 October 2003 (ie the date on which the relevant provisions of the LRA 2002 came into force).

5.43   If the trespasser had been in adverse possession for 12 years before 13 October 2003, he or she has a statutory right to be registered as the owner.[54] Furthermore, he or she has a defence to any claim for possession.[55] Accordingly, he or she is a residential occupier because he or she remains in occupation due to a restriction on the right to recover possession against him or her.

5.44   If a trespasser has not been in adverse possession for 12 years before 13 October 2003, he or she can only become the registered owner through adverse possession in more limited circumstances.

5.45   First, after ten years of adverse possession, he or she can apply to be registered as the owner.[56] The owner will be notified of the

---

51 Limitation Act 1980 s15(1).
52 See above, paras 5.32–5.35.
53 Limitation Act 1980 s17; *Tichborne v Weir* (1892) 678 LT 735, CA.
54 LRA 2002 Sch 12 para 18(1).
55 LRA 2002 Sch 12 para 18(2).
56 LRA 2002 Sch 6 para 1.

application and can ask for the application to be dealt with under LRA 2002 Sch 6 para 5.[57] If the owner does take this option, however, and the trespasser can establish ten years' adverse possession, he or she is entitled to be registered as the owner.

5.46 If the application is dealt with under LRA 2002 Sch 6 para 5, the trespasser has to establish not only that he or she has been in adverse possession for ten years but also that one of a number of very restricted circumstances apply.[58]

5.47 If the trespasser makes this first kind of application but is unsuccessful, he or she may make a second application after a further two years.[59] Assuming that he or she can show that he or she has been in adverse possession for the whole 12 years, he or she is entitled to be registered as the owner. It is not necessary to establish any of the circumstances required in the first application.

5.48 A trespasser who would be entitled to make either one of the applications set out above has a defence to a possession action.[60] Accordingly, such adverse possessors are residential occupiers because of a restriction on the right to recover possession against them.

Special categories[61]

Joint tenants

5.49 A joint tenancy continues so long as the tenancy subsists. Accordingly, a joint tenant remains a residential occupier until either he or she vacates or until the right to occupy determines, whichever is the earlier. If one joint tenant vacates, he or she ceases to be a residential occupier, but this has no bearing on any other joint tenant who continues to reside in the premises.

Assignees[62]

5.50 Where a tenancy has been assigned, the assignee replaces the assignor (ie the contractual tenant). Accordingly, the assignee is a residential occupier on taking up residence.

---

57 LRA 2002 Sch 6 para 3.
58 LRA 2002 Sch 6 para 4. For present purposes, the relevant circumstances are that the trespasser can establish an equity by estoppel or can show some other reason entitling him or her to be registered as the proprietor. In practice, this will rarely be the case.
59 LRA 2002 Sch 6 para 6.
60 LRA 2002 s97.
61 See below, appendix B for explanation of the terms.
62 See below, appendix B, paras B.71–B.74.

Service tenants[63]

5.51   A service tenant is a particular type of tenant. He or she is, there-fore, a residential occupier on the same basis as any other tenant (as considered above), even though he or she may be less likely to have security of tenure.

Tenants of mortgagors

5.52   The tenant of a mortgagor is in the same position as a tenant of any other landlord; it does not matter if the tenancy was granted in con-travention of the mortgage deed.[64]

5.53   Where the mortgagee repossesses as against the mortgagor (for example, for mortgage arrears), the tenant becomes the direct tenant of the mortgagee only if the tenancy is binding on the mortgagee; thus, the tenant remains a residential occupier. If the tenancy is not binding on the mortgagee,[65] the tenant is a trespasser in relation to the mortgagee after the expiry of the possession order obtained against the mortgagor, when he or she will cease to be a residential occupier. The court may, however, on an application by the tenant, postpone the date on which the mortgagor is to give up possession for a period of up to two months.[66] The unauthorised tenant will remain a residential occupier for that period.

Subtenants

5.54   While the mesne tenancy between the landlord (L) and the tenant (T) subsists, a subtenant (ST) is in the same position as the tenant of any other landlord. Whether ST is a residential occupier is determined according to his or her right of occupation in relation to T.

5.55   In general, when the mesne tenancy comes to an end, any sub-tenancy determines automatically;[67] ST has no right to occupy and is a trespasser. This is subject to certain exceptions,[68] whereby ST becomes the direct tenant of L; if so, ST is a residential occupier.

5.56   Where the mesne tenancy is determined and ST does not become the direct tenant of L, ST remains a residential occupier if, at the time

---

63   See below, appendix B, paras B.89–B.90.

64   *Church of England Building Society v Piskor* [1954] 1 Ch 553, CA.

65   For the circumstances where the tenancy is and is not binding on the mortgagee, see appendix B, paras B.75–B.79.

66   Mortgage Repossessions (Protection of Tenants etc) Act 2010 s1(2).

67   *Moore Properties (Ilford) Ltd v McKeon and others* [1976] 1 WLR 1278, ChD.

68   In particular, by surrender of the mesne tenancy (a rule of law) and statutory provisions in respect of assured and regulated tenancies (statutory rights): see appendix B.

of termination of the mesne tenancy, ST was lawfully residing in the premises and the mesne tenancy was neither statutorily protected nor excluded.[69]

Rental purchasers[70]

5.57　Rental purchasers are residential occupiers until the expiry of a possession order because they have statutory protection against eviction without a court order.[71]

Licensees of tenants

5.58　Provided that his or her licence has not been determined by the tenant, a tenant's licensee is a residential occupier until the tenant's interest has been terminated by the landlord.

5.59　Where the tenant had a tenancy which was neither statutorily protected nor excluded, and the licensee was lawfully residing in the premises at the time of termination of the tenant's interest, he or she remains a residential occupier until the possession order obtained by the landlord is executed.[72]

Service occupiers[73]

5.60　A service occupier occupies accommodation under the terms of a contract of employment and is, thus, a residential occupier until it is terminated. A service occupier with exclusive possession of the premises, who remains in occupation after termination of the contract of employment, is a residential occupier until the possession order is executed.[74]

5.61　Agricultural workers in tied accommodation who fall outside the protection afforded by the R(A)A 1976 are residential occupiers until a possession order expires, unless they are excluded licensees.[75] The same applies to such workers who do not qualify as assured agricultural occupiers (under HA 1988).[76]

69　PEA 1977 s3(1) and (2); see para 5.36 above.
70　HA 1980 s88(4); see below, appendix B, paras B.84–B.87.
71　PEA 1977 s3 is applied to these occupiers by HA 1980 Sch 25 para 61.
72　PEA 1977 s3(1) and (2); see para 5.36 above.
73　See below, appendix B, paras B.54–B.56.
74　PEA 1977 s8(2).
75　PEA 1977 s4.
76　If they are tenants of an agricultural holding or they are farm business tenants, they are statutorily protected tenants: PEA 1977 s8(1)(d) and (g).

Spouses and civil partners

5.62　A spouse or civil partner lacking any other right to occupy the home has 'home rights'.[77] These are statutory rights and, accordingly, he or she is a residential occupier for so long as they subsist.[78]

5.63　　A former spouse or civil partner who has been granted an occupation order in respect of the former home[79] is a residential occupier.

Cohabitants

5.64　A cohabitant[80] who has been granted an occupation order over the shared home[81] is a residential occupier, as it is a statutory right.

5.65　　As with a former spouse or civil partner, a former cohabitant with an occupation order in respect of the former shared home[82] is a residential occupier.

Unlawful eviction

5.66　It is an offence where any person:

> ... unlawfully deprives the residential occupier of any premises of his occupation of the premises or any part thereof, or attempts to do so ... [83]

Residential occupier

5.67　The offence can only be committed against a residential occupier (see above, paras 5.3–5.65).

Any person

5.68　The offence is most likely to be committed by a landlord or a landlord's agent, but the defendant may be 'any person', regardless of the relationship to the occupier. Thus, a head landlord who evicts

---

77　Family Law Act (FLA) 1996 s30(2).

78　These rights terminate automatically on the dissolution of the marriage or civil partnership.

79　FLA 1996 s35.

80　'Cohabitants' are two persons who are neither married to each other nor civil partners of each other but are living together as though they were husband and wife or civil partners: FLA 1996 s62(1).

81　FLA 1996 ss33 and 36.

82　FLA 1996 s36.

83　PEA 1977 s1(2).

a subtenant or a tenant's licensee commits the offence (as long as that subtenant or licensee is a residential occupier). Equally, it may be committed by, for example, a landlord's agent, a joint tenant, a co-occupier and even a neighbour. There must, however, be proof of actual participation by the person being prosecuted; a landlord cannot be vicariously liable for the acts of others.[84]

5.69   The definition extends to other legal persons, for example, companies. Where the offence has been committed by a company – in addition to the company itself – any director, manager, secretary or other similar officer may be prosecuted, as may any person 'purporting to act in any such capacity'.[85]

Any premises

5.70   The offence may be committed in relation to 'any premises'. This should be given a broad meaning.[86] It includes all types of residential premises. A single room with the shared use of a kitchen and bathroom is 'premises' for these purposes,[87] as are premises let for mixed residential and business purposes.[88] It extends to a caravan, which, though not attached to the ground, had been static for ten years and could not easily be towed away.[89]

Deprives

5.71   The occupier must be 'deprived' of occupation of the premises, or there must have been an attempt to deprive the occupier of occupation. Whether or not this has occurred is a question of fact for the court to decide.

5.72   Deprivation of part only of the premises (for example, by locking a lavatory door)[90] is sufficient.[91]

---

84 *Peterborough City Council v Quereshi* [2011] EWCA Crim 1584, [2011] HLR 34.
85 PEA 1977 s1(6).
86 *Thurrock UDC v Shina* (1972) 23 P&CR 205, QBD.
87 *Thurrock UDC v Shina* (1972) 23 P&CR 205, QBD. See also the reference to *Uratemp Ltd v Collins*, above at para 5.8. A single room with no cooking facilities should therefore also suffice, assuming the 'residence' element, above, paras 5.5–5.8.
88 *Patel v Pirabakaran* [2006] EWCA Civ 685, [2006] 1 WLR 3112, [2006] HLR 39.
89 *Norton v Knowles* [1969] 1 QB 572, QBD.
90 As in *R v Burke* [1991] 1 AC 135, (1991) 22 HLR 433, HL.
91 See the words of PEA 1977 s1(3).

5.73   Deprivation does not have to be violent; changing the locks may satisfy the requirement.[92]

5.74   Although the definition of the offence does not contain the word 'eviction', any unlawful deprivation of occupation does have to have the character of an eviction.[93] The Court of Appeal regarded the view of Lord Evershed MR in *Crown Lands Commissioners v Page*[94] – that eviction must be permanent – as going too far but nonetheless held that a tenant who was locked out of his accommodation for one night only or for a short period of time, and who was allowed to retain his right of occupation over the premises, had not been deprived of the premises; rather, the incident amounted to harassment (see below from para 5.84 onwards).

5.75   In *Costelloe v Camden LBC*,[95] the question was said to be whether the exclusion was designed to evict the tenant from the premises; if it was, then regardless of whether it was short or long, it was unlawful eviction; if, on the other hand, the object was the deprivation of occupation for a short time, which was what had happened, it was not.

Unlawfully

5.76   The deprivation must be 'unlawful'. This means that the person depriving the residential occupier of the premises does not have the legal right to do so, which in turn relates to the occupier's security, whether by common law or by statute.[96]

5.77   In addition, the PEA 1977 provides:

> Where any premises have been let as a dwelling under a tenancy which is neither a statutorily protected tenancy nor an excluded tenancy and–
> (a) the tenancy ... has come to an end, but
> (b) the occupier continues to reside in the premises or part of them,
> it shall not be lawful for the owner to enforce against the occupier other than by proceedings in court, his right to recover possession of the premises.[97]

5.78   This provision applies to any residential licence except an excluded licence.[98]

---

92 *R v Yuthiwattana* (1984) 16 HLR 49, CA.
93 *R v Yuthiwattana* (1984) 16 HLR 49, CA.
94 [1960] 2 QB 274, 281, CA.
95 [1986] Crim LR 249, QBD.
96 See appendix B.
97 PEA 1977 s3(1).
98 PEA 1977 s3(2A) and (2B); see above, paras 2.118–2.126, and 5.25–5.29.

5.79   Statutorily protected tenancies include protected tenancies, statu-
        tory tenancies, assured tenancies (including assured shortholds),
        protected and assured agricultural occupancies and long leaseholds.[99]
        They are excepted because they enjoy security of tenure under their
        own, other statutes, ie, it would be superfluous to include them here.

5.80   In summary, the combined effect of the common law and statu-
        tory protection is as follows:

   a)   In respect of any residential premises, other than those subject
        to an excluded tenancy or an excluded licence, it is unlawful for a
        landlord to recover possession without a court order.

   b)   In respect of any residential premises subject to an excluded ten-
        ancy or an excluded licence, it is unlawful for a landlord to recover
        possession until it has been validly determined; thereafter, a court
        order is not required.

Defences

5.81   In general, a mistake of fact by the defendant that a person was not a
        residential occupier is a defence to a charge of unlawful eviction.[100]

5.82   If the prosecution establishes that the residential occupier has
        been unlawfully deprived of occupation, it is a specific defence that
        the defendant:

> ... believed, and had reasonable cause to believe, that the residential
> occupier had ceased to reside in the premises.[101]

5.83   It is for the defendant[102] to establish – on a balance of probabilities
        – both the belief and that it was reasonably held.[103] It follows from the
        use of the word 'and' that a purely subjective but unreasonable belief
        that the occupier had left is not sufficient. The existence of such a
        reasonable belief is a question of fact for the magistrates or the jury
        to decide.[104]

---

99   PEA 1977 s8(1).

100 *R v Phekoo* [1981] 1 WLR 1117, CA; *West Wiltshire DC v Snelgrove* (1997) 30
     HLR 57, QBD; although these were decided in relation to harassment, they
     apply equally to illegal eviction (see para 5.122).

101 PEA 1977 s1(2); see, for example, *Islington LBC v Clonis and another* (2000) 80
     P&CR D24, QBD, in which it was held that the magistrates were entitled to
     conclude that the defendant believed the tenant had left the accommodation
     he had occupied under an assured shorthold tenancy, where he was physically
     absent but had left his possessions at the property.

102 Magistrates' Courts Act (MCA) 1980 s101; *R v Hunt* [1987] AC 352, HL.

103 *Blackstone's criminal practice 2012* (Oxford University Press, 2011) at para
     F3.40.

104 *R v Davidson-Acres* [1980] Crim LR 50, CA.

Harassment

5.84   There are two offences of harassment, one where the defendant is the victim's landlord (or an agent of the landlord),[105] the other where the defendant is any person.[106]

5.85   Both offences comprise two elements, each of which must be proved for the defendant to be convicted. These elements are the culpable behaviour (the 'harassing conduct') and the mental intent to do it (the 'intention').

5.86   The harassing conduct is defined in the same way for both. The difference arises in relation to the intention that needs to be proved.[107]

Harassment by a landlord or a landlord's agent[108]

Landlord

5.87   A landlord is the person who would be entitled to possession but for the residential occupier's right to remain or the restriction on the right to recover possession; the definition includes not only the immediate landlord but also any superior landlord from whom the immediate landlord derives title.[109] There must, however, be proof of actual participation by the person being prosecuted; a landlord cannot be vicariously liable for the acts of others.[110]

Agent

5.88   An agent is any person who acts on behalf of the landlord. In the absence of a specific definition in the PEA 1977, it has the meaning ascribed to it by the general law.[111]

5.89   The law of agency is complex and cannot be described here, but it may be noted that agency can be either express or implied. Express

---

105 PEA 1977 s1(3A).

106 PEA 1977 s1(3).

107 The second offence (under PEA 1977 s1(3A)) was created by HA 1988 s29, which amended the PEA 1977, as it was thought that the requirement to prove specific intent in the original offence (under PEA 1977 s1(3)) enabled guilty landlords to escape conviction by placing too high a burden on the prosecution.

108 PEA 1977 s1(3A).

109 PEA 1977 s1(3C).

110 *Peterborough City Council v Quereshi* [2011] EWCA Crim 1584, [2011] HLR 34.

111 See generally, *Bowstead and Reynolds on agency* (19th edn, Sweet & Maxwell, 2010).

agency is specific authorisation by the landlord of another person to act on his or her behalf. There is no requirement that this is evidenced in writing. Agency is implied where the state of affairs gives rise to the implication that one person is acting on behalf of another.

Residential occupier

5.90 The offence can only be committed against a residential occupier (see above, paras 5.3–5.65).

The harassing conduct

5.91 This may be one of two acts:

(a) ... acts likely to interfere with the peace and comfort of a residential occupier or members of his household; or
(b) ... persistently withdraw[ing] or withhold[ing] services reasonably required for the occupation of the premises ... as a residence.[112]

Interfering with peace and comfort

5.92 PEA 1977 does not define these words. It is neither possible nor particularly helpful to compile a list of possible acts; it would never be comprehensive, an omission might mislead, and an incident might be misunderstood in a different context.

5.93 Interference with peace and comfort can comprise, for example, excessive noise or threats of violence. More specific illustrations are: removing fittings, knocking holes in walls and ceilings and leaving rubble about;[113] and ordering a member of a tenant's household to remove his clothes from the premises.[114] It is a question of fact in each case whether the behaviour complained about interfered with the peace and comfort of the residential occupier.

5.94 The qualification provided by the word 'likely' (to interfere) injects an element of objectivity but – because there will be a specific residential occupier in mind – it does not allow a defendant to escape conviction on the basis that some other occupier would not have been affected.

---

112 PEA 1977 s1(3A).
113 *R v Bokhari* (1974) 59 Cr App R 303, CA.
114 *R v Spratt* [1978] Crim LR 102, CA.

5.95   Although the statute refers to 'acts' (ie in the plural), a single act is sufficient.[115]

5.96   Where more than one act is alleged, they are preferably specified in separate counts on the indictment.[116] Where a count on an indictment consists of more than one act, and there is a danger that individual members of the jury may be satisfied that different acts have been proved, the judge should direct them that they may only return a guilty verdict if they are unanimously satisfied in respect of the same act or acts alleged against the defendant.[117]

5.97   There is no requirement – or precondition – that the act or acts complained of should give the occupier a civil cause of action (for example, breach of contract or tort), provided that, as a matter of fact, they are likely to interfere with the occupier's peace or comfort.[118] Thus, while tenants had no contractual right to use a particular bathroom and lavatory (because there were others in the house which they were permitted to use), or to a bell, a landlord who prevented tenants from using a bathroom and lavatory on the same floor as their room and disconnected a doorbell had nonetheless performed acts within the prohibition.[119]

5.98   It is, however, necessary to prove positive action rather than mere omission. An offence is not committed if the landlord fails to act. In *R v Zafar Ahmad*,[120] the landlord started works to a flat without the intention required to constitute an offence. The works rendered the tenant's flat uninhabitable and the landlord refused to do the work necessary to make it habitable again. It was held that his omission to take steps to complete the work was not the doing of an act for the purposes of harassment.

---

115 *R v Evangelos Polycarpou* (1978) 9 HLR 129, CA, applying Interpretation Act 1978 s6(c), which states: 'In any Act unless the contrary intention appears ... words in the singular include words in the plural and words in the plural include the singular'.

116 Or in separate charges in summary proceedings.

117 *R v Mitchell* (1993) 26 HLR 394, CA; although this case concerned an offence under PEA 1977 s1(3A), the decision applies equally to PEA 1977 s1(3).

118 *R v Yuthiwattana* (1984) 16 HLR 49, CA (contrary to the dictum of Ormrod LJ in *McCall v Abelesz* [1976] 1 QB 585, 591, CA). The landlord refused to supply a replacement key, thereby preventing the tenant who had lost it from getting into his accommodation. This conclusion was approved in *R v Burke* [1991] 1 AC 135, 22 HLR 433, HL.

119 *R v Burke* [1991] 1 AC 135, (1991) 22 HLR 433, HL.

120 (1986) 18 HLR 416, CA.

5.99   The question for the court is whether the act or acts alleged by the prosecution are likely to interfere with the peace or comfort of the residential occupier, individually or cumulatively.[121]

5.100   The interference may not only be with the occupier's peace and comfort but also with that of members of his or her household. The word 'household' is wider than family and includes lodgers and flat-sharers.

Persistently withdrawing or withholding services

5.101   'Services' is not defined in the PEA 1977, but must be:

> ... reasonably required for occupation of the premises as a residence.[122]

5.102   Notwithstanding this lack of definition in the PEA 1977, the supply of a utility, such as gas, electricity or water has been held to be a service.[123] From the wording of section 1(3A)(b), it is clear that the court must first determine whether what was withdrawn or withheld was a service and, second, whether it was reasonably required for the occupation of the premises.

5.103   The word 'persistently' qualifies both withdrawing services and withholding services.[124] It requires more than one incident or some element of 'deliberate continuity'.[125]

5.104   It appears unlikely that a mere failure by a landlord to pay a gas or electricity bill, without an intention to harass, and which results in those services being cut off by the supplier, amounts to an offence under section 1.[126]

---

121 *R (McGowan) v Brent JJ* [2001] EWHC Admin 814, (2002) 16 JP 29 per Tuckey LJ at 23.

122 PEA 1977 s1(3A)(b).

123 *Westminster City Council v Peart* (1968) 19 P&CR 736, QBD.

124 *Westminster City Council v Peart* (1968) 19 P&CR 736, QBD.

125 *R v Abrol* [1972] Crim LR 318, CA. In *Hooper v Eaglestone* (1977) 34 P&CR 311, QBD, the question whether cutting off supplies was persistent was not argued but was assumed to be so; the case was brought under Caravan Sites Act 1968 s3, the relevant provision being very similar to PEA 1977 s1(3).

126 See *McCall v Abelesz* [1976] 1 QB 585, CA. In *Westminster City Council v Peart* (1968) 19 P&CR 736, QBD, the landlord failed to pay the gas and electricity accounts to the suppliers, which resulted in disconnection; the Divisional Court left open the question whether, in so doing, the landlord had withheld a service. If disconnection occurs, local housing authorities have the power to make arrangements for the restoration or continuation of supplies of water, gas or electricity for the benefit of the occupiers of the premises: Local Government (Miscellaneous Provisions) Act 1976 s33.

5.105   In *McCall v Abelesz*,[127] it was suggested that the offence cannot be committed where the landlord withholds or withdraws a service that he or she had been providing voluntarily, as opposed to one provided contractually under the terms of the letting. This would no longer seem to be good law. First, it conflicts with the wording of the statute, which provides that it is the withdrawal or withholding of any service 'reasonably required' that constitutes the offence. Second, the proposition was based on the requirement that the defendant had breached a legal right enjoyed by the occupier, which was subsequently held in the House of Lords[128] not to be necessary (albeit in relation to interference with peace and comfort. In principle, it would seem anomalous if this did not also apply to withdrawing and withholding services).

The intention

5.106   The prosecution must prove that the defendant committed the harassing conduct:

> ... know[ing] or [having] reasonable cause to believe either that [the] conduct [was] likely to cause the residential occupier to give up the occupation of the whole or part of the premises or to refrain from exercising any right or pursuing any remedy in respect of the whole or part of the premises.[129]

5.107   Whether the defendant had knowledge of the requisite consequences of his or her actions or had reasonable cause for believing the same is a question of fact for the court to ascertain from what he or she said or how he or she acted. The use of the word 'reasonable' indicates that that belief should be determined objectively.[130]

Defences

5.108   In general, a mistake of fact by the defendant that a person was not a residential occupier is a defence to a charge of unlawful eviction.[131]

---

127 [1976] 1 QB 585 at 596G–H, CA, per Ormrod LJ.

128 *R v Burke* [1991] AC 135, (1991) 22 HLR 433, HL, see above, para 5.97.

129 PEA 1977 s1(3A).

130 See also *R (McGowan) v Brent JJ* [2001] EWHC Admin 814 (QB), (2002) 16 JP 29, Tuckey LJ at 24–25.

131 *R v Phekoo* [1981] 1 WLR 1117, CA; *West Wiltshire DC v Snelgrove* (1997) 30 HLR 57, QBD; although these were decided in relation to charges of harassment by any person, the defence applies equally to harassment by a landlord or an agent (see below para 5.122).

5.109   It is a defence for the defendant to show that he or she had reasonable grounds for interfering with the peace and comfort of the residential occupier or for withdrawing or withholding the services.[132]

5.110   Where a defence is raised, it is for the defendant[133] to establish it on the balance of probabilities.[134] Whether this can be done is a matter of fact for the magistrates or jury to decide.

Harassment by any person[135]

Residential occupier

5.111   The offence can only be committed against a residential occupier (see above, paras 5.3–5.65).

Any person

5.112   As with unlawful eviction, this offence may be committed by 'any person' (see above, paras 5.68–5.69).

The harassing conduct

5.113   This is the same as where the offence is committed by a landlord or a landlord's agent (see above, paras 5.91–5.105).[136]

The intention

5.114   The prosecution must prove that the defendant committed the harassing conduct with the intention of causing the residential occupier either:

(a) to give up occupation of the premises or any part thereof; or
(b) to refrain from exercising any right or from pursuing any remedy in respect of the premises or part thereof ...[137]

---

132 PEA 1977 s1(3B).
133 MCA 1980 s101; *R v Hunt* [1987] AC 352, HL.
134 *Blackstone's criminal practice 2012* (Oxford University Press, 2011) at para F3.40.
135 PEA 1977 s1(3).
136 As originally enacted, PEA 1977 s1(3) required the prosecution to prove that the defendant did 'acts calculated to interfere with the peace and comfort ... [etc]'. HA 1988 s29 substituted 'likely' for 'calculated'; although it is still necessary to prove intent; s1(3) is strengthened because the requirement of proving an ulterior motive has been removed and the court may decide, objectively, whether acts were likely to interfere with the peace and comfort of the occupier.
137 PEA 1977 s1(3).

5.115   The two parts of the subsection do not constitute two separate offences. The harassing conduct may be performed with one of two intentions. If it is unclear on the facts whether a case falls within (a) or (b), there is no reason why the offence should not be expressed in one charge with alternative intentions.[138]

5.116   The intention is, thus, the same as that required for harassment by a landlord or agent subject to the important difference that the prosecution must prove that the defendant had specific intent to achieve the stated effect (give up occupation, refrain from exercising right/pursuing remedy), as opposed to knowledge or belief of the likely consequences of his or her actions.

5.117   In general, where specific intent is an element of an offence, it must be proved that the defendant either intended a particular result or, if not intending it, foresaw it.[139] In the latter case, it cannot be assumed that the defendant intended the natural consequences of his or her actions; the defendant's foresight is to be judged subjectively and:

> ... the probability, however high, of a consequence is only a factor ... to be considered with all the other evidence in determining whether the accused intended to bring it about.[140]

5.118   Intention must be construed within the context of the requirement that the defendant had the purpose of causing the occupier to give up occupation or to refrain from exercising a right or pursuing a remedy.[141] The court is not entitled automatically to draw the conclusion that the defendant had the necessary intent just because the harassing conduct caused the victim to give up occupation (or refrain from the exercise or pursuit).

5.119   Thus, the carrying out of building works, which caused disruption, did not of itself demonstrate the presence of the necessary intent, because it did not automatically follow that the defendant intended the occupier to leave.[142]

5.120   Likewise, indifference by a landlord to the plight of an occupier whose gas had been disconnected by the supplier because of the landlord's failure to pay for it was insufficient to establish the necessary intent under PEA 1977 s1(3)(a),[143] nor was an intention to persuade

---

138   *Schon v Camden LBC* (1986) 18 HLR 341, CA.
139   Criminal Justice Act 1967 s8.
140   *R v Hancock* [1986] AC 455, 474, HL.
141   *R v Burke* [1991] AC 135, (1991) 22 HLR 433, HL.
142   *R v AMK (Property Management) Ltd* [1985] Crim LR 600, CA.
143   *McCall v Abelesz* [1976] QB 585, 598, CA, obiter, per Ormrod LJ.

the occupier to leave for a limited period of time to enable works to be done and thereafter to return.[144] The nature and extent of the harassing conduct is, however, a factor, albeit only a factor, to be taken into account when deciding whether the necessary intent was present.

5.121 The position can be summarised as follows. First, where the evidence clearly establishes that the defendant wanted an event to result, it is a straightforward issue of fact. Thus, where the evidence is that the defendant says that he or she will smash windows if the tenant does not leave, the court must decide whether those words were spoken; if so, the intent will be proved. Second, however, where the evidence is that the defendant may not have wanted the event to occur for its own sake but may have foreseen that it would result as a by-product of his or her actions, the court must go on to consider how likely this was in the light of all the other evidence.

Defences

5.122 In *R v Phekoo*,[145] it was held that a mistaken belief, honestly and reasonably held, that a person was not a residential occupier afforded a defence to a charge of harassment; the mistake was that the defendant believed the occupiers to be trespassers and did not know that they were lawful subtenants of his own tenant.[146] In *West Wiltshire DC v Snelgrove*,[147] the court characterised the mistake in *Phekoo* as a mistake of fact, because a mistake in law can never amount to a defence to a criminal offence.[148]

5.123 Where a defence is raised, it is for the defendant[149] to establish it on the balance of probabilities.[150] Whether this can be done is a matter of fact for the magistrates or jury to decide.

5.124 It should be noted that, unlike in relation to the offence of harassment by a landlord or agent, there is no defence to harassment by any

---

144 *Schon v Camden LBC* (1986) 18 HLR 341, CA. It would be sufficient for PEA 1977 s1(3)(b), but the charge did not refer to this and so the defendant was acquitted.

145 [1981] 1 WLR 1117, CA.

146 The decision would apply equally to illegal eviction; see *Wandsworth LBC v Osei-Bonsu* [1999] 1 WLR 1011, (1998) 31 HLR 515, CA.

147 (1997) 30 HLR 57, 63, QBD, per Simon Brown LJ.

148 Nevertheless, although ignorance of the criminal law is not a defence, a mistake as to the civil law may have the effect of negating the criminal intent: *Wandsworth LBC v Osei-Bonsu* [1999] 1 WLR 1011, (1998) 31 HLR 515, CA, per Simon Brown LJ at 1019H.

149 MCA 1980 s101; *R v Hunt* [1987] AC 352, HL.

150 *Blackstone's criminal practice 2012* (Oxford University Press, 2011) at para F3.40.

person that the defendant had reasonable grounds for committing the harassing conduct.

Penalties

5.125   Unlawful eviction and both harassment offences can be tried in a magistrates' court or the Crown Court. The maximum penalty for any of the offences in a magistrates' court is six months' imprisonment and/or a fine not exceeding £5,000[151] and in the Crown Court two years' imprisonment and/or an unlimited fine.[152]

5.126   In *R v Brennan*,[153] the Court of Appeal remarked that, at least in cases dealt with by the Crown Court, it was proper for those convicted of unlawful eviction to be sent to prison even for a first offence, although the period of imprisonment should be determined in the light of the defendant's overall record and past behaviour.

Identifying the landlord

5.127   An agent or person who receives rent may be served with notice requiring him or her to disclose the full name and place of abode or business address of the landlord in order to bring proceedings[154] under the PEA 1977.[155] For these purposes, the notice must be served with the fixed intention of bringing proceedings, not merely in contemplation of the possibility of bringing proceedings in the future.[156]

5.128   'Landlord' is not defined but includes:[157]

a) any person from time to time deriving title under the original landlord;

b) in relation to any dwelling house, any person other than the tenant who is entitled to possession of the dwelling house;[158] and

---

151   PEA 1997 s1(4) and MCA 1980 s32(2), (9).

152   PEA 1977 s1(4). In *R v Pittard* (1994) 15 Cr App R (S) 108, the Court of Appeal decided that a fine of £1,000 was the appropriate sentence where the defendant broke into his tenant's home, changed the locks and remained there for 12 hours.

153   (1979) 1 Cr App R (S) 103, CA.

154   Criminal or civil.

155   PEA 1977 s7(1).

156   *Lewisham LBC v Ranaweera* [2000] JHL D70, Crown Court.

157   PEA 1977 s7(3).

158   Or – in the case of a protected tenancy – would be entitled to possession but for the security of tenure afforded by the RA 1977.

c) any person who grants to another the right to occupy the dwelling in question as a residence and any person directly or indirectly deriving title from the grantor.

5.129 A failure or refusal to comply with a notice seeking the identity of the landlord is a criminal offence, unless the accused can show that he or she did not know the information sought and could not have acquired it with reasonable diligence.[159] It is triable only in the magistrates' court and the maximum penalty is a fine not exceeding level 4 on the standard scale (currently £2,500).[160]

159 PEA 1977 s7(2).
160 CJA 1982 s37, as amended by CJA 1991 s17.

CHAPTER 6

Harrassment – Protection from Harassment Act 1997

Introduction

6.1   The Protection from Harassment Act (PHA) 1997 and the Criminal Justice and Police Act (CJPA) 2001 prohibit harassment, breach of which is actionable in the civil and criminal courts. The provisions are not specifically directed at landlords (or their agents) but so much of what they provide catches harassment in its Protection from Eviction Act (PEA) 1977, landlord-tenant meaning, that there is as much reason to consider their applicability in the criminal context as there is in the civil.[1]

6.2   The provisions create six criminal offences:[2]

a) harassment of an individual;
b) harassment of two or more persons;
c) harassment of a person in his or her home;
d) putting another person in fear of violence;
e) breach of a restraining order; and
f) breach of an injunction.

6.3   Additionally, PHA 1997 gives a criminal court the power to make a restraining order, which has a similar effect to an injunction.

6.4   The full text of PHA 1997 and the relevant provisions of CJPA 2001 are set out in appendix C.

Harassment

6.5   Section 1(1) of PHA 1997 prohibits a person from:

... pursuing a course of conduct–
(a) which amounts to harassment of another, and
(b) which he or she knows or ought to know amounts to harassment of the other.[3]

6.6   Section 1(1A) of PHA 1997 prohibits a person from:

... pursuing a course of conduct–
(a) which involves harassment of two or more persons, and
(b) which he knows or ought to know involves harassment of those persons, and

---

1 For the civil cause of action, see above, paras 2.71–2.72.
2 Additional offences of stalking (PHA 1997 s2A) and stalking involving fear of violence or serious alarm or distress (PHA 1997 s4A) are to be added by Protection of Freedoms Act 2012 Part 7 s111(2), once brought into force; these offences are not considered here.
3 PHA 1997 s1(1).

(c) by which he intends to persuade any person (whether or not one of those mentioned above) –
(i) not to do something that he is entitled or required to do, or
(ii) to do something that he is not under any obligation to do.[4]

6.7   References to a 'person', in the context of the harassment of a person, are references to an individual.[5] It is unlikely that the offence covers the harassment of a company.[6] An employer may, however, be vicariously liable for harassment committed by one of its employees in the course of his or her employment.[7]

6.8   There is no definition of harassment.[8] It includes, but is not limited to, alarming or causing distress to a person.[9] Conduct need not therefore cause actual alarm or distress,[10] although it must be targeted at an individual and have been calculated to cause that person alarm or distress.[11] The conduct must be oppressive and unacceptable and sufficiently serious to warrant a criminal conviction; unreasonable conduct that merely irritates, annoys or causes a small measure of upset will not amount to harassment.[12] It is for the court, on the facts of the particular case, to assess whether behaviour is unacceptable and unreasonable. The context in which the conduct occurred is

---

4 PHA 1997 s1(1A), as inserted by Serious Organised Crime and Police Act (SOCPA) 2005 s125(2).
5 PHA 1997 s7(5), as inserted by SOCPA 2005.
6 *Daiichi Pharmaceuticals UK Ltd v Stop Huntingdon Animal Cruelty* [2003] EWHC 2337, [2004] 1 WLR 1503, at [20] per Owen J and *Director of Public Prosecutions v Dziurzynski* [2002] EWHC 1380 (Admin), [2002] ACD 88. In *Huntingdon Life Sciences v Curtin and others* [1998] Env LR D9, CA, the Court of Appeal held that a person did include a company. This decision, however, was not followed in *Daiichi* or *Dziurzynski* on the basis that it had been reached following an appeal from an ex parte injunction in which there had not been argument from both sides.
7 *Majrowski v Guy's and St Thomas's NHS Trust* [2006] UKHL 34, [2007] 1 AC 224.
8 The government chose not to include one, taking the view that harassment as a concept had been interpreted regularly by the courts under Public Order Act 1986 s4A: Home Secretary, *Hansard*, HC vol 287 col 784, 17 December 1996.
9 PHA 1997 s7(2); *Director of Public Prosecutions v Ramsdale* (2001) *Independent* 19 March, QBD.
10 *Majrowski v Guy's and St Thomas's NHS Trust* [2006] UKHL 34, [2007] 1 AC 224 at [66] per Lady Hale.
11 *Thomas v News Group Newspapers Ltd.* [2001] EWCA Civ 1233 at [29]–[30] per Lord Philips MR. (This approach has subsequently been doubted, however, in a dissenting judgment in *Allen v Southwark LBC* [2008] EWCA Civ 1478 at [27] per Arden LJ who held that conduct might be harassment even though no alarm or distress was in fact caused.)
12 *Majrowski* at [30] per Lord Nicholls.

likely to assist the court in determining if the conduct amounted to harassment.[13]

6.9   In *Tuppen and another v Microsoft Corporation Ltd and another*,[14] the PHA 1997 was said to be directed at the prevention of stalking, anti-social behaviour by neighbours and racial harassment. In *DPP v Selvanayagam*,[15] however, Collins J observed that, whatever its purpose, the words of PHA 1997 were clear and could cover harassment of any sort. There is little doubt that it would encompass the sort of conduct with which this book is concerned.

6.10   The prosecution must also prove that the defendant was aware that the conduct amounted to or involved harassment or, if not, that he or she 'ought to have known'.

6.11   A person ought to know that a course of conduct amounts to or involves harassment if:

> ... a reasonable person in possession of the same information would think [it] amounted to or involved harassment of [another].[16]

6.12   This indicates a broadly objective approach with no allowance for the defendant's own mental health,[17] belief or culture.[18] The reasonable person, however, is assumed to have the knowledge of the victim;[19] thus, for example, the seemingly innocent act of standing on the pavement looking into a house could be harassment if the notional reasonable person knew what the victim knew, eg that it had occurred every night for the previous week.

Course of conduct

6.13   It is an offence to pursue a course of conduct in breach of the prohibition of harassment set out in PHA 1997 s1(1) or s1(1A).[20] Where the course of conduct is racially or religiously aggravated, the perpetrator is guilty of an offence under Crime and Disorder Act (CDA)

---

13   *Conn v Sunderland CC* [2007] EWCA Civ 1492, (2007) *Times* 23 November, at [12] per Gage LJ.

14   (2000) *Times* 15 November, QBD.

15   (1999) *Times* 23 June, QBD.

16   PHA 1997 s1(2), as amended by SOCPA 2005.

17   *R v Colohan* [2001] EWCA Crim 1251, [2001] 2 FLR 757.

18   *Crawford v Crown Prosecution Service* [2008] EWHC 148 (Admin) at [64] per Thomas LJ.

19   In contrast to the offence of intentional harassment under Public Order Act 1986 s4A, where it is sufficient to show that the victim was affected; that is, however, an offence which requires specific intent.

20   PHA 1997 s2(1).

1998 s32(1)(a), rather than PHA 1997 s2. At least one of the acts constituting the course of conduct must have been committed in the six months before the complaint to the magistrates' court is made.[21]

6.14 'Conduct' is not defined, but it includes speech.[22]

6.15 A 'course of conduct' must involve conduct[23] on a minimum of two occasions.[24] There is no requirement, however, for the conduct to comprise acts of the same nature; it is the course of conduct that must amount to harassment, as opposed to the individual instances of conduct.[25] This means that a course of conduct may amount to harassment even if it involves acts that would not in isolation amount to harassment.

6.16 While the number of incidents required to constitute a course of conduct need not exceed two, where there is only a small number of incidents the conduct will need to be more severe to sustain a conviction.[26] Likewise, the wider apart the incidents are spread, the less likely it is that a finding of harassment can reasonably be made,[27] although it is conceivable that incidents occurring, say, a year apart could constitute a course of conduct, for example, threats made on the complainant's birthday each year.[28] Acts which are not sufficiently

---

21 Magistrates' Courts Act (MCA) 1980 s127; *Director of Public Prosecutions v Baker* [2004] EWHC 2782 (Admin), (2005) 169 JP 140.

22 PHA 1997 s7(4).

23 Acts done on behalf of the Crown, which the Home Secretary has certified relate to national security, the economic well-being of the UK or the prevention or detection of serious crime are specifically excluded from being 'conduct' for these purposes: PHA 1997 s12.

24 PHA 1997 s7(3). This is a more restrictive alternative to 'persistent', which is used in both offences of harassment under PEA 1977 s1(3) and (3A), in which context it has been held to mean both more than once and one occurrence followed by 'deliberate continuity': *R v Abrol* [1972] Crim LR 318, CA.

25 *Iqbal v Dean Manson (Solicitors)* [2011] EWCA Civ 123, [2011] CP Rep 26 per Rix LJ at [45].

26 *Jones v Director of Public Prosecutions* [2010] EWHC 523 (Admin), [2011] 1 WLR 833 at [35] per Ouseley J.

27 *Baron v Crown Prosecution Service* (CO/1569/00) unreported, QBD.

28 *Lau v Director of Public Prosecutions* [2000] 1 FLR 799, QBD and *R v Patel* [2005] 1 Cr App R 27, CA. In *Pratt v Director of Public Prosecutions* [2001] EWHC 483(Admin), (2001) *Times* 22 August, the High Court held that two incidents almost three months apart were 'close to the line, but sufficient to establish a course of conduct'. See also *R v Hills* [2001] 1 FLR 580, CA, and *R v Sahin* [2009] EWCA Crim 2616. In *Kelly v Director of Public Prosecutions* [2002] EWHC 1428 (Admin), (2002) 166 JP 621, three telephone calls made in a five minute period constituted a 'course of conduct'.

connected in type and context, however, will not constitute a course of conduct.[29]

6.17　　There is no requirement that the course of conduct is communicated to the victim by the perpetrator directly. If a person pursues a course of conduct and the detail of his or her actions is relayed to the victim by a third party then the perpetrator will have committed the offence.[30]

6.18　　Conduct may be directed at more than one person.[31] In such circumstances, there is a course of conduct where the perpetrator commits one act against both people separately.[32] Likewise, where the harassment is carried out by two or more people, it is not a requirement that both persons commit two acts separately; one act each is sufficient.[33]

6.19　　Furthermore, where one person's conduct is aided, abetted, counselled or procured[34] by another, it is deemed:

a) to be conduct of the other person (as well as conduct of the first person whose conduct it is); and

b) to be conduct in relation to which the other's knowledge and purpose[35] are the same as they were in relation to what was contemplated or reasonably foreseeable at the time of the aiding, abetting, counselling or procuring.[36]

6.20　A course of conduct does not, however, amount to harassment in any of the following three circumstances.[37]

a) It is pursued to prevent or detect crime – this exception is necessary to prevent law enforcement agencies being caught by the provision, but it is not limited to action by the police. So, for example, a tenancy relations officer pursuing a landlord during the course of an investigation into allegations of harassment of a tenant, can rely on it, as can a private individual.

29　*Pratt v Director of Public Prosecutions* [2001] EWHC 483 (Admin), (2001) *Times* 22 August.

30　*Kellett v Director of Public Prosecutions* [2001] EWHC 107 (Admin) at [16] per Penry-Davey J.

31　PHA 1997 s1(1A); *Director of Public Prosecutions v Dunn* [2001] 1 Cr App R 22.

32　PHA 1997 s7(3)(b).

33　PHA 1997 s7(3A), as amended by Criminal Justice and Police Act 2001.

34　The concepts of aiding, abetting, counselling and procuring are familiar to criminal lawyers. See *Blackstone's criminal practice 2012* (Oxford University Press, 2011) at para A4.1.

35　Including what he or she ought to have known.

36　PHA 1997 s7(3A).

37　PHA 1997 s1(3).

b) It is pursued under any statute or rule of law or to comply with a condition or requirement imposed by any person under a statute; if the law permits certain conduct, such as the service of a notice seeking possession, it may not amount to harassment.[38]

c) In the particular circumstances, it was reasonable to pursue it – this is an open category allowing a court to decide on the facts of the particular case that the defendant's behaviour was not harassment. For example, the mere reporting of a person's wrongdoing to an employer is likely to be reasonable, but will cease to be reasonable if the person doing the reporting goes beyond the simple reporting of the fact, ie, by adding other unfounded allegations.[39]

Penalty

6.21 The offence under PHA 1997 s2 is triable only in the magistrates' court. The maximum penalty is six months' imprisonment and/or a fine not exceeding level 5 on the standard scale (currently £5,000).[40] In addition, on conviction, the court may make a restraining order[41] (see below, paras 6.34–6.36).

6.22 The offence under CDA 1998 s32 is triable in either the magistrates' court or the Crown Court. If tried in the magistrates' court, the maximum penalty is the same as for the offence under PHA 1997 s2.[42] If tried in the Crown Court, the maximum penalty is two years' imprisonment and/or an unlimited fine.[43]

---

38 The issue of five sets of proceedings against a person seeking possession orders on essentially the same ground might, however, be considered to be conduct that amounted to harassment: *Allen v Southwark LBC* [2008] EWCA Civ 1478.

39 *Kellett* at [18].

40 PHA 1997 s2(2); Criminal Justice Act (CJA) 1982 s37, as amended by CJA 1991 s17. *The magistrates' courts guidelines* (2012) set out aggravating features – which can increase the sentence imposed – which include: contact at night, threatening violence, taking photographs, sending offensive material, attempts to enter a victim's home, planning, using contact arrangements with a child to instigate the offence, the involvement of others, where the action is over a long period and where the victim needs medical help or counselling.

41 PHA 1997 s5(1).

42 CDA 1998 s32(3)(a); CJA 1982 s37. *The magistrates' courts guidelines* indicate that the sentence should be greater than for an offence under PHA 1997 s2 to reflect the racially or aggravated element (see above, para 6.13).

43 CDA 1998 s32(3)(b). *The magistrates' courts guidelines* indicate that the offence should be heard in the Crown Court where there are sexual threats or a vulnerable person has been targeted.

Harassment of a person in his or her home

6.23   Section 42A of CJPA 2001 provides that:

(1) A person commits an offence if –

(a) that person is present outside or in the vicinity of any premises that are used by any individual ('the resident') as his dwelling;

(b) that person is present there for the purpose (by his presence or otherwise) of representing to the resident or another individual (whether or not one who uses the premises as his dwelling), or of persuading the resident or such another individual –

(i)   that he should not do something he is entitled or required to do; or

(ii) that he should do something that he is not under any obligation to do.

6.24   In addition, the person must intend, know or ought to know that his or her presence is likely to result in the harassment of, or to cause alarm or distress to the resident.[44] A person ought to know the likely effect of his or her conduct if a reasonable person would think that the person's presence was likely to have that effect.[45] The conduct must also amount to, or be likely to, result in harassment, alarm or distress of the resident.[46]

Penalty

6.25   The offence is triable in the magistrates' court only.[47] The maximum penalty is six months' imprisonment or a fine not exceeding level 4 on the standard scale (currently £2,500).[48]

---

44 CJPA 2001 s42A(1)(c).
45 CJPA 2001 s42A(4).
46 CJPA 2001 s42A(1)(d).
47 CJPA 2001 s42A(4).
48 CJA 1982 s37, as amended by CJA 1991 s17.

Putting another in fear of violence

6.26   It is an offence to pursue a course of conduct[49] which:

> ... causes another to fear, on at least two occasions, that violence will be used against him ... if he knows or ought to know that his course of conduct will cause the other so to fear on each occasion.[50]

6.27   'Course of conduct' has the same meaning as it does in relation to the offence of harassment (see above, paras 6.13–6.20) with the additional requirement that the conduct must have caused another person to fear that violence will be used against him or her.[51]

6.28   A person 'ought to know' that a course of conduct would cause another to fear violence if a reasonable person possessed of the same information would think so.[52] Unlike with the offence under PHA 1997 s2,[53] each act must cause fear that violence will be used.[54] The conduct itself must be such that there is fear that violence *will* be used against another; conduct which causes a person to be frightened about what *might* happen is insufficient.[55] Accordingly, while a fear of violence may be inferred from a person's conduct, direct evidence ordinarily needs to be adduced to prove that a person actually feared that violence would be used against him or her.[56]

6.29   Where the course of conduct is racially or religiously aggravated, the perpetrator is guilty of an offence under CDA 1998 s32(1)(b) rather than PHA 1997 s4.

6.30   If the defendant is acquitted by the Crown Court of this offence under PHA 1997 s4, he or she may, nevertheless, be convicted of harassment.[57]

---

49 Acts done on behalf of the Crown, which the Home Secretary has certified relate to national security, the economic well-being of the UK or the prevention or detection of serious crime are specifically excluded from being 'conduct' for these purposes: PHA 1997 s12.
50 PHA 1997 s4(1).
51 *R v Curtis* [2010] EWCA Crim 123, [2010] 1 WLR 2770 at [20] per Pill LJ.
52 PHA 1997 s4(2); ie, the same guidance to the meaning of constructive knowledge as in s1(2) in relation to whether a person knows a course of conduct amounts to harassment (see paras 6.10–6.12 above).
53 Above, para 6.15.
54 *Kelly v Director of Public Prosecutions* [2002] EWHC 1428 (Admin) at [24] per Burton J.
55 *R v Henley* [2000] Crim LR 582, CA at [13] per Burton J.
56 *R (a child) v Director of Public Prosecutions* [2001] EWHC 17 (Admin) at [19] per Newman J.
57 PHA 1997 s4(5); but not if acquitted in a magistrates' court.

Defences

6.31   A defence to a charge of putting a person in fear of violence is available in any of the following three circumstances:[58]

a) the course of conduct was pursued to prevent or detect crime;

b) the course of conduct was pursued under any statute or rule of law or to comply with a condition or requirement imposed by a person under a statute;

c) the pursuit of the course of conduct was reasonable for the protection of him or herself or of another or for the protection of his or her or another's property.

6.32   It follows that the circumstances in which a person will have a specific defence to a charge of putting a person in fear of violence are broadly the same as the circumstances in which a course of conduct will not amount to harassment.[59] It is for the defendant[60] to establish the defence on the balance of probabilities.[61] Whether this has been done is a matter of fact for the magistrates or the jury to decide.

Penalty

6.33   The offence can be tried in either a magistrates' court or the Crown Court. The maximum penalty in a magistrates' court is six months' imprisonment and/or a fine not exceeding level 5 on the standard scale (currently £5,000)[62] and in the Crown Court five years' imprisonment and/or an unlimited fine.[63] On conviction, the court may make a restraining order.[64] (See para 6.34 below.)

Restraining orders

6.34   The court may impose a 'restraining order' on a defendant to protect the victim or victims (or any other specified person(s)) from

58   PHA 1997 s4(3).

59   See above, para 6.20. Note, however, that, in relation to harassment, it is sufficient to show that the conduct was reasonable per se, whereas for this offence it is necessary to prove that it was reasonable specifically for the protection of the person or property.

60   MCA 1980 s101; *R v Hunt* [1987] AC 352, HL.

61   *Blackstone's criminal practice 2012* (Oxford University Press, 2011) at para F3.40.

62   CJA 1982 s37, as amended by CJA 1991 s17.

63   PHA 1997 s4(4).

64   PHA 1997 s5(1).

further conduct which may amount to harassment or causing a fear of violence.[65]

6.35   The power arises where:

A court [is] sentencing or otherwise dealing with the person ('the defendant') convicted of an offence (as well as sentencing him or dealing with him in any other way).[66]

6.36   A court can impose a restraining order on or after conviction.[67] In addition, a court may impose a restraining order on a person who is acquitted of an offence if it considers it necessary to do so to protect a person from harassment by the defendant.[68] The order must describe the prohibited conduct and may be for a specified period or until a further order is made.[69]

Breach of a restraining order

6.37   It is an offence for a person to do anything prohibited under a restraining order, without reasonable excuse.[70] When determining if an individual has breached the terms of a restraining order, the court is required to give the words used in the order their ordinary English meaning and not to construe them narrowly simply because they are being applied in a criminal context.[71]

6.38   Whether an excuse is reasonable is to be determined objectively. It is for the defendant[72] to establish – on the balance of probabilities – both the excuse and that it was reasonable.[73] The existence of a reasonable excuse is a question of fact for the magistrates or the jury to decide.

---

65 PHA 1997 s5(1) and (2).
66 PHA 1997 s5(1).
67 Prior to conviction, a similar result can be achieved by the court remanding the defendant on bail, subject to a condition not to interfere with a witness, in this case, the victim: Bail Act (BA) 1976 s3(6).
68 In either the magistrates' court or Crown Court. PHA 1997 s5A, as inserted by Domestic Violence, Crime and Victims Act 2004.
69 PHA 1997 s5(2) and (3).
70 PHA 1997 s5(5).
71 *R v Evans* [2004] EWCA Crim 3102, [2005] 1 WLR 1435 at [15] and [18] per Dyson LJ.
72 MCA 1980 s101; *R v Hunt* [1987] AC 352, HL.
73 *Blackstone's criminal practice 2012* (Oxford University Press, 2011) at para F3.40.

Penalty

6.39 The offence can be tried in either a magistrates' court or the Crown Court. The maximum penalty in a magistrates' court is six months' imprisonment and/or a fine not exceeding level 5 on the standard scale (currently £5,000)[74] and in the Crown Court five years' imprisonment and/or an unlimited fine.[75]

Breach of an injunction

6.40 Where a civil court has granted an injunction to prevent further harassment in civil proceedings for breach of the prohibition of harassment,[76] it is an offence if the defendant:

> ... without reasonable excuse ... does anything which he is prohibited from doing by the injunction.[77]

6.41 The penal notice in an injunction must therefore indicate that a failure to comply with the order will constitute a criminal offence under PHA 1997.[78] As to 'reasonable excuse', see above, para 6.38. The defendant cannot be convicted of this offence if he or she has been punished for contempt of court[79] for breach of the injunction.[80]

Penalty

6.42 The offence can be tried in either a magistrates' court or the Crown Court. The maximum penalty in a magistrates' court is six months' imprisonment and a fine not exceeding level 5 on the standard scale (currently £5,000)[81] and in the Crown Court five years' imprisonment and/or an unlimited fine.[82]

---

74 CJA 1982 s37, as amended by CJA 1991 s17.

75 PHA 1997 s5(6).

76 Under PHA 1997 s3(3), and see above, paras 2.71–2.72. Note that it is not an offence to breach an injunction made in relation to any other cause of action.

77 PHA 1997 s3(6). This is entirely novel. The normal way in which an injunction is enforced is by proceedings for contempt of court in the civil courts, see above, paras 4.16–4.24.

78 *Jefferies v Robb*, unreported, 28 June 2012, CA.

79 See above, paras 4.16–4.24.

80 PHA 1997 s3(8).

81 CJA 1982 s37, as amended by CJA 1991 s17.

82 PHA 1997 s3(9).

CHAPTER 7

Violent entry to premises – Criminal Law Act 1977

Introduction

7.1   Before 1977, there was no offence of criminal trespass; it had been a matter solely for the civil law. The genesis of the change was a Law Commission Report,[1] recommending the modernisation of the law on forcible entry, much of which had remained the same since the Forcible Entry Act 1381, and the abolition of the offence of conspiracy to commit a tort.[2]

7.2   The proposals for reform were brought into focus by two contemporary phenomena, residential squatting and 'sit-ins'.[3] The Criminal Law Act (CLA) 1977 created two criminal offences relating to entry to premises, whether by lawful owners or strangers:[4] where land is occupied, an owner with an immediate right to possession against a trespasser is expected to use the summary possession procedure in the High Court or the county court.[5] It is the fact that the offences can be committed even by a lawful owner which means that the provisions are relevant in the context of this book.

7.3   The two offences are:

a) using violence to secure entry to premises; and
b) threatening violence to secure entry to premises.

7.4   The Legal Aid, Sentencing and Punishment of Offenders Act (LASPO) 2012 s144 criminalises all those who live in residential buildings without permission. Accordingly, it could also catch, eg, a landlord who unlawfully evicted a tenant and moved into the premises himself or herself, or someone else put in by a landlord following an unlawful eviction.

7.5   The full text of the relevant sections is set out in appendix C.

---

1   *Conspiracy and criminal law reform* (Law Com No 76 (1976)). For commentaries, see Dashwood and Trice [1976] Crim LR 500 and A T H Smith [1977] Crim LR 139.

2   Thereby reversing the House of Lords decision in *Kamara v Director of Public Prosecutions* [1974] AC 104, HL.

3   The occupation of industrial or academic premises, usually for political reasons.

4   Although there are exemptions for owner-occupiers and certain persons who intend to take up occupation (see below – 'displaced residential occupiers' and 'protected intended occupiers' – paras 7.22–7.32).

5   Civil Procedure Rules (CPR) Part 55.

Using violence to secure entry to premises

7.6 It is an offence if:

> ... any person ... without lawful authority, uses ... violence for the purpose of securing entry into any premises for himself or any other person ... provided that –
>
> (a) there is someone present on those premises who is opposed to the entry which the violence is intended to secure; and
>
> (b) the person using or threatening the violence knows that that is the case.[6]

7.7 Certain occupiers, known as 'displaced residential occupiers' and 'protected intended occupiers' – and persons acting on their behalf – (see below, paras 7.22–7.32) are, however, exempt from the provisions of this section.[7]

Lawful authority

7.8 CLA 1977 does not define 'lawful authority'. Instead, it states what is *not* lawful authority, namely, merely being the owner or having a right of possession or occupation of the premises.[8]

7.9 Examples of persons having lawful authority are a displaced residential occupier,[9] a protected intended occupier,[10] a court bailiff executing a possession order, and a police officer entering to exercise a power of arrest or search under the criminal law.

7.10 The wording of the section means that the burden lies on the prosecution to prove an absence of lawful authority, rather than on the defendant to prove that he or she had it.

Premises

7.11 This term is widely defined. It includes not only buildings, but also land ancillary[11] to a building and even the whole of a site that comprises a building or buildings with ancillary land.[12]

---

6 CLA 1977 s6(1).

7 CLA 1977 s6(1A).

8 CLA 1977 s6(2).

9 By virtue of having or having been given a right over the property and who are expressly disapplied from CLA 1977 s6(1) by s6(1A).

10 Ibid.

11 For instance, adjacent to a building and used in connection with its occupation: CLA 1977 s12(2).

12 CLA 1977 s12(1).

7.12   If parts of a building are separately occupied, however, they constitute different premises,[13] so that a person already lawfully in one part of the building can commit the offence by entering another (separately occupied) part.

7.13   The term also encompasses any fixed structure used for whatever purpose and any movable structure, vehicle or vessel, designed or adapted for use for residential purposes.[14] Thus, caravans, houseboats and converted buses are within the definition.

Violence

7.14   Violence[15] is not defined in CLA 1977 and so it is a question of fact and degree in any one case whether violence was used. It should be construed in its ordinary, everyday sense.

7.15   It is immaterial whether the violence is directed against a person or against property.[16] It is not enough, however, that the person in the premises opposed to entry feared or apprehended violence. The prosecution must prove that actual violence was used.[17]

For the purposes of securing entry to the premises

7.16   The violence must be committed with the objective in the mind of the person acting violently of securing entry to the premises. It is not essential that actual entry into the premises be achieved.

7.17   It is irrelevant whether the purpose of the entry is to acquire possession or for any other purpose;[18] it is as much an offence to gatecrash a party violently as it is to evict a squatter – all that is needed is the intention to secure entry.

---

13   CLA 1977 s12(1) and (2).

14   CLA 1977 s12(2).

15   This word was chosen rather than 'force', which is perhaps more common in criminal statutes, on the basis that it covers any application of force against the person, but carries a somewhat restricted meaning in relation to property; splintering a door or window would be violent but forcing a window catch would not: *Conspiracy and criminal law reform* (Law Com No 76 (1976)) at para 2.61.

16   CLA 1977 s6(4)(a).

17   There is, of course, the offence of threatening violence to secure entry (see below, paras 7.33–7.36) and conduct falling short of actual violence may be sufficient to constitute a threat.

18   CLA 1977 s6(4)(b).

Someone on the premises opposed to the entry

7.18 It does not matter what the status of the person on the premises is. The occupier may be an owner, a tenant, a licensee or a trespasser. As long as there is someone present and opposed to the entry, the person seeking to secure entry violently commits the offence.

7.19 It is unclear whether the person opposed to entry has to know that the defendant is intending to secure entry to the premises. The test is whether he or she opposes the entry. This does not appear to import a requirement for an active display of opposition, merely the factual question whether someone on the premises does oppose.[19]

7.20 If nobody is on the premises, however, no offence is committed.

Knowledge that there is someone on the premises

7.21 There is some older authority for the proposition that knowledge includes 'wilfully shutting one's eyes to the truth',[20] but the modern view is that nothing short of actual knowledge will suffice.[21] In the final analysis, it is a question of evidence whether the accused knew that somebody was on the premises opposed to entry.

Displaced residential occupier

7.22 CLA 1977 exempts from the offence someone who has been prevented from entering his or her own home. This is not a warrant to commit violence, because an offence against the person of the trespasser could still be committed, but prevents such a person being caught by this offence.

---

19 It would seem bizarre if no offence was committed where someone was too ill or frail to oppose the entry or, indeed, even asleep or unaware of the entry.

20 *Warner v Metropolitan Police Commissioner* [1969] 2 AC 256, HL, 279 per Lord Reid.

21 See eg, *Westminster City Council v Croyalgrange Ltd* [1986] 1 WLR 674, HL, 682C per Lord Bridge. See generally *Blackstone's criminal practice 2012* (Oxford University Press, 2011).

7.23   For the purposes of CLA 1977, such a person is known as a 'displaced residential occupier' and is defined as:[22]

> ... any person who was occupying any premises as a residence[23] immediately before being excluded by anyone who entered those premises, or any access to those premises,[24] as a trespasser.

7.24   A person remains a displaced residential occupier while excluded from occupation by the trespasser or any subsequent trespasser.[25]

7.25   A trespasser cannot benefit from the privilege given to a displaced residential occupier. A person is not a displaced residential occupier if he or she was occupying the premises as a trespasser immediately before being excluded from occupation.[26] For these purposes, a person who occupies by virtue of any title derived from a trespasser, or permission given by a trespasser,[27] is treated as a trespasser.[28]

7.26   Displaced residential occupiers cannot commit the offence of violent entry.[29] The exemption extends to anyone acting on behalf of a displaced residential occupier.

7.27   It is a question of fact whether one person is 'acting on behalf of' another. There appears to be no need for an express agreement; it can be inferred from the circumstances.

7.28   If a defendant adduces sufficient evidence of being a displaced residential occupier,[30] it creates a rebuttable presumption that he or she is such an occupier which, should the issue arise by way of trial, the prosecution will have to disprove.[31]

Protected intended occupier

7.29   The second class of persons who cannot commit the offence is known as 'protected intended occupiers'.

---

22   CLA 1977 s12(3).
23   See paras 5.5–5.8 for a discussion on occupying as a residence.
24   Access means any part of a site or building in which the premises are situated, which constitutes an ordinary means of access to those premises: CLA 1977 s12(1)(b).
25   CLA 1977 s12(3).
26   CLA 1977 s12(4).
27   Or from a person who himself or herself derived title from a trespasser.
28   CLA 1977 s12(6).
29   CLA 1977 s6(2).
30   Or acting on behalf of a displaced residential occupier.
31   CLA 1977 s6(1A).

7.30   Although not resident, a protected intended occupier intends to become so, but cannot because he or she is prevented from taking up occupation by a trespasser.

7.31   There are three types of such occupier, defined[32] as an individual,[33] who requires the premises for his or her own occupation, who is excluded from occupation by a trespasser and who is one of the following:

a) a freeholder or a leaseholder (whose lease has at least two years to run) with a sworn statement to this effect;[34]

b) a tenant or licensee of a local authority,[35] a registered provider of social housing or a registered social landlord with a certificate[36] from the landlord to this effect;[37]

c) any other tenant or a licensee of a freeholder or a leaseholder (whose lease has at least two years to run) with a sworn statement to this effect.[38]

7.32   As in the case of a displaced residential occupier, a protected intended occupier cannot commit the offence of violent entry.[39] Similarly, the exemption extends to anyone acting on behalf of a protected intending occupier.

Threatening violence to secure entry to premises

7.33   It is also an offence to threaten violence to secure entry to premises.[40] Threats may be made in any number of ways, for instance, spoken to someone in his or her presence of or over the telephone, put into writing or implied by behaviour.

---

32 CLA 1977 s12A.

33 Compare the definition of a displaced residential occupier in CLA 1977 s12(3), which refers to 'any person'. Presumably this is to avoid another type of legal person, eg, a company, from benefiting. It is unnecessary to make the distinction for displaced residential occupiers because a company cannot be resident: *Hiller v United Dairies* [1934] 1 KB 57, CA.

34 CLA 1977 s12A(2). The statement must be sworn by both landlord and tenant before a Justice of the Peace or a commissioner for oaths: CLA 1977 s12A(3).

35 Or a similar body: see Rent Act (RA) 1977 s14 for the complete list. It also applies where the landlord is the Regulator of Social Housing.

36 That is a statement in writing.

37 CLA 1977 s12(6).

38 CLA 1977 s12A(4) and (5).

39 CLA 1977 s6(2).

40 CLA 1977 s6(1).

7.34   The offence is committed only where the threat is of violence. Acts which cause the occupier to fear violence but which, on an objective view, do not amount to a threat of violence are not sufficient.

7.35   A general threat of violence towards an occupier is not enough; it must be for the purpose of securing entry to the property.

7.36   All the other elements of the offence – and the disapplications for displaced residential occupiers and protected intended occupiers and persons acting on their behalf – are the same as in relation to the offence of using violence to secure entry. (See paras 7.6–7.32 above.)

Penalties

7.37   These offences are triable only in a magistrates' court. The maximum penalty is six months' imprisonment and/or a fine of up to level 5 on the standard scale[41] (currently £5,000).[42]

Trespass in a residential building

7.38   LASPO 2012 s144 provides that it is a criminal offence where a person:

(a) is in a residential building as a trespasser having entered it as a trespasser,
(b) knows or ought to know that he or she is a trespasser, and
(c) is living in the building or intends to live there for any period.[43]

7.39   A building is 'residential' if it is designed or adapted, before the time of entry, for use as a place to live.[44]

7.40   A person who remains in a residential building after his or her tenancy or licence has determined is not guilty of the offence.[45]

7.41   A person who remains as a trespasser in a residential building at the time section 144 is brought into force will commit the offence.[46]

---

41 CLA 1977 s6(5).
42 Criminal Justice Act (CJA) 1982 s37, as amended by CJA 1991 s17.
43 LASPO 2012 s144(1).
44 LASPO 2012 s144(3).
45 LASPO 2012 s144(2) .
46 LASPO 2012 s144(7).

Penalties

7.42 This offence is triable only in the magistrates' court. The maximum penalty is a sentence for imprisonment of six months[47] and/or a fine of up to level 5 on the standard scale (currently £5,000).[48]

47 When CJA 2003 s281(5) is introduced, the maximum sentence will be 51 weeks' imprisonment: LASPO 2012 s144(5), (6).
48 LASPO 2012 s144(5), (6); CJA 1982 s37, as amended by CJA 1991 s17.

CHAPTER 8

Bringing criminal proceedings

Introduction

8.1   This chapter provides an outline of criminal procedure as it is relevant to the offences discussed in the previous chapters. It is primarily aimed at those advisers[1] who are unfamiliar with the criminal court process. It is not intended to be a comprehensive guide and practitioners are referred to the standard texts for detailed guidance on practice in both magistrates' courts and the Crown Court.

8.2   The most serious criminal offences ('indictable offences') must be heard by a Crown Court, where trial is by jury. Less serious cases ('summary offences') may only be heard by a magistrates' court. There are other offences (called 'either way offences') which can be dealt with by either court, depending variously on the wish of the prosecution, the defence or the court itself.

8.3   Unlawful eviction and harassment under the Protection from Eviction Act (PEA) 1977 are either way offences,[2] as are putting another in fear of violence and breach of a restraining order or an injunction under the Protection from Harassment Act (PHA) 1997. The other offences discussed in this book are summary offences.

Who may prosecute?

8.4   As a general rule, there is no restriction on who may institute criminal proceedings.[3] In practice, however, a magistrates' court is unlikely to issue proceedings unless the person has a sufficient interest. In general, therefore, prosecutions are usually taken by one of the following: the police, the victim or another body empowered to take proceedings because of a special interest. A local authority will almost invariably be considered to have a sufficient interest (see below, para 8.8 onwards).

The police

8.5   Although the police are commonly thought of as responsible for enforcing the totality of the criminal law, they have a wide discretion

---

1 Most housing practitioners, whether lawyers or non-lawyers, will have far more experience of the civil justice system, ie, county courts.

2 The defendant has a right to elect trial by jury in the Crown Court.

3 They can be started by 'any person': Prosecution of Offences Act (POA) 1985 s6.

as to both the investigation and prosecution[4] of criminal offences. The exercise of this discretion varies substantially between neighbouring police areas, reflecting different local priorities.

8.6 The police rarely, if ever, take action in relation to offences under PEA 1977, which, although criminal offences, tend to be perceived as disputes between landlords and occupiers and therefore more suitable for civil proceedings. That is not to say that the police should not be encouraged to bring criminal proceedings; they are, however, unlikely to participate beyond keeping opposing parties apart, eg where there is a risk of a breach of the peace, or worse.[5]

The victim

8.7 It is always open to a victim of any crime to take a private prosecution. This is not, however, recommended for a number of reasons (see above, para 1.32).[6]

Local authorities

8.8 Certain local authorities[7] are authorised to institute criminal proceedings for harassment or unlawful eviction under PEA 1977.[8]

8.9 Local authorities in any event have power to bring prosecutions if they 'consider it expedient for the promotion or protection of the inhabitants of their area',[9] which allows authorities to bring prosecutions, despite having no express power to do so, against persons for using violence to enter premises under the Criminal Law Act (CLA) 1977 or any offence created by PHA 1997 or Criminal Justice and Police Act (CJPA) 2001 s42A.

---

4 All police prosecutions in England and Wales are now conducted by the Crown Prosecution Service: POA 1985 ss1 and 3.

5 In *Cowan v Chief Constable of Avon and Somerset* [2001] EWCA Civ 1699, [2002] HLR 44, the Court of Appeal held that the police did not owe a tenant a duty of care to prevent his unlawful eviction.

6 It might be added that many magistrates' courts view private prosecutions with some suspicion; sometimes, the court clerk will try to avoid proceedings going ahead by suggesting that the prosecutor withdraws the proceedings if the defendant agrees to be bound over to keep the peace.

7 District councils, London boroughs, Welsh county councils, Welsh county boroughs, the Common Council of the City of London and the Council of the Isles of Scilly: PEA 1977 s6. A unitary authority which is a county council has the powers of a district council: Local Government Changes for England Regulations 1994 SI No 867 reg 5(7).

8 PEA 1977 s6.

9 Local Government Act 1972 s222.

8.10   A decision that it is expedient does not comprise a heavy burden to discharge and, accordingly, there will rarely be circumstances
where an authority cannot justify prosecuting under either of these
two statutes, particularly if the police have declined to take action.[10]

8.11   Local housing authorities are under a duty to take reasonable
steps to ensure that accommodation does not cease to be available
for occupation by a person who has become unintentionally threatened with homelessness.[11] As homelessness may often be the result
of unlawful eviction or harassment, the swift institution of criminal
proceedings by a local authority may be exactly the reasonable steps
or appropriate assistance which is needed.

8.12   Although authorities possess the legal powers to investigate and
prosecute alleged incidents, they are under no duty to do so and many
choose not to exercise them.[12]

8.13   In many cities and large towns, however, where unlawful eviction
and harassment tend to be more prevalent, councils employ officers
(commonly called 'harassment' or 'tenancy relations officers'), whose
job is to deal with the problem.

8.14   Those councils that do treat these incidents seriously only prosecute in a small percentage of cases.[13] Reasons for this include victims'
reluctance to give evidence against their landlords, internal council
procedures, and the hesitation of many local authority legal depart-
ments to issue proceedings unless virtually certain of a conviction.

8.15   Regardless of whether civil proceedings are also to be taken, it is,
nonetheless, advisable to contact the relevant official or department
and invite the local authority to investigate and prosecute.

Starting proceedings

8.16   Criminal proceedings must be commenced in the magistrates' court
for the area in which the offence is alleged to have been committed.
This applies whether or not the offence will eventually be tried in that
court or the Crown Court.

10 Where the police are willing to act, it could be more difficult to argue that it
was 'expedient' for the authority to prosecute.
11 Housing Act (HA) 1996 s195(2). A person is threatened with homelessness if
'it is likely that he will become homeless within 28 days': s175(4).
12 Advice to local authorities on these issues is set out in DoE Circular 3/89
(Housing Act 1988: Protection of Residential Occupiers), reproduced in
Encyclopaedia of housing law and practice, Vol 4 (Sweet & Maxwell).
13 Only 38 prosecutions were brought in 2011.

8.17 A person accused of an offence may be brought before a court in one of three ways: by charge, which is only available to the police, by summons or by warrant; the last two methods can be used regardless of who prosecutes.

By charge

8.18 This is how the police[14] formally accuse a person of an offence and require him or her to attend court. They are not required to obtain the prior approval of the court to start proceedings.

By summons

8.19 An 'information' must be laid before a magistrate (or more commonly a magistrates' court clerk) by the prosecutor.[15] It must give details of both the prosecutor and the accused, brief particulars of the alleged offence and, if contrary to statute, details of that statutory provision.[16] The information can be provided orally or in writing, but need not be under oath.[17]

8.20 The decision to issue a summons is judicial, not merely administrative. The magistrate or clerk issuing the summons must be satisfied that the information alleges an offence known to the law. There is, however, no requirement that the magistrate or clerk should inquire into whether there is a prima facie case or examine the evidence upon which the allegation is based.[18] There is a discretion to refuse to issue a summons, but this may only be exercised if there is a compelling reason to do so.[19]

8.21 The summons is usually sent to the accused by post at his or her last known or usual address[20] requiring attendance at the magistrates' court on a given date to answer the accusation. This procedure is available for the prosecution of any offence and is the most

---

14 This procedure is not available to any other 'organ of the state'.

15 If the prosecutor is a corporate body (eg a local authority), it can be laid by another person, such as an employee, provided that he or she has written authorisation to do so: Criminal Procedure Rules r2.5(1)(b).

16 Criminal Procedure Rules rr7.3(1) and 7.7(1).

17 Criminal Procedure Rules r7.2(1).

18 *R v Gateshead Justices ex p Tesco Stores Ltd* [1981] QB 470, CA.

19 There is a discretion to refuse to issue a summons if the magistrate or court clerk believes that the application is frivolous, vexatious or an abuse of process: *R v Bros* (1901) 66 JP 54, QBD.

20 Criminal Procedure Rules r4.4(1), (2)(a). Service may also be effected by leaving it at this address or personally: r4.3(1)(a).

common way for harassment and unlawful eviction proceedings to be commenced.

By warrant

8.22 Wherever there is jurisdiction to issue a summons, a magistrate may instead issue a warrant for the arrest of the person named in the information provided the information is in writing and the offence is either indictable or is punishable with a sentence of imprisonment.[21]

8.23 The warrant directs the police to bring the person before the court as soon as possible when the court may either hear the matter or adjourn the case. The magistrate has a power to 'back the warrant for bail', in which case, having been arrested, the accused will be released by the police to attend court on a particular date.[22]

8.24 Harassment and unlawful eviction are offences which carry a sentence of imprisonment,[23] as does an offence for harassment of a person in his or her home,[24] any offence under PHA 1997[25] and violent entry to premises.[26] Warrants can, accordingly, be issued in respect of these offences.

8.25 The advantage of using the warrant procedure is that the police are obliged to arrest the accused, even if he or she is subsequently released on bail.

The hearing

8.26 If the defendant[27] pleads not guilty, the case is unlikely to be tried at the first hearing and will be adjourned to another date. It may be adjourned more than once because of a shortage of time, or because of the absence of witnesses.

8.27 At the trial, the prosecution must prove the case on the criminal standard of proof (ie, 'beyond reasonable doubt') and is responsible for putting the evidence before the court. This can include

---

21 Magistrates' Courts Act (MCA) 1980 s1(1), (3), (4).
22 MCA 1980 s117.
23 Up to six months in a magistrates' court and two years in the Crown Court: PEA 1977 s1(4).
24 Up to six months: CJPA 2001 s42A(4).
25 See chapter 6.
26 Up to six months: CLA 1977 s6(5).
27 Who may apply for legal aid; because of the possibility of a custodial sentence on conviction, it should be granted, subject to means.

any witnesses, such as police officers, local authority officials, or an adviser who attempted to persuade the landlord to readmit the occupier or desist from harassing him or her. The occupier's evidence is likely to be of prime importance.

Compensation

8.28 On conviction, the court can order the defendant to pay compensation to the victim for 'personal injury, loss or damage resulting from [an] offence'.[28]

8.29 The power has been described[29] as 'a convenient and rapid means of avoiding the expense of resort to civil litigation when the criminal clearly has means that would enable the compensation to be paid'. Magistrates' courts are encouraged to order compensation wherever possible. In deciding to whether to make an award, justices should not have regard to the availability of other sources of compensation, such as civil litigation or the Criminal Injuries Compensation scheme.[30]

8.30 When making a compensation order, the court must have regard to the means of the person against whom the order is to be made.[31] Where the court considers it appropriate both to impose a fine and to make a compensation order, but the defendant has insufficient means to pay both, the compensation order should be made in preference to the fine.[32]

8.31 In the magistrates' court, compensation is limited to a maximum of £5,000 per convicted offence.[33] The Magistrates' Courts Sentencing Guidelines afford general guidance as to the amount to be awarded for certain injuries.[34] There is no limit in the Crown Court.

8.32 In *Bond v Chief Constable of Kent*,[35] it was held that anxiety and distress directly caused by the defendant's offence could be either 'personal injury' or 'damage' for the purposes of a compensation order.

28 Powers of Criminal Courts (Sentencing) Act (PCC(S)A) 2000 s130(1).
29 Scarman LJ in *R v Inwood* (1974) 60 Cr App 70, 73, CA of the previous provisions of the Powers of Criminal Courts Act 1973 s35.
30 *Magistrates' courts sentencing guidelines 2012*, para 4, p165.
31 *R v Daly* [1974] 1 WLR 133, CA.
32 PCC(S)A 2000 s130(12).
33 PCC(S)A 2000 s131(1).
34 For example, the suggested award for a bruise is £100, whereas the suggested award for a broken arm is £3,300.
35 [1983] 1 WLR 40, QBD.

8.33   Compensation is not restricted to personal injury and may therefore also be suitable for losses such as the cost of emergency accommodation or the value of damaged or destroyed belongings. Any award
must, however, be based on evidence before the court.[36] The victim
should be advised to bring to court supporting evidence, such as
photographs and bills for repairs to damaged goods or for temporary
accommodation, as appropriate. It is not the role of a criminal court,
however, to embark on a complex inquiry into the scale of the loss if
it is not obvious from the evidence before it. Compensation orders
will therefore only be made in clear cases.[37] It is, therefore, unlikely
to be awarded to compensate the victim for, say, the loss of the right
of occupation, injured feelings, distress or inconvenience.[38]

8.34   It does not matter whether the prosecutor is the individual occupier, the police or a local authority,[39] compensation may still be
claimed on behalf of the injured party.[40]

8.35   If compensation is awarded, it does not bar the victim from taking
civil proceedings, but any award by a criminal court will be deducted
from any damages subsequently awarded in civil proceedings.[41]

---

36 *R v Horsham Justices ex p Richards* [1985] 1 WLR 986, CA.
37 See *Blackstone's criminal court practice 2012* (Oxford University Press, 2011) at
    para E18.2.
38 If the victim wants compensation, the civil court is far better placed to award a
    realistic and substantial sum (see chapter 3).
39 It is important for authorities bringing prosecutions to consult the victim about
    compensation and to remember that his or her role in the process is not merely
    as a witness.
40 In addition, a magistrates' court may, of its own volition and after considering
    any evidence and representations made to it, make any order it considers
    appropriate: PCC(S)A 2000 s130(1) and (4).
41 PCC(S)A 2000 s134(2).

APPENDICES

APPENDIX A

Other remedies

Introduction

A.1   Harassment and other forms of nuisance experienced by an occupier of residential premises – whether or not committed by or on behalf of his or her landlord – may additionally or alternatively be addressed outside the law governing the landlord/tenant relationship. This appendix outlines a number of statutory provisions and common law remedies additional to those in the main body of this book,[1] which may nonetheless usefully be borne in mind. It focuses on powers aimed at broader anti-social behaviour and other kinds of conduct, eg noise, which are generally available only to local authorities or private registered providers of social housing. Even where occupiers do not have standing to bring actions themselves, however, they may nonetheless be able to persuade their landlord or local authority to do so.

A.2   There are three parts to this appendix:

a) public nuisance;
b) environmental and noise controls;
c) anti-social behaviour orders (ASBOs) and anti-social behaviour injunctions (ASBIs).

Nuisance

Public nuisance

A.3   A nuisance is conduct or an activity that unduly interferes with the use or enjoyment of land. Nuisance is actionable as a tort (see above at paras 2.58–2.70), but may also be punishable as a common-law,[2]

---

1 See para 1.8, above. Andrew Dymond, *Anti-social behaviour: law and practice*, LAG, forthcoming, will address these provisions in more detail.
2 *R v Rimmington* [2005] UKHL 63, [2006] 1 AC 459.

criminal offence if the interference is with exercise or enjoyment of a right to which a person is entitled as a member of the public: this is public nuisance. For public nuisance, the act or omission must be shown to 'materially affect the reasonable comfort and convenience of a class of Her Majesty's subjects'.[3]

A.4   Examples of public nuisance include: interference with the public highway;[4] sending a large number[5] of separate postal packages containing racially offensive material;[6] a series of hoax phone calls to the emergency services;[7] 1,000 phone calls in two weeks to 15 complainants;[8] organising illegal raves;[9] allowing pigeons to roost under a railway bridge;[10] and, permitting land to become covered with waste.[11]

A.5   A defendant is guilty of an offence if he or she knew, or ought to have known, that as a result of his or her acts or omissions, the probable outcome is that the public would be affected.[12] If the act or omission is authorised by statute, the defendant has a complete defence.[13]

A.6   The offence of public nuisance is triable either way.[14]

Environmental and noise controls

Waste

A.7   Activities involving waste are governed by Part 2 of the Environmental Protection Act (EPA) 1990.[15] It is an offence for a person to deposit controlled or extractive waste,[16] or knowingly to cause or permit controlled waste to be deposited, treated, kept, or disposed of in,

---

3   *Attorney-General v PYA Quarries Ltd* [1957] 2 QB 169, CA.
4   *Attorney-General v PYA Quarries Ltd* [1957] 2 QB 169, CA.
5   538.
6   *R v Rimmington* [2005] UKHL 63, [2006] 1 AC 459.
7   *R v Lowrie* [2004] EWCA Crim 2325, [2005] 1 Cr App R (S) 95.
8   *R v Eskdale* [2001] EWCA Crim 1159, [2002] 1 Cr App R (S) 28.
9   *R v Shorrock* [1994] QB 279, CA.
10 *Wandsworth LBC v Railtrack plc* [2001] EWCA Civ 1236, [2002] QB 756.
11 *Attorney-General v Heatley* [1897] 1 Ch 560, CA.
12 *R v Shorrock* [1994] QB 279, CA.
13 Principles of statutory authorisation apply.
14 Magistrates' Courts Act (MCA) 1980 s17(1) and Sch 1.
15 Note also, however, the offence of carrying controlled waste under Control of Pollution (Amendment) Act 1989 s1.
16 Meaning household, industrial, commercial waste or any such waste: EPA 1990 s75(4).

or on, any land that is not authorised by licence: EPA 1990 s33(1). An offence is also caused if a person treats, keeps or disposes of controlled or extractive waste in a manner likely to cause pollution or the environment or harm to human health: EPA 1990 s33(1)(c).

A.8   It is a defence if the defendant either:

(a) took all reasonable precautions and exercised due diligence to prevent the offence from occurring; or

(b) the acts were conducted in an emergency in order to avoid danger to human health and all reasonably practicable steps were taken to minimise the pollution of the environment and harm to human health, provided that particulars of the acts were furnished to the waste regulation authority as soon as reasonably practicable after they were done.[17]

A.9   An offence under section 33(1) is triable either way.[18]

A.10   In cases of breach of EPA 1990 s33(1) caused or permitted by an owner or occupier, an authority may, by service of notice on him or her, require that the waste is removed from the land within a specific period not less than 21 days after service of notice and/or take specified steps to eliminate or reduce the consequences of the waste deposit within a specific period.[19] An owner or occupier who fails to comply with the requirement(s) without reasonable excuse may be liable on summary conviction to a fine not exceeding level 5 on the standard scale (currently £5,000)[20] and to a further fine of one-fifth of a fine not exceeding level 5 each day that the non-compliance continues.

Statutory nuisance

A.11   The EPA 1990 s79 imposes a duty on every local authority to cause its area to be inspected from time to time to detect any statutory nuisances. Where a complaint of a statutory nuisance is made to it by a person living within its area, a local authority is under a duty to take such steps as are reasonably practicable to investigate the complaint.[21] Failure to comply with the duty may lead to the secretary of

---

17 EPA 1990 s33(7).
18 Liable on summary conviction to imprisonment for a term not exceeding 12 months or a fine not exceeding £50,000 or both; or liable on indictment to imprisonment for a term not exceeding five years or an unlimited fine or both: EPA 1990 s33(8).
19 EPA 1990 s59.
20 Criminal Justice Act (CJA) 1982 s37, as amended by CJA 1991 s17.
21 EPA 1990 s79.

state ordering the local authority to investigate a potential statutory nuisance.[22] A person suffering from a nuisance may compel the local authority to fulfil its duty by judicial review.[23]

A.12   The following matters constitute statutory nuisances:[24]

a) any premises in such state as to be prejudicial to health or a nuisance;

b) smoke emitted from premises so as to be prejudicial to health or a nuisance;

c) fumes or gases emitted from premises so as to be prejudicial to health or a nuisance;

d) any dust, steam, smell arising on industrial, trade or business premises and being prejudicial to health or a nuisance;

e) any accumulation or deposit which is prejudicial to health or a nuisance;

f) any animal kept in such a place or manner as to be prejudicial to health or a nuisance;

g) any insects emanating from relevant industrial, trade or business premises and being prejudicial to health or a nuisance;

h) artificial light emitted from premises so as to be prejudicial to health or a nuisance;

i) noise emitted from premises so as to be prejudicial to health or a nuisance;

j) noise that is prejudicial to health or a nuisance and is emitted from or caused by a vehicle, machinery or equipment in a street;

k) any other matter declared by any enactment to be a statutory nuisance.

A.13   'Prejudicial to health' is defined at EPA 1990 s79(7), as injurious or likely to cause injury to health. This may include problems caused by mould growth;[25] unsealed drains;[26] loss of sleep.[27] The test is an objective one.

A.14   The definition of 'nuisance' is the same as that for common law nuisance.[28]

---

22   EPA 1990 Sch 3 para 4(2).

23   *R (Anne) v Test Valley BC* [2002] EWHC Admin 1019, [2002] Env LR 22.

24   *R (Anne) v Test Valley BC* [2002] EWHC Admin 1019, [2002] Env LR 22.

25   *Birmingham City Council v Oakley* [2001] 1 AC 617, HL.

26   *Salford City Council v McNally* [1976] AC 379, HL.

27   *Lewisham LBC v Fenner* (1995) 248 ENDS Report 44.

28   *National Coal Board v Thorn* [1976] 1 WLR 543, DC. See paras 2.58–2.70 above.

A.15   Examples of statutory nuisance include noise[29] from premises or the street that does not arise from military forces, traffic or aircraft.[30] There is no minimum noise level that needs to be met before a nuisance is caused for the purposes of EPA 1990. Indeed, it is not necessary to provide evidence of measurements of noise, although such evidence is preferable.[31] Whether noise is a nuisance may depend on factors other than volume such as pitch and nature.[32]

A.16   When a local authority identifies that a statutory notice exists, or is likely to occur, it must either serve[33] an abatement notice or take such other action it thinks appropriate to cause the appropriate person to abate the nuisance. The abatement notice should identify the nuisance complained of and what is required of the person served with the notice.[34] The notice must identify the (reasonable)[35] time for compliance with the requirements.[36] The time for appeal (21 days from service) must be specified in the notice.[37]

A.17   Failure to comply with the requirements set out in an abatement notice without reasonable excuse is an offence under EPA 1990 s80(4) liable on summary conviction to a fine not exceeding level 5 on the standard scale (currently £5,000)[38] plus a further fine of up to £500 for each day that the offence continues.[39]

A.18   In addition to the local authority's power to take action to abate a statutory nuisance,[40] it is open to the person aggrieved[41] by the statutory nuisance to institute proceedings him or herself.[42] He or she

---

29 Can include vibrations: EPA 1990 s79(7).

30 EPA 1990 ss6 and 6A.

31 *Lewisham LBC v Yvonne Hall* [2002] EWHC 960 (Admin), [2003] Env LR 4 and *Gillbard v Caradon District Council* [2006] EWHC 3233 (Admin), [2007] Env LR D5, DC. There are fewer evidential requirements for proving statutory noise nuisance than under Noise Act 1996 (see below at paras A.19–A.25.)

32 *Cambridge City Council v Douglas* [2001] Env LR 41, DC.

33 In accordance with the rules of service EPA 1990 s160 or Local Government Act 1972 s233.

34 EPA 1990 s80(1).

35 Statutory Nuisance (Appeals) Regulations 1995 SI No 2644 reg 2(2)(c); *R v Tunbridge Wells Justices ex p Tunbridge Wells BC* [1996] Env LR 88, QBD.

36 EPA 1990 s80(1).

37 EPA 1990 s80(3) and Sch 3 para 6.

38 CJA 1982 s37 as amended by CJA 1991 s17.

39 EPA 1990 s80(5).

40 Including the power to serve a fixed penalty notice: EPA 1990 s80(6).

41 A person who has been affected by the statutory nuisance so that prejudice is caused to his or her health or whose reasonable enjoyment has been affected.

42 EPA 1990 s82(1).

cannot issue an abatement notice as can the local authority, but may make an application to a magistrates' court for an order requiring the defendant to abate the nuisance. The proceedings should be brought against the person causing the nuisance.[43] If the nuisance is caused by a structural defect or the person responsible cannot be found, proceedings should be instigated against the owner or occupier. If the magistrates' court is satisfied that the statutory nuisance exists, or is likely to occur or recur, it may make an order requiring the defendant to abate the nuisance and/or require that specified work(s) are carried out within a specific time to prevent a recurrence of the nuisance and/or impose a fine not exceeding level 5 (currently £5,000)[44] on the standard scale.[45]

Noise

A.19   In addition to the remedies already discussed, noise problems can be dealt with under the following statutes:

a) Noise Act (NA) 1996, as amended; and
b) Anti-social Behaviour Act 2003.

A.20   The NA 1996 affords a local authority the power to deal with noise emanating from a dwelling (or licensed premise or a temporary notice) at night[46] using a summary procedure. If a complaint about noise at night is received by the local authority, the authority may arrange for an officer to investigate. If the officer is satisfied that the noise exceeds the permitted levels,[47] he or she may serve a warning notice.[48]

A.21   A warning notice must be served on the person present, at or near the dwelling who appears to be responsible for the noise.[49] It should include the following information:

---

43   Alternatively, if noise nuisance is emitted from a vehicle, machinery or equipment, proceedings should be brought against the person in control of that vehicle, machinery or equipment.
44   CJA 1982 s37, as amended by CJA 1991 s17.
45   EPA 1990 s82(2) and (8).
46   Between the hours of 11pm and 7am: NA 1996 s2(6).
47   As defined in the directions set by the secretary of state, currently set within Permitted Level of Noise (England) Directions 2008. It is not necessary for the levels to be measured by devices; the assessment is one for the investigating officer: NA 1996 s2(5).
48   NA 1996 s2(4).
49   NA 1996 s3(3)(a).

i) that an officer considers that the noise emitted from the dwelling or licensed premises exceeds the permitted level during night hours;

ii) that the person responsible for the noise emitted may be guilty of an offence;

iii) that the period specified must be one beginning at least ten minutes after the service of the notice and ending with the following 7am;

iv) the time the notice was served.[50]

A.22   A person responsible for any noise exceeding permitted levels emitted[51] within the period specified from the dwelling or licensed premises following service of a warning notice is guilty of an offence.[52] There is a defence of reasonable excuse for such noise emitted from a dwelling, but no such defence for similar noise from licensed premises.[53]

A.23   The penalty on summary conviction arising from dwellings is a fine not exceeding level 3 (currently £1,000)[54] on the standard scale. Summary conviction from licensed premises has a penalty of a fine not exceeding level 5 (currently £5,000)[55] on the standard scale.

A.24   As an alternative to trial and possible conviction, a fixed penalty notice may be issued and served for this offence.[56]

A.25   By virtue of NA 1996, an officer of a local authority has the power to enter and seize equipment used to make unlawful noise after a warning notice has been served and breached.[57] A warrant is not necessary before the officer can take such action, although one may be sought if entry is refused. Any person wilfully obstructing an officer from entering and seizing equipment is guilty of an offence liable on summary conviction to a fine not exceeding level 3 (currently £1,000)[58]

---

50 See NA 1996 s3(1) and (2).

51 As measured by an approved device: NA 1996 s5(2). If an unapproved device is used, that evidence is inadmissible for prosecution purposes: s4 and as currently governed by Measuring Devices (Noise Act 1996) (England) Approval 2008.

52 NA 1996 s4(2).

53 NA 1996 s4(2).

54 CJA 1982 s37 as amended by CJA 1991 s17.

55 CJA 1982 s37 as amended by CJA 1991 s17.

56 NA 1996 s4 or s4A.

57 NA 1996 s10.

58 CJA 1982 s37 as amended by CJA 1991 s17.

on the standard scale.[59] If a court convicts the defendant, it may also make an order for forfeiture of the seized equipment.[60]

Noisy premises closure orders

A.26 Section 40 of the Anti-social Behaviour Act (ASBA) 2003 allows local authorities immediately to close noisy premises in circumstances where it is reasonably believed[61] that the noise is causing a public nuisance[62] and that it is necessary[63] to close the premises to prevent the nuisance from occurring. Where an officer decides that a closure order is necessary, he or she must serve the order on the person responsible for the premises requiring him or her to close the premises for a period of up to 24 hours from the time the written notice was received.[64] If a person keeps premises open in contravention of the closure order without reasonable excuse, he or she commits a criminal offence punishable summarily by a term of imprisonment of up to 51 weeks or a fine not exceeding £20,000 or both.[65] An officer may cancel the notice as soon as reasonably practicable after he or she comes to believe that the order is no longer necessary to prevent a public nuisance.[66]

Anti-social behaviour

A.27 There is a number of measures which can be used to combat anti-social behaviour, not least because that is a description which lends itself to a wide range of conduct, including, of course, all the conduct addressed above. Under this heading, we consider three further measures:

a) closure orders under ASBA 2003, as amended;
b) anti-social behaviour orders (ASBOs) under Crime and Disorder Act (CDA) 1998, as amended; and
c) anti-social behaviour injunctions (ASBIs) under Housing Act (HA) 1996, as amended.

---

59 NA 1996 s10(8).
60 NA 1996 Sch 1 para 4.
61 By the chief executive officer of the relevant local authority: ASBA 2003 s40(1)(a).
62 See discussion and definition of 'public nuisance' above at paras A.3–A.6.
63 ASBA 2003 s40(1)(b).
64 ASBA 2003 s40(3).
65 ASBA 2003 s41(5).
66 ASBA 2003 s41(5). Any notice of cancellation must be in writing.

Closure orders[67]

A.28   Additional to the provisions for noisy premises considered above, Part 1A of ASBA 2003 affords powers for the closure of premises associated with persistent disorder or nuisance. In order to close premises, a police officer, not below the rank of superintendent, must have reasonable grounds for believing[68] that at any time during the relevant period[69] the premises is associated with significant and persistent disorder or persistent serious nuisance to members of the public.[70] Although there is no prescribed form for closure notice, it must contain the following information:[71]

(a) notice that an application will be made for the closure of the premises;

(b) a statement that access to the premises by any person other than a person who habitually resides in the premises or the owner of the premises is prohibited;

(c) the date and time when and the place at which the application will be heard;

(d) the effects of an order;

(e) that failure to comply with the notice amounts to an offence;

(f) information about relevant advice providers.

A.29   Service of the notice must be effected by a constable[72] or an employee of the local authority[73] by fixing a copy to at least one prominent place on the premises.[74] The application for the closure order must be heard at the magistrates' court no later than 48 hours after service of the notice.[75] The magistrates may make a closure order if they are satisfied – to the civil standard[76] – of the following:

---

67 It is also possible for premises to be closed if they are used for drug use (ASBA 2003 Part 1) and/or for prostitution or pornography (Sexual Offences Act 2003 s136B): see footnotes 132 to 133 below. These powers are beyond the scope of this book and are, thus, not discussed in detail here.

68 *R (Errington) v Metropolitan Police Authority* [2006] EWHC 1155 (Admin).

69 Period of three months ending with the day on which the officer considers whether to issue a closure notice: ASBA 2003 s11A(11).

70 ASBA 2003 s11A(1).

71 ASBA 2003 s11A(5). If a notice does not contain the required information, a magistrate is unlikely to hear any application made until the notice is correct: *R (Errington) v Metropolitan Police Authority* [2006] EWHC 1155 (Admin).

72 If a notice is properly issued by an authorising officer: ASBA 2003 s11A(6)(a).

73 If a notice is authorised by the local authority: ASBA 2003 s11A(6).

74 Or by one of the means listed at ASBA 2003 s11A(7).

75 ASBA 2003 s11B(2).

76 *Chief Constable of Cumbria Constabulary v Wright* [2006] EWHC 3574 (Admin), [2007] 1 WLR 1407.

(i) a person has engaged in anti-social behaviour on the premises in respect of which the Part 1A closure notice was issued;

(ii) use of the premises is associated with the significant and persistent disorder or persistent serious nuisance to members of the public;

(iii) the making of the order is necessary to prevent the occurrence of such disorder or serious nuisance for the period specified in the order.[77]

A.30   A closure order may close the premises for up to three months and may include any provision relating to access which the court considers appropriate.[78] A person affected by the closure order may, at any time while it has effect, apply to the magistrates' court for an order relating to access to the premises.[79] The police may make an application[80] at any time before the end for an extension of the closure order if an officer has reasonable grounds for believing that it is necessary to extend the order for the purpose of preventing the occurrence of disorder or serious nuisance and has consulted the relevant local authority.[81] A closure order can only be discharged by order once the court is satisfied that closure is no longer necessary.[82]

A.31   Contravention of a closure order is a criminal offence punishable by summary conviction to a term of imprisonment up to six months, to a fine not exceeding level 5 (currently £5,000)[83] on to the standard scale or both.[84]

Anti-social behaviour orders

A.32   Anti-social behaviour orders are civil remedies containing terms or prohibitions, which are considered necessary to protect others from anti-social behaviour. Breach of an ASBO is a criminal offence. An ASBO can be applied for by a relevant authority, usually the local

---

77 ASBA 2003 s11B(4). In addition, as a closure order may result in a person being dispossessed from his or her home, article 8 of the European Convention on Human Rights may be engaged, thus any order must be considered to be necessary and proportionate: *R (Cleary) v Highbury Corner Magistrates' Court* [2006] EWHC 1869 (Admin), [2007] 1 WLR 1272.

78 ASBA 2003 s11B(5) and (6).

79 ASBA 2003 s11B(7).

80 To the appropriate justice of the peace.

81 ASBA 2003 s11B(1).

82 ASBA 2003 s11B.

83 CJA 1982 s37 as amended by CJA 1991 s17.

84 ASBA 2003 s11D(1), (2) and (3).

authority or police,[85] in either the magistrates' court[86] or the county court.[87] In addition, any criminal court has the power to make an ASBO following conviction in criminal proceedings.[88]

A.33   A relevant authority can apply for an ASBO if it considers[89] that:

i)   a person aged over ten has acted in an anti-social manner, ie in a manner that caused or was likely to cause harassment, alarm or distress to one or more persons not of the same household as him or herself, which he or she cannot show was reasonable in the circumstances;[90] and

ii) such an order is necessary to protect relevant persons[91] from further anti-social acts by him or her.[92]

A.34   The terms sought to be contained within an ASBO must be necessary to prevent further anti-social behaviour.[93] Before application, the relevant authority must consult other agencies in accordance with CDA 1998 s1E[94] and provide written evidence of such consultation.[95]

A.35   Prior to the final determination of an ASBO application, a relevant authority may apply for an interim ASBO. An interim order should be granted if the court is satisfied that it is 'just' to make an interim order. Interim ASBOs have the same effect as a full ASBO. An interim ASBO may be applied for without giving notice to the defendant provided the justices' clerk is satisfied that such an

---

85 Also includes chief constable of the British Transport Police, a registered provider of social housing, a registered social landlord (in Wales), a housing action trust or any other relevant authority added by the order of the secretary of state: CDA 1998 s1(1A).

86 CDA 1998 s1.

87 CDA 1998 s1B.

88 CDA 1998 s1C.

89 Partner agencies should have protocols for considerations. See also Home Office Guidance, 'A guide to anti-social behaviour orders', August 2006.

90 CDA 1998 s1(5).

91 Who is relevant will depend on who the applying authority is, ie for a local authority applicant, it will be people in that local authority's area.

92 CDA 1998 s1(1).

93 CDA 1998 s1(6).

94 Councils and the police must consult each other. Any other relevant authority must consult both the council and the police who deal with the area that the defendant resides. Failure to consult may invalidate the ASBO application: *Manchester City Council v Muir* [2006] EWCA Civ 423 at [21]. Substantial compliance with the duty to consult, however, may be sufficient for an ASBO application: *McClarty v Wigan BC*, unreported, 30 October 2005, High Court at Liverpool.

95 Civil Procedure Rules (CPR) 65.25.

application is 'necessary'.[96] When considering whether an ex parte application is 'necessary', the clerk should consider the following non-exhaustive list:[97]

a) the likely response of the defendant on receiving notice of such application;

b) whether such response is liable to prejudice the complainant having regard to the complainant's vulnerability;

c) the gravity of the conduct complained of within the scope of conduct tackled by ASBOs in general as opposed to the particular locality;

d) the urgency of the matter;

e) the nature of the prohibition sought in the interim ASBO;

f) the right of the defendant to know about the proceedings against him or her;

g) the counterbalancing protections for the rights of the defendant.

A.36　When an interim ASBO is made without notice, the order and the application must be served on the defendant in person as soon as possible[98] and will not take effect until such service is carried out.[99] Once served, a defendant is entitled to apply to the court to discharge or vary the order.[100]

A.37　Free-standing applications for ASBOs made to the magistrates' court are civil proceedings.[101] There must have been an allegation of anti-social behaviour made within 6 months of the application,[102] although not all allegations must fall within this time period.

A.38　Applications for ASBOs made to the county court must be brought as part of other proceedings to which the relevant authority or the defendant are a party,[103] eg in possession proceedings.

A.39　ASBOs made following criminal conviction may be made by application or by the court's own motion if it is deemed appropriate.[104]

96　Magistrates' Courts (Anti-social Behaviour Orders) Rules 2002 SI No 2784 r5(2).

97　*R (Manchester City Council) v Manchester Magistrates' Court* [2005] EWHC 253 (Admin) at [23] and [24].

98　2002 SI No 2784 r5(3). If an interim without notice ASBO is not served within seven days of being made, it expires and a fresh application will be necessary if the relevant authority wishes to obtain another one.

99　2002 SI No 2784 r5(4).

100　2002 SI No 2784 r5(8).

101　*R v Manchester Crown Court ex p McCann* [2002] UKHL 39, [2003] 1 AC 787.

102　MCA 1980 s127.

103　CDA 1998 s1B(1).

104　CDA 1998 s1C(1).

Part 50 of the Criminal Procedure Rules govern the procedure in such cases, although proceedings are still civil in nature.

A.40 In order to make an ASBO, the court must be satisfied that the defendant acted in an anti-social manner[105] and that an order is necessary to protect others from further anti-social acts by the defendant.[106] The court must then consider what terms should be included within the order to control the defendant's behaviour.[107]

A.41 An ASBO must last for a minimum of two years from the date the order was made.[108] It is open to both parties to apply to vary or discharge an ASBO.[109]

A.42 Breaches of an ASBO are dealt with by way of criminal proceedings and are punishable on summary conviction to a term of imprisonment up to six months or a fine or both. A breach is punishable on indictment to a term of imprisonment up to five years or a fine or both.[110]

Anti-social behaviour injunctions

A.43 Sections 153A–E of the HA 1996 provide the court[111] with powers to impose an anti-social behaviour injunction (ASBI) on a person to prohibit him or her from engaging in acts of nuisance or annoyance.

A.44 HA 1996 s153A provides that a court may grant an ASBI, on application by a relevant landlord,[112] against a person who has engaged in or threatens to engage in housing-related conduct[113] which is capable of causing a nuisance or annoyance to a relevant person.[114]

A.45 A relevant landlord may apply for an ASBI to prevent a person from engaging in or threatening to engage in using premises for an unlawful purpose, pursuant to HA 1996 s153B.

---

105 To the criminal standard of proof.
106 No standard of proof applies to the test of 'necessity'; it is a matter for the court's judgment: *McCann*.
107 CDA 1998 ss1(4), 1B(4), 1C(2).
108 CDA 1998 s1(7) and (9).
109 CDA 1998 s1(8). Liberty to vary an ASBO includes an application to extend an ASBO if so advised.
110 CDA 1998 s1(10).
111 Either High Court or County Court, although the County Court is the more usual forum: HA 1996 s153E(6).
112 Ie a housing action trust, local authority, non-profit registered provider of social housing or registered social landlord: HA 1996 s153E(7).
113 Ie directly or indirectly related to or affecting the housing management function of the relevant landlord. The conduct, therefore, need not be confined to behaviour in the premises: HA 1996 s153E(7).
114 HA 1996 s153A(4).

A.46   HA 1996 s153D enables a relevant landlord to apply for an ASBI if its tenant has breached or is likely to breach a term of his or her tenancy. A court may make an ASBI under section 153D if it is satisfied that by such breaches or anticipated breaches, the tenant[115] is engaging in or threatening to engage in conduct that is capable of causing nuisance or annoyance to any person.

A.47   The procedural rules governing ASBIs are contained in CPR Part 65 and the corresponding Practice Direction. An application for an ASBI must be made on form N16A.[116] An application notice and any accompanying evidence must be served on the defendant personally.[117]

A.48   An application may be considered without notice to the defendant.[118] If an application is made without notice, a witness statement must also be provided explaining why the application has been made ex parte.[119]

A.49   Although there is no specific requirement to serve an ASBI on the defendant personally,[120] personal service is – in practice – necessary for the ASBI to be enforceable.[121]

A.50   An ASBI may be granted for a specified period or until varied or discharged.[122] An ASBI granted without notice, however, should be made for an initial period and an on notice hearing should be listed to take place as soon as practicable after the first hearing.[123]

A.51   An ASBI may include a term excluding the defendant from any premises[124] or any area[125] where the defendant's conduct has consisted of or includes the use or threatened use of violence, or there is

---

115 Or any other person allowed, incited or encouraged by the tenant.

116 CPR Part 65 PD 1.1. If the application is in conjunction with a claim for possession, then the claim form for possession proceedings should be used in accordance with CPR Part 55.

117 CPR 65.3(5).

118 For guidance, see *Moat Housing Group-South Limited v Harris & Hartless* [2006] EWCA Civ 287, [2006] QB 606, [2005] HLR 33.

119 CPR 65.3(3).

120 Unlike ASBOs where personal service is a requirement: CDA 1998 s1B(4).

121 See above, paras 4.16–4.24.

122 HA 1996 s153E(2) and (3).

123 See *Moat Housing Group-South Limited v Harris & Hartless* [2006] EWCA Civ 287, [2006] QB 606, [2005] HLR 33: an initial period of six months was acceptable so long as an on notice hearing is listed as soon as practicable after the first hearing.

124 HA 1996 s153C(2)(a).

125 HA 1996 s153C(2)(b).

significant risk of harm to a relevant person.[126] The area of exclusion should be clearly described and/or a map delineating the area should be attached to the ASBI order.

A.52   If an ASBI is granted, the court may also attach a power of arrest to the order or specified term(s) in the order if it is satisfied that the conduct consists of or includes the use or threatened use of violence, or there is a significant risk of harm to a relevant person.[127] A power of arrest may be attached if, in all the circumstances, the court thinks it is appropriate.[128]

A.53   Breaches of ASBIs are dealt with by way of application for committal.[129] A committal application should be accompanied by affidavit evidence setting out the date and detail of any alleged breach(es). If the court finds that a person has been in contempt of court, it has the power to imprison him or her for a term up to two years and/or to impose an unlimited fine.[130]

Proposed anti-social behaviour reform[131]

A.54   The government intends to replace ASBOs and ASBIs with Crime Prevention Injunctions (CPIs). The CPI will be available to a wide range of public bodies. To grant a CPI, the court will have to be satisfied that the perpetrator has been found, on the balance of probabilities, to have engaged in conduct that is capable of causing a nuisance or annoyance and that it is just and convenient to make the order. Applicants will also be able to apply for interim orders without giving notice to the perpetrator. Unlike ASBOs and ASBIs a court will be able to impose positive obligations on the perpetrator requiring him or her to do so something, eg attend a drug rehabilitation programme, as well as prohibiting anti-social conduct.

A.55   Under the proposals, orders may be made for as long as necessary and there will be no minimum or maximum duration. A power of arrest may be attached to an order where the perpetrator has used, or threatened the use of, violence or there is a risk of significant harm to the victim.

A.56   Breach of a term of a CPI will be by contempt of court and will carry a fine or a term of imprisonment for up to two years. Breaches

126 As described in HA 1996 s153A(3).
127 HA 1996 s153C(3).
128 HA 1996 s154.
129 CCR Order 29.
130 Contempt of Court Act 1981 s14.
131 *Putting victims first: more effective responses to anti-social behaviour*, May 2012.

by children will not be a criminal offence and may be punished either by the imposition of a curfew, activity or supervision requirement. In cases where there are repeated breaches and their conduct has caused serious harm, children between 14 and 17 may be detained for up to three months.

A.57   Criminal Behaviour Orders (CBOs) will replace the ASBOs on conviction and drink banning orders[132] on conviction. A local authority, as well as the police, may request that the Crown Prosecution Service (CPS) apply for such an order on conviction and an order may be made where it would prevent harassment, alarm or distress to a member of the public. Again like the CPI, CBOs may impose positive as well as prohibitive requirements. Unlike the CPI, such orders must last for at least two years for adults and one year for children. A breach of a CBO will be an offence.

A.58   Community Protection Order (Closure) will replace the premises closure order,[133] crack house closure order,[134] the noisy premises closure order[135] and the closure order.[136] A CPO (Closure) may be applied for by both the police and local authorities. An order cannot be made unless there has been consultation between the owner, landlord, licensee and anyone who appears to be residing in the premises. The court must be satisfied that there is a public nuisance or there is likely to be disorder imminently in the vicinity and related to the premises and that the order is necessary to prevent the occurrence of such disorder or behaviour. An order will last for up to 48 hours unless extended by the magistrates' court. Those persons who are

132 Drink banning orders impose terms prohibiting the individual against whom they are made from engaging in specified criminal or disorderly conduct while under the influence of alcohol: Violent Crime Reduction Act 2006 s1.

133 Closure orders applied for where there is reason to believe that during the relevant period premises have been used for activities related to one or more specified prostitution or pornography offences and closure is necessary to prevent the premises being used for such purposes: Sexual Offences Act 2003 s136B.

134 Ie closure orders applied for if there are reasonable grounds for believing that at any time during the relevant period the premises have been used in connection with the unlawful use, production or supply of a Class A controlled drug, and that the use of the premises is associated with the occurrence of disorder or serious nuisance to members of the public: ASBA 2003 s1.

135 Closure orders applied for in respect of premises where a premises licence or a temporary event notice has effect, it is reasonably believed that a public nuisance is being caused by noise coming from the premises and it is necessary to prevent the nuisance: ASBA 2003 s40.

136 General closure orders applied for if there has been anti-social behaviour on the premises such that the use of the premises is associated with significant and persistent disorder or serious nuisance: ASBA 2003 s11B.

habitually resident at the premises may enter the premises during this time.

A.59   A magistrates' court may extend the order if satisfied that a person has engaged in disorder or anti-social or criminal behaviour on the premises, which has caused disorder or serious nuisance to members of the public and that the order is necessary in order to prevent the occurrence of such disorder or behaviour. Breach of the order without a reasonable excuse will be a criminal offence.

APPENDIX B

Classification of occupation

Introduction

B.1   Whether or not an occupier can use the remedies and causes of action described in this book is affected by his or her status, ie his or her right of occupation at common law and statutory security of tenure. This appendix provides a short guide to status of occupation and the security of tenure enjoyed by different occupiers in private sector housing; it is important to stress (a) that it is only a brief outline, directed to the urgency of harassment and illegal eviction,[1] and (b) that it does not cover every different type of occupation: at its fullest, the subject of status is one of considerable complexity.[2]

B.2   There are three parts to this appendix:

a) right of occupation, setting out the ways in which land[3] can be occupied;

b) security of tenure (including statutory protection) which, in this context, broadly means the legal right to remain in occupation; and

c) special categories.

Right of occupation

Freehold

B.3   A freeholder has an 'interest in land', in effect, rights as an owner. The extent of this ownership is not limited in time, that is, it is indefinite.

---

1   Ie if possession proceedings are issued, including by way of response to a claim for harassment or illegal eviction, more detailed consideration will be required.

2   For a fuller guide, see Arden and Dymond, *Manual of housing law* (9th edn, Sweet & Maxwell, 2012) or Arden, Partington, Hunter and Dymond, *Housing law* (looseleaf, Sweet & Maxwell).

3   Including buildings on land.

Tenancy

B.4   Like a freeholder, a tenant (normally) has an interest in land, but, unlike freehold ownership, a tenancy is limited in time. Many tenancies are, however, for such a long period of time that they are considered a form of owner-occupation, ie long leaseholders. There will, however, still be a landlord (not uncommonly, a company formed by a group of long leaseholders, eg in a block of flats) and there will still be rent and, invariably, service charges payable, and payment of such sums can give rise to disputes which can even ultimately (and on rare occasion) result in evictions.

B.5   In *Street v Mountford*,[4] the House of Lords identified the 'hallmarks' of a tenancy as the grant of exclusive possession for a term in exchange for the payment of rent.[5] The term is the time element and may be expressed either as a fixed term or by reference to a period (for example, week to week, month to month, etc).[6]

B.6   A tenancy granted for an uncertain term (eg a tenancy which purports to be a periodic tenancy but which cannot, under its terms, be determined by a notice to quit) is deemed to be held for a term of 90 years determinable on the tenant's death.[7]

Licence

B.7   A tenancy does not arise where the parties do not intend to enter into binding legal relations, in which case the arrangement is a licence.[8]

B.8   A licence is permission to occupy and confers no rights of ownership on the occupier. A licence arises where one or more of the

---

4 [1985] AC 809, (1985) 17 HLR 402, HL; see also *Bruton v London & Quadrant Housing Trust* [2000] 1 AC 406, (2000) 31 HLR 902, HL.

5 It is theoretically possible to create a tenancy at no rent: *Ashburn Anstalt v Arnold* [1989] Ch 1, CA. In relation to residential occupation, however, such an arrangement would usually be regarded as a licence, the absence of rent evidencing a lack of intention to enter legal relations.

6 Where a tenancy has statutory protection, it is generally irrelevant whether it is fixed term or periodic.

7 Law of Property Act (LPA) 1925 s149(6); *Mexfield Housing Co-operative Ltd v Berrisford* [2011] UKSC 52, [2011] 3 WLR 1091, [2012] HLR 15.

8 See, for instance, *Booker v Palmer* [1942] 2 All ER 674, CA (accommodation provided as an act of generosity or friendship); *Facchini v Bryson* [1952] 1 TLR 1386, CA (family arrangement); *Sopwich v Stuchbury* (1984) 17 HLR 50, CA (occupation during negotiations subject to contract, eg, by a purchaser before completion); *Vaughan-Armatrading v Sarsah* (1995) 27 HLR 631, CA, *Westminster City Council v Basson* (1991) 23 HLR 225, CA (sub-occupant continuing in occupation after the expiry of the head tenancy).

hallmarks of the tenancy is absent or where the parties did not intend to enter into binding legal relations.[9]

B.9   Common examples of a licence are occupation of a room in a hostel or a hotel[10] or where one person lives as a lodger in the home of another person,[11] because in neither case does the occupier have exclusive possession; or a family arrangement or where accommodation is provided as an act of generosity or friendship as there is no intention to enter into a legally-binding agreement.

Trespass

B.10   Trespassers have no permission to be on premises from anyone who has authority to give such permission, such as an owner, agent or tenant.

Security of tenure

B.11   Within these categories, there are a number of subdivisions. Currently, a number of statutes[12] limit, to a greater or lesser extent, the ability of an owner to recover his or her property from a person occupying it.

B.12   Protection falls into four distinct groups, ie where the landlord:

a) must prove a ground for possession in order to obtain a possession order;

b) must obtain a possession order but does not have to prove a ground for possession;

c) does not have to obtain a possession order once the right to occupy has been determined;

d) does not have to obtain a possession order at any time.[13]

---

9 See cases referred to in note 8 above.

10 Where a bedsitting-room is provided, this may constitute a licence if the conditions on which the room is made available makes it unrealistic to speak of a transfer of possession: *Marchant v Charters* [1977] 1 WLR 1181, CA.

11 Who retains general control over the whole of the premises: see, eg *Monmouth BC v Marlog* (1994) 27 HLR 30, CA; *Huwyler v Ruddy* (1996) 28 HLR 550, CA; *Parkins v Westminster City Council* (1998) 30 HLR 894, CA.

12 Landlord and Tenant Act (LTA) 1954, Rent (Agriculture) Act (R(A)A) 1976, Rent Act (RA) 1977, Protection from Eviction Act (PEA) 1977, Housing Act (HA) 1985, HA 1988 and Local Government Housing Act (LGHA) 1989.

13 Even though a landlord does not need to obtain a possession order, it may be advisable to do so.

Landlord must prove ground to obtain possession order

B.13   This is the highest protection. It only applies to:

a) long leaseholders;
b) assured tenancies;
c) protected and statutory tenancies;
d) secure tenancies;
e) assured agricultural occupancies and protected occupancies;
f) protected occupancies and statutory tenancies.

B.14   The landlord must obtain a possession order, which the court can only grant if satisfied that one of the grounds for possession set out in the relevant statute has been proved.

Long leaseholders

B.15   Generally, on the expiry of a long lease,[14] the landlord has an immediate right to possession. If, however, at the date of termination, the leaseholder occupies the premises as a residence, he or she has statutory security of tenure.

B.16   For tenancies commencing before 1 April 1990,[15] a periodic tenancy arises by operation of law on termination of the fixed term; the landlord can either seek possession on a ground set out in the LTA 1954[16] or convert it to an assured tenancy under the HA 1988[17] and seek possession in the usual way for such a tenancy.

B.17   For tenancies commencing on or after 1 April 1990, similar protection is afforded.[18]

B.18   During the term, however, the landlord may only bring the lease to an end by forfeiting the lease. A landlord may not, however, exercise a right of forfeiture for the breach of a term (other than for non-payment of rent) unless the breach has been admitted or has been found proved by a court or leasehold valuation tribunal.[19] If the landlord exercises a right of forfeiture the leaseholder can apply to the court for relief from forfeiture.[20]

---

14 A tenancy for a fixed term in excess of 21 years at a low rent: LTA 1954 s2. For tenancies commencing on or after 1 April 1990, see LGHA 1989 s186 and Sch 10 para 1.
15 When the LGHA 1989 came into force.
16 LTA 1954 s12, Sch 3.
17 LGHA 1989 s186 and Sch 10.
18 LGHA 1989 Sch 10.
19 HA 1996 s81 and Commonhold and Leasehold Reform Act 2002 s168.
20 LPA 1925 s146, County Courts Act 1984 s138.

Assured tenancies

B.19   Assured tenancies[21] replaced protected tenancies as the principal vehicle for statutory protection for private sector tenancies commencing on or after 15 January 1989.[22]

B.20   An assured tenancy must satisfy the following conditions:[23]

a) it was granted on or after 15 January 1989;
b) it is a tenancy of a dwelling house let as a separate dwelling;
c) the tenant is an individual occupying the premises as his or her only or principal home;
d) if granted on or after 28 February 1997, it is not an assured shorthold tenancy; and
e) it is not any of the following: a tenancy at a high rent (or with a high rateable value), at a low rent,[24] let to a student by an educational establishment, let for a holiday, let by a resident landlord, let by the Crown or let to provide accommodation for the support of an asylum-seeker[25] and certain other lettings.[26]

B.21   The landlord cannot bring an assured tenancy to an end[27] but must serve a notice seeking possession on the tenant,[28] as a pre-condition[29] of obtaining a possession order.

---

21 See generally, HA 1988 Part 1 Ch I.
22 When HA 1988 Part 1 came into force. Note the exceptions to this general rule in ss34 and 35.
23 HA 1988 s1 and Sch 1.
24 If a tenancy at a low rent is a long leasehold, it is protected by LTA 1954 Part 1 or LGHA 1989 Sch 10. (See paras B.15–B.18 above.)
25 HA 1988 Sch 1 para 12A, added by Immigration and Asylum Act (IAA) 1999 Sch 14 para 88 (with effect from 1 April 2000).
26 In particular, long leases, business and agricultural tenancies and lettings from local authorities (and similar bodies), which enjoy their own schemes of statutory protection.
27 This can only be done by a court order. If the tenant remains in occupation after the fixed term comes to an end, it is automatically converted into a 'statutory periodic tenancy' which continues until ended by court order: HA 1988 s5(1).
28 HA 1988 s8.
29 The court has the power to dispense with the requirement for the notice, if it considers it 'just and equitable' to do so, in respect of any ground except ground 8 (two months' rent arrears): HA 1988 s8(1)(b) and (5).

Protected and statutory tenancies

B.22   Protected tenancies afford the best form of statutory security for private tenancies granted before 15 January 1989.

B.23   A protected tenancy must satisfy the following conditions:[30]

a) it was granted before 15 January 1989;[31]
b) it is of a dwelling house let as a separate dwelling; and
c) it is not any of the following: a tenancy with board or attendance or let by a resident landlord (which is a restricted contract, see below paras B.51–B.52), at a high rent (or with a high rateable value), let at a low rent,[32] let to a student by an educational establishment, let for a holiday or let by the Crown, all of which are unprotected (see below, paras B.53–B.54).[33]

B.24   A protected tenancy is brought to an end or expires in the usual way.[34] When it does, a statutory tenancy[35] arises automatically if the tenant continues to reside in the premises.[36] A landlord must obtain a possession order to bring a statutory tenancy to an end.[37]

Secure tenancies

B.25   Secure tenancies[38] provide statutory protection to occupants of public sector housing. When first introduced by HA 1980, public sector housing included that provided by what were then registered housing

---

30 See generally, RA 1977 Part 1.

31 In limited circumstances, a protected tenancy can be created on or after 15 January 1989, namely, where the tenancy is granted: (a) pursuant to a contract entered into before that date, (b) by the landlord to an existing protected tenant or (c) where a court, granting possession of a protected tenancy on the ground of suitable alternative accommodation, orders that it should be protected: HA 1988 s34.

32 If a tenancy at a low rent is a long leasehold, it is protected by LTA 1954 Part 1. See paras B.15–B.18. above.

33 Also excepted are business and agricultural tenancies and lettings from local authorities (and similar bodies) and housing associations (and similar bodies), which enjoy their own schemes of statutory protection.

34 Eg by notice to quit, forfeiture, effluxion of time, surrender.

35 This is not a true tenancy, ie an interest in land, but a mere personal right to occupy, described by Stephenson LJ in *Jessamine Investments Co v Schwartz* [1978] QB 264, CA, at 276F, as a 'status of irremovability'. Once a statutory tenant ceases to reside in the premises, the statutory tenancy comes to an end.

36 RA 1977 s2.

37 RA 1977 s98.

38 See generally, HA 1985 Part 4.

associations[39] and charitable housing trusts; since 15 January 1989, such bodies have been unable to grant secure tenancies,[40] but are treated in the same way as private landlords.[41]

B.26   A secure tenancy must satisfy the following conditions:[42]

a) it is a tenancy of a dwelling house let as a separate dwelling;
b) the landlord is a local authority[43] (or a housing association,[44] where the tenancy commenced before 15 January 1989);
c) the tenant is an individual occupying the premises as his or her only or principal home; and
d) it is not any of the following: an introductory tenancy, a tenancy connected with certain employment, of development land, let to a homeless person,[45] of temporary accommodation to a person taking up employment, under a short-term arrangement,[46] of temporary accommodation during works, let to a student by an educational establishment, let to provide accommodation for the support of an asylum-seeker,[47] a licence to occupy an almshouse and certain other lettings,[48] all of which are unprotected (see below, paras B.53–B.54).

---

39 In England, now private registered providers of social housing: Housing and Regeneration Act (HRA) 2008 s110.
40 Save in limited circumstances, effectively by way of replacement for earlier, secure tenancies: HA 1988 s38(4A).
41 Other than in very limited circumstances: see HA 1988 s35. Since 15 January 1989, tenancies granted by registered social landlords have generally been assured tenancies. The present position is that a tenancy can be a secure tenancy if granted by a local authority at any time or by a registered social landlord before 15 January 1989.
42 HA 1985 ss79–81 and Sch 1.
43 Or a similar body, eg, an urban development corporation.
44 Or a similar body.
45 Pursuant to a function under HA 1996 Part 7, unless the tenant was notified that it was to be secure.
46 Often referred to as 'private sector leasing'.
47 HA 1985 Sch 1 para 4A, added by Immigration and Asylum Act (IAA) 1999 Sch 14 para 81 (with effect from 1 April 2000).
48 Also excepted are long leases, business and agricultural tenancies and tenancies of licensed premises, which enjoy their own schemes of statutory protection.

B.27   The landlord cannot bring a secure tenancy to an end[49] but must serve a notice seeking possession on the tenant,[50] as a pre-condition[51] of obtaining a possession order.

Assured agricultural occupancies

B.28   Certain agricultural[52] workers (known as 'assured agricultural occupiers') whose right of occupation commenced on or after 15 January 1989 enjoy statutory protection under HA 1988.

B.29   An assured agricultural occupancy must satisfy the following conditions:[53]

a) it was granted on or after 15 January 1989;
b) the occupier is an assured tenant (but not an assured shorthold tenant),[54] or a licensee with exclusive occupation;[55] and
c) the premises occupied are in qualifying ownership and the occupier is a qualifying worker[56] or has been during the subsistence of the licence or tenancy.[57]

B.30   An assured agricultural occupancy, which is not an assured tenancy, is treated as if it were an assured tenancy.[58] The landlord cannot bring an assured agricultural occupancy to an end[59] but must serve a notice

---

49 HA 1985 s82(1). In the case of a fixed-term tenancy, a periodic tenancy arises automatically on expiry: s86(1). Note, however, that this statutory protection does not arise where such a tenancy is brought to an end by the tenant or by surrender.

50 HA 1985 ss83 and 83A.

51 The court has the power to dispense with the requirement for the notice, if it considers it 'just and equitable' to do so: HA 1985 s83(1)(b).

52 And forestry: HA 1988 Sch 3 para 1.

53 HA 1988 s24.

54 Or a tenant who is not an assured tenant solely because there is a low rent or because it is an agricultural holding.

55 HA 1988 s24(1).

56 For instance, the occupier is employed in agriculture and his or her employer is either the owner of the premises or has made arrangements with the owner for them to be used as housing for persons in agriculture: HA 1988 Sch 3 para 2.

57 He or she has worked 'whole time' in agriculture for not less than 91 weeks out of the last 104 weeks: HA 1988 Sch 3 para 1.

58 HA 1988 s24(3).

59 This can only be done by a court order. If the occupier remains in occupation after the fixed term comes to an end, it is automatically converted into a 'statutory periodic tenancy' which continues until ended by court order: HA 1988 s5(1).

seeking possession on the tenant,[60] as a pre-condition[61] of obtaining a possession order.

Protected occupancies and statutory tenancies

B.31 Certain agricultural[62] workers (known as 'protected occupiers') whose right of occupation commenced before 15 January 1989 enjoy statutory protection under the R(A)A 1976.

B.32 A protected occupancy must satisfy the following conditions:[63]

a) it was granted before 15 January 1989;

b) the premises occupied are in qualifying ownership[64] and the occupier is a qualifying worker[65] or has been during the subsistence of the licence or tenancy; and

c) the occupier is a licensee or a tenant of the premises.

B.33 When a protected occupancy comes to an end,[66] a statutory tenancy[67] arises automatically if the occupier continues to reside in the premises,[68] unless the landlord is the Crown, a local authority (or similar body), a charitable housing trust, a private registered provider of social housing, a registered social landlord (in Wales) or a co-operative housing association.[69]

Landlord need not prove ground to obtain possession order

B.34 This applies to:

a) assured shorthold tenancies;

b) introductory tenancies;

---

60 HA 1988 s8.

61 The court has the power to dispense with the requirement for the notice, if it considers it 'just and equitable' to do so, in respect of any ground except ground 8 (two months' rent arrears): HA 1988 s8(1)(b) and (5).

62 And forestry: R(A)A 1976 s1(1).

63 R(A)A 1976 s2(1).

64 The occupier is employed in agriculture and his or her employer is either the owner of the premises or has made arrangements with the owner for it to be used as housing for persons in agriculture: R(A)A 1976 Sch 3 para 3.

65 He or she has worked whole-time in agriculture for not less than 91 weeks out of the last 104 weeks: R(A)A 1976 Sch 3 para 1.

66 For example, by expiry of a notice to quit.

67 It is known as a statutory tenancy, even if it was a licence prior to termination.

68 R(A)A 1976 s4(1).

69 R(A)A 1976 s5.

c) demoted tenancies;
d) demoted assured-shorthold tenancies;
e) flexible tenancies;
f) protected shorthold tenancies;
g) restricted contract tenancies and licences;
h) unprotected tenancies;
i) licences except excluded licences; and
j) service occupancies.

B.35   For these occupancies, the obtaining of a possession order is a formality. If the court is satisfied that the occupancy in question is one of the above, it must grant a possession order and has an extremely limited discretion to postpone the date of expiry of the order.[70]

Assured shorthold tenancies

B.36   An assured shorthold tenancy is a particular type of assured tenancy.[71] There are alternative definitions depending on when it was granted.

B.37   *If granted*[72] *between 15 January 1989 and 27 February 1996,* an assured shorthold tenancy must satisfy the following conditions:[73]

a) it is an assured tenancy for a fixed term of six months or more;
b) the landlord cannot bring it to an end in the first six months;[74] and
c) before grant, the landlord gave the tenant written notice in the prescribed form that it was to be an assured shorthold tenancy.

B.38   When the fixed term expires, the landlord has a right to possession.[75]

B.39   *If granted on or after 28 February 1997,* any assured tenancy is automatically an assured shorthold tenancy unless:

a) the landlord serves notice to the contrary;
b) the tenancy agreement states that it is not a shorthold; or

---

70 Two weeks (or up to six weeks if there is exceptional hardship): HA 1980 s89.
71 As such, many of the assured tenancy provisions apply equally to assured shorthold tenancies.
72 An assured shorthold tenancy cannot be granted to an assured tenant of the same landlord. This applies even if the two tenancies are in respect of different accommodation: HA 1988 s20(3).
73 HA 1988 s20(1), (2).
74 Other than by re-entry or forfeiture: HA 1988 s45(4).
75 HA 1988 s21(1) and (4).

c) it is granted by the same landlord to a person who was previously the tenant under an assured tenancy.[76]

B.40 The court cannot order possession to take effect earlier than six months from the commencement of the tenancy.[77]

Introductory tenancies

B.41 HA 1996 Part 5 enables local authorities and housing action trusts to elect to operate an introductory tenancy scheme.[78] If they do so, subject to certain exceptions, new periodic tenancies granted by them are introductory tenancies.[79] The purpose of the scheme is to provide a probationary period ('the trial period') during which the landlord may determine the tenancy without the need to prove a ground for possession.[80] The general rule is that the trial period lasts for one year from the date on which the tenancy was entered into, at which point it becomes secure.[81] This period may be extended by six months, provided a notice has been served in accordance with the statutory requirements before the expiry of the trial period.[82] If, before then, the landlord has commenced possession proceedings, the tenancy remains an introductory tenancy until the possession proceedings are finally concluded.[83]

B.42 An introductory tenancy must satisfy the following conditions:[84]

a) the landlord has elected to operate the introductory tenancy regime;
b) the tenancy was not entered into or adopted[85] in pursuance of a contract made before the election was made;
c) the tenancy is periodic;
d) the tenancy would otherwise be a secure tenancy; and

76 HA 1988 s19A and Sch 2A: it is also not a shorthold if it is an assured tenancy which was formerly a secure tenancy, if it arises by succession to a regulated tenancy or if it arises at the end of a long lease.
77 HA 1988 s21(5).
78 HA 1996 s124(1).
79 HA 1996 s124(2).
80 As an exception to the normal security of tenure available to secure tenants under HA 1985 Part 4: see HA 1985 Sch 1 para 1A.
81 HA 1996 s125(1).
82 HA 1996 s125A.
83 HA 1996 s130(2).
84 HA 1996 s124.
85 A tenancy is adopted by a person if that person becomes the landlord under the tenancy, whether on a disposal or surrender of the interest of the former landlord: HA 1996 s124(4).

e) immediately before the tenancy was entered into or adopted, the tenant (or, in the case of joint tenants, one or more of them) was neither a secure tenant of the same or another dwelling house, nor an assured tenant of a registered social landlord (otherwise than under an assured shorthold tenancy) in respect of the same or another dwelling house.

B.43   The landlord may only bring an introductory tenancy to an end by obtaining a court order.[86] Before commencing possession proceedings, the landlord must serve the tenant with a notice containing certain information including the reasons for the decision to bring proceedings and that he or she has the right to request a review of the decision under HA 1985 s129.[87] Provided the landlord has served this notice and conducted a review (if requested), the court must make an order for possession.[88]

Demoted tenancies

B.44   Demoted tenancies arise as a result of a demotion order made by a court against a secure tenant.[89] The effect of the order is that the tenant's security of tenure is lost for a period of 12 months.[90] Like the introductory tenancy, a landlord is able to bring the tenancy to an end by obtaining an order of the court.[91] Such an order must be made provided the landlord has, first, served a notice explaining the reasons for bringing the claim for possession and notifying the tenant that he or she has the right to request an internal review of the decision and, second, the landlord has carried out a review, if one has been requested, and, third, the review has upheld the decision to seek possession.[92]

86 HA 1996 s127(1).

87 HA 1996 s128.

88 HA 1996 s127(2); a court may refuse to make an order for possession if the eviction of the tenant would amount to a disproportionate interference with his or her article 8 rights or the decision is one which no reasonable person would consider justifiable: see *Pinnock v Manchester City Council* [2010] UKSC 45, [2011] 2 AC 104, [2011] HLR 7.

89 HA 1996 s143A(4).

90 HA 1996 s143B(1).

91 HA 1996 s143D(1).

92 HA 1996 s143D(2), a court may refuse to make an order for possession if the eviction of the tenant would amount to a disproportionate interference with his or her article 8 rights or the decision is one which no reasonable person would consider justifiable: see *Pinnock v Manchester City Council* [2010] UKSC 45, [2011] 2 AC 104, [2011] HLR 7.

B.45 Unless a demoted tenancy is ended by a court order, the tenancy becomes secure (or assured if the interest of the landlord has been transferred to a private registered provider of social housing)[93] at the end of the demotion period.[94]

Demoted assured shorthold tenants

B.46 Demoted assured shorthold tenancies arise after a court has made a demotion order against an assured tenant who has committed acts of anti-social behaviour.[95] The effect of the order is that the tenant becomes an assured shorthold tenant for a period of 12 months.[96] The rights of a landlord to end a demoted assured shorthold tenancy are identical to other assured shorthold tenancies (see paras B.36–B.40 above). If, however, the assured shorthold tenancy is not brought to an end within 12 months it reverts to an assured tenancy.[97]

Flexible tenancies

B.47 A flexible tenancy is a secure tenancy which is granted for a fixed term of two years or more.[98] At the conclusion of the fixed term, the tenancy is replaced by a statutory periodic tenancy.[99] The landlord may bring the periodic tenancy to an end by obtaining an order of the court. The court must make a possession order provided that:[100]

a) the landlord has given the tenant a notice, six months in advance, informing the tenant that he or she does not intend to grant a further tenancy, its reasons for not doing so and the fact that the tenant has a right to request a review of the decision;[101]

b) the landlord has carried out the review (if requested) in accordance with the law and upheld its decision to seek possession;[102] and

---

93 HA 1996 s143C(2), (3).

94 HA 1996 s143B(1).

95 HA 1988 s20B(1).

96 HA 1988 s6A(3).

97 HA 1988 s20B(2).

98 HA 1985 s107A.

99 HA 1985 s107D(8).

100 HA 1985 s107D(1).

101 HA 1985 s107D(3).

102 HA 1985 s107D(3), (6), a court may refuse to make an order for possession if the eviction of the tenant would amount to a disproportionate interference with his or her article 8 rights or the decision is one which no reasonable person would consider justifiable: see *Pinnock v Manchester City Council* [2010] UKSC 45, [2011] 2 AC 104, [2011] HLR 7.

c) the landlord has given the tenant another notice, on or before the fixed term has expired, that it requires possession of the property within two months of the tenant receiving the notice.[103]

Protected shorthold tenancies

B.48   As it has been impossible to create new protected shorthold tenancies since 15 January 1989[104] and a new agreement after this date between the landlord and an existing protected shorthold tenant gives rise to an assured shorthold tenancy,[105] these are now very rare.

B.49   A protected shorthold tenancy is a particular type of protected tenancy,[106] but subject to a special mandatory ground for possession.[107]

Restricted contract tenancies and licences[108]

B.50   Restricted contracts are also becoming increasingly rare, as, with one exception,[109] it has been impossible to create any since 15 January 1989 and any variation in rent (other than in accordance with a rent tribunal registration) of an existing restricted contract after this date is deemed to be a new agreement at the date of variation.[110]

B.51   A restricted contract must satisfy the following conditions:[111]

a) it was granted before 15 January 1989;[112]
b) the occupant has exclusive occupation of at least some part of the premises for use as a residence;[113]

103 HA 1985 s107D(4), (5).

104 HA 1988 s34(2).

105 HA 1988 s34(3).

106 It must fulfil the 'shorthold conditions': HA 1980 s52 (now repealed by HA 1988 Sch 19).

107 RA 1977 Sch 15 case 19; although technically this type of occupancy requires the landlord to prove a ground for possession, it is merely to satisfy the court that the tenancy is a protected shorthold and the notice was served at the correct time.

108 A restricted contract licensee whose licence was entered into before 28 November 1980 becomes a trespasser on termination of the contract and thus a possession order is not necessary, cf PEA 1977 s3(2A), which takes into s3(1) (so as to eviction without a court order) those holding over after licences created on or after this date.

109 Where the agreement was entered into before 15 January 1989: HA 1988 s36(1).

110 HA 1988 s36(2), and see *Rowe v Matthews* (2001) 33 HLR 921, CA. Where it is a restricted contract because of a resident landlord, the occupancy becomes an excluded tenancy or licence if there is shared accommodation (see below, Excluded tenancies and licences, paras B.61–B.69).

111 RA 1977 ss12, 19–21 and Sch 2.

112 Or pursuant to an agreement entered into before this date: HA 1988 s36(1).

113 The occupant can be a tenant or a licensee.

c) there is a resident landlord[114] or the rent includes a payment for furniture or services; and

d) it is not any of the following:[115] a contract for premises with a high rateable value,[116] let with substantial board,[117] let for a holiday[118] or let by the Crown,[119] all of which are unprotected tenancies or non-excluded licences (see below, paras B.53–B.54 and B.55–B.56).

B.52   If it is periodic and was entered into before 28 November 1980,[120] the rent tribunal can defer the operation of any notice to quit for up to six months at a time.[121] Whether fixed term or periodic, if it was entered into on or after 28 November 1980, the county court may delay possession for up to three months.[122]

Unprotected tenancies

B.53   This refers to a tenancy which is neither a statutorily-protected tenancy nor an excluded tenancy.[123]

B.54   Examples are:

a) a tenancy at no or a low rent;[124]

b) a tenancy at a high rent or of property with a high rateable value;[125]

c) a tenancy which has ceased to be assured because the tenant no longer occupies as his or her only or principal home;

d) a letting to a student by an educational establishment;[126]

e) an excluded tenancy entered into before 15 January 1989;[127]

---

114 Provided the tenancy was granted on or after 14 August 1974: RA 1977 s12(1).

115 Also excepted under RA 1977 s19(5) are 'old-style' assured tenancies, ie under HA 1980 s56 (para (f)), protected tenancies (para (a)), protected occupancies under the R(A)A 1976 (para (d)), occupancies where the landlord is a local authority or similar body (para (aa)) and housing association tenancies under RA 1977 Pt 6 (para (e)), which enjoy their own schemes of statutory protection.

116 RA 1977 s19(3) and (4).

117 RA 1977 s19(5)(c).

118 RA 1977 s19(7).

119 RA 1977 s19(5)(b).

120 When HA 1980 came into force.

121 RA 1977 s104.

122 RA 1977 s106A.

123 See paras 2.116 and B.61–B.69.

124 HA 1988 Sch 1 para 3.

125 For the limits, see RA 1977 s4 and HA 1988 Sch 1 para 2.

126 HA 1988 Sch 1 para 8.

127 PEA 1977 s3(2C).

f) a tenancy granted by a resident landlord on or after 15 January 1989 where the landlord and the occupier do not share accommodation;

g) a family intervention tenancy (ie a tenancy granted by a local authority, a private registered provider of social housing or registered social landlord[128] to a tenant who has been, or could have been, made subject to a possession order on the grounds of anti-social behaviour);[129]

h) a tenant of a fully mutual housing association.[130]

Non-excluded licences

B.55 This refers to any licence which is not an excluded licence.[131]

B.56 Examples are:

a) a licence from a resident landlord granted on or after 15 January 1989 where the landlord and occupier do not share accommodation;

b) a licence to occupy a private hostel granted on or after 15 January 1989.

Service occupancies

B.57 A service occupancy arises where the right of occupation is granted so that the occupier can perform his or her duties as an employee.

B.58 There are alternative tests.[132] Either:

a) it is an express term of the contract of employment that the employee must occupy the premises in order to better perform his or her duties to a material degree; or

b) it is an implied term of the contract of employment that the employee must occupy the premises to perform the duties; this will occur where the employee's duties cannot be carried out unless he or she occupies the premises.[133]

---

128 In Wales.

129 HA 1985 Sch 1 para 4ZA and HA 1988 Sch 1 para 12ZA.

130 HA 1988 Sch 1 para 12(1)(h). Some tenants of fully mutual housing associations may have a tenancy for a term of 90 years determinable on their death if the terms of their tenancy agreement provides that a notice to quit may only be served in prescribed circumstances: *Mexfield Housing Co-Operative v Berrisford* [2011] UKSC 52, [2012] 3 WLR 1091, [2012] HLR 15, and see para B.6 above.

131 See paras B.61–B.69.

132 *Smith v Seghill Overseers* (1875) LR 10 QB 422.

133 *Glasgow Corporation v Johnstone* [1965] AC 609, HL; see also *Northern Ireland Commissioner of Valuation v Fermanagh Protestant Board of Education* [1969] 1 WLR 1708, HL. In order for a term to be implied, there has to be a compelling reason for deeming that term to form part of the contract: *Hughes v Greenwich LBC* [1994] 1 AC 170, (1994) 26 HLR 99, HL. In *Surrey CC v Lamond* (1999)

B.59 Service occupiers with exclusive occupation of their accommodation are entitled to remain in occupation until a court order is made.[134]

Possession order not necessary after right to occupy ends

B.60 No possession order is necessary after termination of an excluded tenancy or excluded licence entered into on or after 15 January 1989.[135] Such an occupier enjoys security of tenure up until the landlord determines his or her right of occupation (for example, by giving notice to quit to a periodic tenant). Thereafter, he or she is a trespasser if he or she remains.

Excluded tenancies and licences

B.61 A right of occupation is an excluded tenancy or excluded licence if it is one of the following:[136]

a) sharing with a resident landlord;
b) sharing with a member of a resident landlord's family;
c) temporary expedient to a trespasser;
d) holiday accommodation;
e) other than for money or money's worth;
f) granted to an asylum-seeker by the secretary of state;
g) licence to occupy a public sector hostel.

Sharing with a resident landlord

B.62 The following conditions must be fulfilled:

a) it is a tenancy or a licence under the terms of which the occupier is obliged to share accommodation[137] with the landlord; and

31 HLR 105, CA, it was held that the court must discover the duties that the employee is required to perform and then, having regard to the nature of those duties, ask itself whether or not it is really practical for the duties to be carried out if the employee did not live in the property in question. If it is really impractical for the employee to carry out the duties unless he or she is living in the property, then the necessary term can be implied into the contract of employment.

134 PEA 1977 s8(2).
135 PEA 1977 ss3(2C) and 3A. See para 2.118 above.
136 PEA 1977 s3A. See paras 2.118–2.126 above.
137 'Sharing' means having the use of the accommodation in common with another person; 'accommodation' is anything other than the common parts (ie, stairs, passageways, etc) or a storage area: PEA 1977 s3A(4) and (5).

b) the landlord occupied as his or her only or principal home[138] premises which include the shared accommodation both immediately before the right of occupation was granted and when it comes to an end.

Sharing with a member of a resident landlord's family

B.63   The following conditions must be satisfied:

a) it is a tenancy or a licence under the terms of which the occupier is obliged to share accommodation with a member of the landlord's family;[139]
b) the member of the landlord's family occupied as his or her only or principal home premises which include the shared accommodation both immediately before the right of occupation was granted and when it comes to an end; and
c) both immediately before the occupancy was granted and when it comes to an end, the landlord occupied premises as his or her only or principal home in the same building[140] as the shared accommodation.

Temporary expedient to a trespasser

B.64   This refers to a tenancy or licence granted as a temporary expedient to an occupier who had entered the premises or any other premises as a trespasser,[141] for example, a squatter who later receives permission to stay in the premises.

Holiday accommodation

B.65   This applies where the right of occupation was granted for a holiday.[142]

---

138 In *Crawley BC v Sawyer* (1987) 20 HLR 98, CA, the court held that there was no material difference between occupying premises as a home and as a residence.
139 'Family member' is a spouse, civil partner, cohabitant, parent, grandparent, child, grandchild, brother, sister, uncle, aunt, nephew or niece: HA 1985 s113.
140 Not being a purpose-built block of flats: PEA 1977 s3A(3)(c).
141 This follows the terminology of HA 1985 s79, excluding from security of tenure former squatters who may subsequently have been granted short-life licences of the properties. The phrase 'any other premises' is extremely wide but it seems clear that there must be some nexus between the original squat and the current tenancy or licence, even if there have been one or more intervening tenancies or licences.
142 If a holiday let is a sham, the letting will not be excluded: see *R v Rent Officer for Camden LBC ex p Plant* (1980) 7 HLR 15, QBD and *Buchmann v May* (1978) 7 HLR 1, CA.

Other than for money or money's worth

B.66 This applies where, under the terms of the tenancy or licence, the occupier is not obliged to pay for the accommodation, for example, a family arrangement or a weekend guest.

Asylum-seekers

B.67 This applies where the right of occupation was granted in order to provide accommodation to an asylum-seeker (and/or a dependant) under IAA 1999 Part 6 (Support for Asylum-seekers).[143]

Licence to occupy a public sector hostel

B.68 This applies to a licence to occupy a hostel[144] provided by a public sector landlord.[145]

B.69 Excluded tenants are entitled to a common law notice to quit, that is, the notice must be at least the length of the period of the tenancy and must expire on the first or last day of a period of the tenancy. An excluded tenant is not, however, entitled to the additional protection afforded by PEA 1977 s5,[146] which provides for notice to be not less than four weeks, in writing and containing prescribed information as to the tenant's rights.[147] Excluded licensees are entitled to reasonable notice.[148]

---

143 PEA 1977 s3A, as amended by IAA 1999 Sch 14 para 73 (with effect from 1 April 2000).

144 A hostel is a building in which residential accommodation and either meals or facilities for the preparation of meals are provided to persons generally or to some class of persons, but where the accommodation is not separate or self-contained: HA 1985 s622.

145 A local authority, a private registered provider of social housing or a registered social landlord or housing trust, the regulator of social housing, the secretary of state, a combined authority, a development corporation, an economic prosperity board, an urban development corporation, a Mayoral development corporation, a housing action trust, or any other person or body specified by the secretary of state: PEA 1977 s3A(8). To date, the secretary of state has specified the London Hostels Associations Ltd (Protection from Eviction (Excluded Licences) Order 1991 SI No 1943), the Shaftesbury Society (Protection from Eviction (Excluded Licences) (Shaftesbury Society) Order 1999 SI No 1758) and the Royal British Legion Industries Ltd (Protection from Eviction (Excluded Licences) (Royal British Legion Industries Ltd) (England) Order 2003 SI No 2436).

146 PEA 1977 s5(1B).

147 See Notice to Quit etc (Prescribed Information) Regulations 1988 SI No 2201.

148 *Minister of Health v Bellotti* [1944] KB 298, CA; how long is reasonable depends on all the circumstances such as, the purpose for which the licence was granted, the behaviour of the parties, how long the occupier has lived on the premises and the availability of alternative accommodation.

Possession order not necessary at any time

Trespass

B.70   Trespassers have no contractual rights and no statutory protection giving them a right of occupation. They have only limited rights under the Criminal Law Act (CLA) 1977 preventing a person with an immediate right of possession from using violence to gain entry.[149] Even these limited rights will be reduced by the Legal Aid, Sentencing and Punishment of Offenders Act (LASPO) 2012 s144(1) when it is brought into force: trespassers who live in a residential building, and who enter a building as a trespasser, will be capable of being removed by a police officer[150] as they will be committing a criminal offence.[151]

Special categories

Joint tenancies

B.71   If the tenant's interest in the property is held by more than one person, the tenancy is a joint tenancy. For an arrangement to be a joint tenancy it must exhibit the 'four unities': [152]

   a) unity of title – each tenant claims title under the same act or document;
   b) unity of time – the interest of each tenant commences at the same time;
   c) unity of interest – the interest of each tenant is the same in extent, nature and duration;
   d) unity of possession – each tenant is as much entitled to possession of the land as any of the others.

B.72   The shared legal interest is not divisible; no one joint tenant owns an identifiable part of the property, nor generally can such a part be disposed of without the termination of the whole joint tenancy.

---

149 See chapter 7.
150 Police and Criminal Evidence Act (PACE) 1984 s17(1)(c)(vi) (to be brought into force at a date to be appointed).
151 LASPO 2012 s144(1) (to be brought into force at a date to be appointed). See paras 7.38–7.41 above.
152 *AG Securities v Vaughan* [1988] 2 WLR 689 at 700D–701B, (1988) 20 HLR 212, CA, per Fox LJ at 227.

B.73   Joint tenants have 'joint and several liability' in respect of all the obligations of the tenancy. One joint tenant cannot be excluded by any other(s). On the death of a joint tenant his or her legal interest is absorbed into the interest(s) of the remaining joint tenant(s) (the 'right of survivorship'), and this occurs automatically even if a contrary intention is expressed in the deceased tenant's will.[153]

Assignment

B.74   An assignment arises when the interest of the tenant (the 'assignor') is transferred to another (the 'assignee'). By this process, the assignee effectively steps into the shoes of the assignor.

B.75   An assignment must be by deed.[154] It will not otherwise bind the landlord, ie it will not establish the relationship of landlord and tenant between the landlord and the assignee.[155]

B.76   The right of a tenant to assign a tenancy may be prohibited or limited by the terms of the tenancy (for example, a covenant against sub-letting) or the law (for example, a periodic assured tenancy cannot be assigned without the landlord's express permission).[156]

B.77   If there is no such prohibition, assignment is lawful. Even if there is a restriction (for example, obtaining the landlord's prior consent), the assignment is lawful if the assignor complies with the restriction. An unlawful assignment is a breach of the tenancy agreement.

Tenancies from mortgagors

B.78   The power of a mortgagor (ie a borrower) to grant a tenancy can only be exercised where no contrary intention is expressed in the mortgage deed.[157] Most mortgage deeds contain a term preventing the mortgagor from granting a tenancy.

---

153 Note also that a joint tenant may be freed from his or her obligations to the other joint tenant(s) by the execution between them of a deed of release. The released tenant will continue to be a tenant until the expiry of a fixed term or the commencement of the next period of a periodic tenancy; but see *Burton v Camden LBC* [2000] 2 AC 399, (2000) 32 HLR 625, HL in respect of secure tenancies.

154 LPA 1925 s52; see Law of Property (Miscellaneous Provisions) Act 1989 s1 for the requirements of a deed.

155 *Crago v Julian* [1992] 1 WLR 372, (1992) 24 HLR 306, CA.

156 HA 1988 s15.

157 LPA 1925 s99.

B.79   If the tenancy is granted in breach of the mortgage deed, it is, nevertheless, binding as between the mortgagor and the tenant.[158]

B.80   The position of the tenant of a mortgagor as against the mortgagee depends on two factors:

a) whether the tenancy commenced before or after the property was mortgaged; and

b) whether the mortgagee (ie, the lender) gave its consent.

B.81   The tenancy does not bind the mortgagee if there is a term preventing its grant, or a term with which the landlord does not comply restricting its grant (for example, to obtain the mortgagee's prior consent), and the tenancy was created after the mortgage.[159] The tenancy binds the mortgagee where it was granted either before the mortgage[160] or afterwards but in accordance with its terms, ie no prohibition, or only with consent.

B.82   Nonetheless, if a mortgagee brings proceedings for possession against the mortgagor, an unauthorised tenant may apply to a court to postpone the date on which the mortgagee can recover possession of the premises for a period of up to two months.[161]

Sub-tenancies

B.83   A sub-tenant (ST) is a person whose immediate landlord is a tenant (T). T's landlord (L) is known as the 'head landlord'. The tenancy between L and T is known as the 'mesne tenancy' and the tenancy between T and ST as the 'sub-tenancy'. L has no direct relationship with ST and, during the subsistence of the mesne tenancy, can take no action against ST.

B.84   It is common for the mesne tenancy either to require T to obtain L's prior consent to the grant of any sub-tenancy (known as a qualified prohibition) or else to prohibit sub-letting absolutely.[162] If T is permitted to sub-let, it is a 'lawful' sub-tenancy. If T sub-lets without permission, it is an 'unlawful' sub-tenancy.[163] The creation of an unlawful

---

158 *Church of England Building Society v Piskor* [1954] 1 Ch 553, CA.

159 *Dudley and District Benefit Building Society v Emerson* [1949] Ch 707, CA.

160 *Rogers v Humphreys* [1835] 4 Ad & El 299, KB.

161 Mortgage Repossessions (Protection of Tenants etc) Act 2010 s1(2).

162 In the case of an assured periodic tenancy, it is an implied term that the tenant must not sub-let without the landlord's consent: HA 1988 s15.

163 It might be thought that this meant sub-letting at all in the case of an absolute prohibition, or without prior consent in the case of a qualified prohibition. In practice, however, if T procured L's consent in the case of an absolute prohibition, L would be estopped from relying on the breach, either by being

sub-tenancy is a breach[164] of the mesne tenancy and leaves T vulnerable to action by L, for example, for damages and/or possession.

B.85   When the mesne tenancy comes to an end, any sub-tenancy usually determines automatically;[165] so that ST has no rights to occupy and becomes a trespasser. This is, however, subject to exceptions:

a) ST may become the direct tenant of L if the mesne tenancy is surrendered (even if the sub-letting was unlawful);[166]

b) there are statutory provisions in respect of assured and regulated tenancies;[167] and

c) if a lawful sub-tenancy, L will still need to comply with PEA 1977 s3.[168]

B.86   If L exercises a right to forfeit the mesne tenancy, ST may seek relief against forfeiture.[169] If granted, the court may vest the mesne tenancy in ST.[170]

Rental purchase

B.87   A rental purchaser is one who enters into occupation of premises, as a licensee, under a contract of purchase, the terms of which provide that the purchase price is to be paid in three or more instalments.[171]

---

treated as having varied the nature of the prohibition on that occasion, or as having waived the breach: *Moore Properties (Ilford) Ltd v McKeon and others* [1976] 1 WLR 1278, ChD.

164 Unless L 'waives' the breach, ie unequivocally affirms the continuation of the tenancy with knowledge of the breach, in which case L can no longer rely on it in any proceedings against T.

165 *Moore Properties (Ilford) Ltd v McKeon and others* [1976] 1 WLR 1278, ChD.

166 *Mellor v Watkins* (1874) 9 QB 400, QB; *Parker v Jones* [1910] 2 KB 32, KBD; see also *Barrett v Morgan* [2000] 2 AC 264, HL per Lord Millett at 273C. This is so whether the sub-tenancy is lawful or unlawful, but only if the mesne tenancy remains contractual: *Solomon v Orwell* [1954] 1 WLR 629, CA. Note, however, that this rule does not apply (as it was for a time believed) where the mesne tenancy is ended by a tenant's notice to quit: *Barrett v Morgan*, above; *Pennell v Payne* [1995] QB 192, CA.

167 In both cases the provisions are similar, namely, when the mesne tenancy determines, a lawful sub-tenant will usually become the tenant of the head landlord by operation of law: see HA 1988 s18, RA 1977 s137; *Wellcome Trust Ltd v Hammad* [1998] QB 638, CA.

168 But not a lawful excluded sub-tenancy, to which PEA 1977 s3 does not apply (see above, para 2.118).

169 LPA 1925 s146(4).

170 *Factors (Sundries) Ltd v Miller* [1952] 2 All ER 630, CA.

171 HA 1980 s88(4); ie more than just on exchange and completion, which is the norm where there is a simple conveyance of a freehold or grant of a long leasehold interest.

B.88   Under a rental purchase agreement, completion is deferred until the whole or a specified part of the purchase price is paid. The purchase may be of a freehold or of a leasehold interest.

B.89   Although it is not necessary for the landlord to prove a ground of possession, the county court has wide powers to defer the expiry of a possession order,[172] and rental purchasers have statutory protection against eviction without a court order.[173]

B.90   Rental purchase agreements were generally designed to avoid statutory protection under RA 1977. They have become increasingly rare since the introduction of assured shorthold tenancies by HA 1988.

Licence from a tenant

B.91   As against the tenant, the licensee is in no better nor worse position than any licensee (see above, Licence, paras B.8–B.9). As against the head landlord, the licensee's right of occupation is dependent on the existence of the tenancy; once it has been determined, the licensee becomes a trespasser.

Service accommodation

B.92   An employee occupying property provided by his or her employer may do so as an ordinary tenant or licensee[174] or as a 'service tenant' or a 'service occupier'.[175] Whether the occupier is a service occupier or a service tenant depends on the reason for the occupation.[176]

B.93   A service tenant is a tenant whose occupation is in consequence of the employment, ie results from his or her employment. A service

---

172 HA 1980 s88(1): the same power that can be exercised on the making of a possession order based on a discretionary ground in respect of an assured or a regulated tenancy.

173 PEA 1977 s3 is applied to these occupiers by HA 1980 Sch 25 para 61.

174 Where, in either case, occupation is merely incidental to the employment and the employee's occupation is either a tenancy or licence according to the usual rules (see above – Status of occupation, paras B3–B10).

175 Service occupation is not a form of a licence arising as an exception to the general rule that a tenancy is created where the occupier has exclusive possession at a rent for a term (see above, paras B.54–B.56). The essence of service occupation is that exclusive possession is never given to the employee as against his or her employer; the employee occupies on behalf of the employer, ie as the employer's representative: *Street v Mountford* [1985] AC 809, (1985) 17 HLR 402, HL.

176 See above, para B.54.

tenant is generally entitled to the same protection as is available to any tenant.[177]

Spouses and civil partners

B.94   Spouses and civil partners are in a special position. If a spouse or civil partner does not otherwise have a right of occupation[178] (for example, as a joint tenant), he or she automatically has 'home rights' – ie a right to occupy – over the home he or she occupies with his or her spouse or civil partner,[179] without having to apply to the court for an order.[180]

B.95   Former spouses or civil partners can apply to a court for an occupation order in respect of the home.[181]

Cohabitants

B.96   Cohabitants[182] do not enjoy automatic rights over the home they share in the way that married couples do, but either may apply to a court for an occupation order[183] if he or she does not otherwise have a right of occupation.

B.97   As with former spouses and civil partners, former cohabitants can apply to a court for an occupation order in respect of the former shared home.[184]

---

177 In the case of service tenants who are assured or regulated tenants, there are special grounds for possession: RA 1977 Sch 15 case 8, HA 1988 Sch 2 ground 16.

178 Ie by virtue of a beneficial estate or interest or contract, or by virtue of a statutory right: Family Law Act (FLA) 1996 s30(1).

179 This applies whether it is, or was intended to be, the matrimonial home: FLA 1996 s30(7).

180 FLA 1996 s30(2).

181 FLA 1996 s35.

182 'Cohabitants' are two persons who are neither married to each other nor civil partners of each other but are living together as though they were husband and wife or civil partners: FLA 1996 s62(1).

183 FLA 1996 ss33 and 36.

184 FLA 1996 s36.

Legislation

Protection from Eviction Act 1977

PART I: UNLAWFUL EVICTION AND HARASSMENT

Unlawful eviction and harassment of occupier

1(1) In this section 'residential occupier', in relation to any premises, means a person occupying the premises as a residence, whether under a contract or by virtue of any enactment or rule of law giving him the right to remain in occupation or restricting the right of any other person to recover possession of the premises.

(2) If any person unlawfully deprives the residential occupier of any premises of his occupation of the premises or any part thereof, or attempts to do so, he shall be guilty of an offence unless he proves that he believed, and had reasonable cause to believe, that the residential occupier had ceased to reside in the premises.

(3) If any person with intent to cause the residential occupier of any premises–
  (a) to give up the occupation of the premises or any part thereof; or
  (b) to refrain from exercising any right or pursuing any remedy in respect of the premises or part thereof;
does acts [likely] to interfere with the peace or comfort of the residential occupier or members of his household, or persistently withdraws or withholds services reasonably required for the occupation of the premises as a residence, he shall be guilty of an offence.

[(3A) Subject to subsection (3B) below, the landlord of a residential occupier or an agent of the landlord shall be guilty of an offence if–
  (a) he does acts likely to interfere with the peace or comfort of the residential occupier [or members of his household, or]
  (b) he persistently withdraws or withholds services reasonably required for the occupation of the premises in question as a residence,
and (in either case) he knows, or has reasonable cause to believe, that that conduct is likely to cause the residential occupier to give up the occupation of the whole or part of the premises or to refrain from exercising any right or pursuing any remedy in respect of the whole or part of the premises.

(3B) A person shall not be guilty of an offence under subsection (3A) above if he proves that he had reasonable grounds for doing the acts or withdrawing or withholding the services in question.

(3C) In subsection (3A) above 'landlord,' in relation to a residential occupier of any premises, means the person who, but for–
  (a) the residential occupier's right to remain in occupation of the premises, or
  (b) a restriction on the person's right to recover possession of the premises,
would be entitled to occupation of the premises and any superior landlord under whom that person derives title.]

(4) A person guilty of an offence under this section shall be liable–
  (a) on summary conviction, to a fine not exceeding [level 5 on the standard scale] or to imprisonment for a term not exceeding 6 months or to both;
  (b) on conviction on indictment, to a fine or to imprisonment for a term not exceeding 2 years or to both.

(5) Nothing in this section shall be taken to prejudice any liability or remedy

to which a person guilty of an offence thereunder may be subject in civil proceedings.

(6) Where an offence under this section committed by a body corporate is proved to have been committed with the consent or connivance of, or to be attributable to any neglect on the part of, any director, manager or secretary or other similar officer of the body corporate or any person who was purporting to act in any such capacity, he as well as the body corporate shall be guilty of that offence and shall be liable to be proceeded against and punished accordingly.

Amendments

The word in square brackets in s1(3) was substituted by Housing Act 1988 s29(1). Section 1(3A), (3B) and (3C) were added by Housing Act 1988 s29(2). Section 1(4) is printed as amended by Criminal Justice Act 1982 s46.

Restriction on re-entry without due process of law

2 Where any premises are let as a dwelling on a lease which is subject to a right of re-entry or forfeiture it shall not be lawful to enforce that right otherwise than by proceedings in the court while any person is lawfully residing in the premises or part of them.

Prohibition of eviction without due process of law

3(1) Where any premises have been let as a dwelling under a tenancy which is [neither a statutorily protected tenancy nor an excluded tenancy] and–

(a) the tenancy (in this section referred to as the former tenancy) has come to an end, but

(b) the occupier continues to reside in the premises or part of them,

it shall not be lawful for the owner to enforce against the occupier, otherwise than by proceedings in the court, his right to recover possession of the premises.

(2) In this section 'the occupier', in relation to any premises, means any person lawfully residing in the premises or part of them at the termination of the former tenancy.

[(2A) Subsections (1) and (2) above apply in relation to any restricted contract (within the meaning of the Rent Act 1977) which–

(a) creates a licence; and

(b) is entered into after the commencement of section 69 of the Housing Act 1980;

as they apply in relation to a restricted contract which creates a tenancy.]

[(2B) Subsections (1) and (2) above apply in relation to any premises occupied as a dwelling under a licence, other than an excluded licence, as they apply in relation to premises let as a dwelling under a tenancy, and in those subsections the expressions 'let' and 'tenancy' shall be construed accordingly.

(2C) References in the preceding provisions of this section and section 4(2A) below to an excluded tenancy do not apply to–

(a) a tenancy entered into before the date on which the Housing Act 1988 came into force, or

(b) a tenancy entered into on or after that date but pursuant to a contract made before that date,

but, subject to that, 'excluded tenancy' and 'excluded licence' shall be construed in accordance with section 3A below.]

(3) This section shall, with the necessary modifications, apply where the owner's right to recover possession arises on the death of the tenant under a statutory tenancy within the meaning of the Rent Act 1977 or the Rent (Agriculture) Act 1976.

Amendments

Section 3(2A) was added by Housing Act 1980 s69(1), below. The words in square brackets in s3(1) were substituted and ss3(2B) and 3(2C) were added by Housing Act 1988 s30.

Excluded tenancies and licences

[3A(1) Any reference in this Act to an excluded tenancy or an excluded licence is a reference to a tenancy or licence which is excluded by virtue of any of the following provisions of this section.

(2) A tenancy or licence is excluded if–
- (a) under its terms the occupier shares any accommodation with the landlord or licensor; and
- (b) immediately before the tenancy or licence was granted and also at the time it comes to an end, the landlord or licensor occupied as his only or principal home premises of which the whole or part of the shared accommodation formed part.

(3) A tenancy or licence is also excluded if–
- (a) under its terms the occupier shares any accommodation with a member of the family of the landlord or licensor;
- (b) immediately before the tenancy or licence was granted and also at the time it comes to an end, the member of the family of the landlord or licensor occupied as his only or principal home premises of which the whole or part of the shared accommodation formed part; and
- (c) immediately before the tenancy or licence was granted and also at the time it comes to an end, the landlord or licensor occupied as his only or principal home premises in the same building as the shared accommodation and that building is not a purpose-built block of flats.

(4) For the purposes of subsections (2) and (3) above, an occupier shares accommodation with another person if he has the use of it in common with that person (whether or not also in common with others) and any reference in those subsections to shared accommodation shall be construed accordingly, and if, in relation to any tenancy or licence, there is at any time more than one person who is the landlord or licensor, any reference in those subsections to the landlord or licensor shall be construed as a reference to any one of those persons.

(5) In subsections (2) to (4) above–
- (a) 'accommodation' includes neither an area used for storage nor a staircase, passage, corridor or other means of access;
- (b) 'occupier' means, in relation to a tenancy, the tenant and, in relation to a licence, the licensee; and
- (c) 'purpose-built block of flats' has the same meaning as in Part III of Schedule 1 to the Housing Act 1988;

and section 113 of the Housing Act 1985 shall apply to determine whether a person who is for the purposes of subsection (3) above a member of another's family as it applies for the purposes of Part IV of that Act.

(6) A tenancy or licence is excluded if it was granted as a temporary expedient to a person who entered the premises in question or any other premises as a trespasser (whether or not, before the beginning of that tenancy or licence, another tenancy or licence to occupy the premises or any other premises had been granted to him).

(7) A tenancy or licence is excluded if–

    (a) it confers on the tenant or licensee the right to occupy the premises for a holiday only; or

    (b) it is granted otherwise than for money or money's worth.

[(7A) A tenancy or licence is excluded if it is granted in order to provide accommodation [under section 4 or Part VI of the Immigration and Asylum Act 1999].]

[(7C) A tenancy or licence is excluded if it is granted in order to provide accommodation under the Displaced Persons (Temporary Protection) Regulations 2005.]

(8) A licence is excluded if it confers rights of occupation in a hostel, within the meaning of the Housing Act 1985, which is provided by–

    (a) the council of a county, [county borough,] district or London Borough, the Common Council of the City of London, the Council of the Isles of Scilly, the Inner London Education Authority, [the London Fire and Emergency Planning Authority,] a joint authority within the meaning of the Local Government Act 1985 or a residuary body within the meaning of that Act;

    [(aa) an economic prosperity board established under section 88 of the Local Democracy, Economic Development and Construction Act 2009;

    (ab) a combined authority established under section 103 of that Act;]

    (b) a development corporation within the meaning of the New Towns Act 1981;

    (c) the [new towns residuary body] ;

    (d) an urban development corporation established by an order under section 135 of the Local Government, Planning and Land Act 1980;

    [(da) a Mayoral development corporation;]

    (e) a housing action trust established under Part III of the Housing Act 1988;

    [...]

    (g) the [Regulator of Social Housing] [...] ;

    [(ga) the Secretary of State under section 89 of the Housing Associations Act 1985;]

    [(h) a housing trust (within the meaning of the Housing Associations Act 1985) which is a charity [, a private registered provider of social housing] or a registered social landlord (within the meaning of the Housing Act 1985); or]

    (i) any other person who is, or who belongs to a class of person which is, specified in an order made by the Secretary of State.

[(8A) In subsection (8)(c) above 'new towns residuary body' means–

    (a) in relation to England, the Homes and Communities Agency so far as exercising functions in relation to anything transferred (or to be transferred) to it as mentioned in section 52(1)(a) to (d) of the Housing and Regeneration Act 2008 [or the Greater London Authority so far as exercising its new towns and urban development functions]; and

(b) in relation to Wales, means the Welsh Ministers so far as exercising functions in relation to anything transferred (or to be transferred) to them as mentioned in section 36(1)(a)(i) to (iii)of the New Towns Act 1981.]

(9) The power to make an order under subsection (8)(i) above shall be exercisable by statutory instrument which shall be subject to annulment in pursuance of a resolution of either House of Parliament.']

Amendments

Section 3A was added by Housing Act 1988 s31. Section 3A(7A) was added by Immigration and Asylum Act 1999 Sch 14 para 73. The words in square brackets in s3A(8)(a) were added by Local Government (Wales) Act 1994 Sch 8 para 4(1) and Greater London Authority Act 1999 Sch 29(l) para 27. Sections 3A(8)(aa) and (ab) were added by Local Democracy, Economic Development and Construction Act 2009 Sch 6 para 47. The words in square brackets in s3A(8)(c) were substituted by Housing and Regeneration Act 2008 Sch 8 para 24(2). Section 3A(8)(da) was added by Localism Act 2011 Sch 22 para 6. Section 3A(8)(h) was substituted by Housing Act 1996 (Consequential Provisions) Order 1996 SI No 2325 Sch 2 para 7. Section 3A(8)(f) and the words omitted in s3A(8)(g) were repealed by, and s3A(8)(ga)was added by, Government of Wales Act 1998 Schs 16 and 18. Section 3A(7B) was added by Nationality, Immigration and Asylum Act 2002 s32(5). Section 3A(7C) was added by Displaced Persons (Temporary Protection) Regulations 2005 SI No 1379. The words in double square brackets in s3A(7A) were substituted by Immigration, Asylum and Nationality Act 2006 s43(4). Section 3A(8A) and the words in square brackets in s3A(8A) were inserted or substituted with effect from 1 December 2008, by Housing and Regeneration Act 2008 Sch 8 para 24. The words in triple square brackets in s3A(8) were substituted by Housing and Regeneration Act 2008 (Consequential Provisions) Order 2010 SI No 866 Sch 2. The words in double square brackets in s3A(8A) were inserted by Localism Act 2011 Sch 19 para 6 with effect from 1 April 2012 (Localism Act 2011 (Commencement No 4 and Transitional, Transitory and Saving Provisions) Order 2012 SI No 628 art 6(i) subject to transitional provisions in arts 9, 11, 14, 15 and 17 of the same order).

Special provisions for agricultural employees

4(1) This section shall apply where the tenant under the former tenancy (within the meaning of section 3 of this Act) occupied the premises under the terms of his employment as a person employed in agriculture, as defined in section 1 of the Rent (Agriculture) Act 1976, but is not a statutory tenant as defined in that Act.

(2) In this section 'the occupier' , in relation to any premises, means–
(a) the tenant under the former tenancy; or
(b) the [surviving spouse or surviving civil partner] of the tenant under the former tenancy residing with him at his death or, if the former tenant leaves no such [surviving spouse or surviving civil partner], any member of his family residing with him at his death.

[(2A) In accordance with section 3(2B) above, any reference in subsections (1) and (2) above to the tenant under the former tenancy includes a reference to the licensee under a licence (other than an excluded licence) which has come to an end (being a licence to occupy premises as a dwelling); and in the following provisions of this section the expressions 'tenancy' and 'rent' and any other expressions referable to a tenancy shall be construed accordingly.]

(3) Without prejudice to any power of the court apart from this section to postpone the operation or suspend the execution of an order for possession, if in proceedings by the owner against the occupier the court makes an order for the possession of the premises the court may suspend the execution of the order on such terms and conditions, including conditions as to the payment by the occupier of arrears of rent, mesne profits and otherwise as the court thinks reasonable.

(4) Where the order for possession is made within the period of 6 months beginning with the date when the former tenancy came to an end, then, without prejudice to any powers of the court under the preceding provisions of this section or apart from this section to postpone the operation or suspend the execution of the order for a longer period, the court shall suspend the execution of the order for the remainder of the said period of 6 months unless the court—

(a) is satisfied either—
    (i) that other suitable accommodation is, or will within that period be made, available to the occupier; or
    (ii) that the efficient management of any agricultural land or the efficient carrying on of any agricultural operations would be seriously prejudiced unless the premises are available for occupation by a person employed or to be employed by the owner; or
    (iii) that greater hardship (being hardship in respect of matters other than the carrying on of such a business as aforesaid) would be caused by the suspension of the order until the end of that period than by its execution within that period; or
    (iv) that the occupier, or any person residing or lodging with the occupier, has been causing damage to the premises or has been guilty of conduct which is a nuisance or annoyance to persons occupying other premises; and

(b) considers that it would be reasonable not to suspend the execution of the order for the remainder of that period.

(5) Where the court suspends the execution of an order for possession under subsection (4) above it shall do so on such terms and conditions, including conditions as to the payment by the occupier of arrears of rent, mesne profits and otherwise as the court thinks reasonable.

(6) A decision of the court not to suspend the execution of the order under subsection (4) above shall not prejudice any other power of the court to postpone the operation or suspend the execution of the order for the whole or part of the period of 6 months mentioned in that subsection.

(7) Where the court has, under the preceding provisions of this section, suspended the execution of an order for possession, it may from time to time vary the period of suspension or terminate it and may vary any terms or conditions imposed by virtue of this section.

(8) In considering whether or how to exercise its powers under subsection (3) above, the court shall have regard to all the circumstances and, in particular, to—

(a) whether other suitable accommodation is or can be made available to the occupier;

(b) whether the efficient management of any agricultural land or the efficient carrying on of any agricultural operations would be seriously prejudiced unless the premises were available for occupation by a person employed or to be employed by the owner; and

(c) whether greater hardship would be caused by the suspension of the execution of the order than by its execution without suspension or further suspension.

(9) Where in proceedings for the recovery of possession of the premises the court makes an order for possession but suspends the execution of the order under this section, it shall make no order for costs, unless it appears to the court, having regard to the conduct of the owner or of the occupier, that there are special reasons for making such an order.

(10) Where, in the case of an order for possession of the premise to which subsection (4) above applies, the execution of the order is not suspended under that subsection or, the execution of the order having been so suspended, the suspension is terminated, then, if it is subsequently made to appear to the court that the failure to suspend the execution of the order or, as the case may be, the termination of the suspension was–

(a) attributable to the provisions of paragraph (a)(ii) of subsection (4), and

(b) due to misrepresentation or concealment of material facts by the owner of the premises,

the court may order the owner to pay to the occupier such sum as appears sufficient as compensation for damage or loss sustained by the occupier as a result of that failure or termination.

Amendments

Section 4(2A) was added by Housing Act 1988 s30(3). The words in square brackets in s4(2)(b) were substituted by Civil Partnership Act 2004 Sch 8.

PART II: NOTICE TO QUIT

Validity of notices to quit

5(1) [Subject to section (1B) below] no notice by a landlord or a tenant to quit any premises let (whether before or after the commencement of this Act) as a dwelling shall be valid unless–

(a) it is in writing and contains such information as may be prescribed, and

(b) it is given not less than 4 weeks before the date on which it is to take effect.

[(1A) Subject to subsection (1B) below, no notice by a licensor or a licensee to determine a periodic licence to occupy premises as a dwelling (whether the licence was granted before or after the passing of this Act) shall be valid unless–

(a) it is in writing and contains such information as may be prescribed, and

(b) it is given not less than 4 weeks before the date on which it is to take effect.

(1B) Nothing in subsection (1) or subsection (1A) above applies to–

(a) premises let on an excluded tenancy which is entered into on or after the date on which the Housing Act 1988 came into force unless it is entered into pursuant to a contract made before that date; or

(b) premises occupied under an excluded licence.]

(2) In this section 'prescribed' means prescribed by regulations made by the Secretary of State by statutory instrument, and a statutory instrument containing any such regulations shall be subject to annulment in pursuance of a resolution of either House of Parliament.

(3) Regulations under this section may make different provision in relation to different descriptions of lettings and different circumstances.

Amendments

The words in square brackets in subs(1) and subs(1A) and (1B) were added by Housing Act 1988 s32.

PART III: SUPPLEMENTAL PROVISIONS

Prosecution of offences

6 Proceedings for an offence under this Act may be instituted by any of the following authorities–

(a) councils of districts and London boroughs;

[(aa) councils of Welsh counties and county boroughs]

(b) the Common Council of the City of London;

(c) the Council of the Isles of Scilly.

Amendment

The words in square brackets were added by Local Government (Wales) Act 1994 Sch 8 para 4(2).

Service of notices

7(1) If for the purpose of any proceedings (whether civil or criminal) brought or intended to be brought under this Act, any person serves upon–

(a) any agent of the landlord named as such in the rent book or other similar document, or

(b) the person who receives the rent of the dwelling,

a notice in writing requiring the agent or other person to disclose to him the full name and place of abode or place of business of the landlord, that agent or other person shall forthwith comply with the notice.

(2) If any such agent or other person as is referred to in subsection (1) above fails or refuses forthwith to comply with a notice served on him under that subsection he shall be liable on summary conviction to a fine not exceeding [level 4 on the standard scale], unless he shows to the satisfaction of the court that he did not know, and could not with reasonable diligence have ascertained, such of the facts required by the notice to be disclosed as were not disclosed by him.

(3) In this section 'landlord' includes–

(a) any person from time to time deriving title under the original landlord,

(b) in relation to any dwelling-house, any person other than the tenant who is or, but for Part VII of the Rent Act 1977 would be, entitled to possession of the dwelling-house, and

(c) any person who, [...] grants to another the right to occupy the dwelling in question as a residence and any person directly or indirectly deriving title from the grantor.

Amendment

Section 7(2) is printed as amended by Criminal Justice Act 1982 ss39, 46 and Sch 3 (see further, notes to s7(2), below). The words omitted in s7(3)(c) were repealed by Housing Act 1988 Sch 17 para 26.

Interpretation

8(1) In this Act 'statutorily protected tenancy' means–

(a)   a protected tenancy within the meaning of the Rent Act 1977 or a tenancy to which Part I of the Landlord and Tenant Act 1954 applies;

(b)   a protected occupancy or statutory tenancy as defined in the Rent (Agriculture) Act 1976;

(c)   a tenancy to which Part II of the Landlord and Tenant Act 1954 applies;

(d)   a tenancy of an agricultural holding within the meaning of the [Agricultural Holdings Act 1986] [[which is a tenancy in relation to which that Act applies]];

[(e)   an assured tenancy or assured agricultural occupancy under Part I of the Housing Act 1988];

[(f)   a tenancy to which Schedule 10 to the Local Government and Housing Act 1989 applies];

[(g)   a farm business tenancy within the meaning of the Agricultural Tenancies Act 1995].

(2) For the purposes of Part I of this Act a person who, under the terms of his employment, had exclusive possession of any premises other than as a tenant shall be deemed to have been a tenant and the expressions 'let' and 'tenancy' shall be construed accordingly.

(3) In Part I of this Act 'the owner', in relation to any premises, means the person who, as against the occupier, is entitled to possession thereof.

[(4) In this Act 'excluded tenancy' and 'excluded licence' have the meaning assigned by section 3A of this Act.

(5) If, on or after the date on which the Housing Act 1988 came into force, the terms of an excluded tenancy or excluded licence entered into before that date are varied, then–

(a) if the variation affects the amount of the rent which is payable under the tenancy or licence, the tenancy or licence shall be treated for the purposes of sections 3(2C) and 5(1B) above as a new tenancy or licence entered into at the time of the variation; and

(b) if the variation does not affect the amount of the rent which is so payable, nothing in this Act shall affect the determination of the question whether the variation is such as to give rise to a new tenancy or licence.

(6) Any reference in subsection (5) above to a variation affecting the amount of the rent which is payable under a tenancy or licence does not include a reference to–

(a) a reduction or increase effected under Part III or Part VI of the Rent Act 1977 (rents under regulated tenancies and housing association tenancies), section 78 of that Act (power of rent tribunal in relation to restricted contracts) or sections 11 to 14 of the Rent (Agriculture) Act 1976; or

(b) a variation which is made by the parties and has the effect of making the rent expressed to be payable under the tenancy or licence the same as a rent for the dwelling which is entered in the register under Part IV or section 79 of the Rent Act 1977.]

Amendments

Para(e) in subs(1) and subs(4), (5) and (6) were added by the Housing Act 1988 s33. Para (f) in subs(1) was added by Local Government and Housing Act 1989 Sch 11 para 54. The words in square brackets in subs(1)(d) were substituted by Agricultural Holdings Act 1986 Sch 14 para 61. Those in double square brackets were added by Agricultural Tenancies Act 1995 Sch para 29, as was subs(1)(g).

The court for purposes of Part I

9(1) The court for the purposes of Part I of this Act shall, subject to this section, be–

(a) the county court , in relation to premises with respect to which the county court has for the time being jurisdiction in actions for the recovery of land; and

(b) the High Court , in relation to other premises.

(2) Any powers of a county court in proceedings for the recovery of possession of any premises in the circumstances mentioned in section 3(1) of this Act may be exercised with the leave of the judge by any registrar of the court, except in so far as rules of court otherwise provide.

(3) Nothing in this Act shall affect the jurisdiction of the High Court in proceedings to enforce a lessor's right of re-entry or forfeiture or to enforce a mortgagee's right of possession in a case where the former tenancy was not binding on the mortgagee.

(4) Nothing in this Act shall affect the operation of–

(a) section 59 of the Pluralities Act 1838;

(b) section 19 of the Defence Act 1842;

(c) section 6 of the Lecturers and Parish Clerks Act 1844;

(d) paragraph 3 of the Schedule 1 to the Sexual Offences Act 1956; or

(e) section 13 of the Compulsory Purchase Act 1965.

Application to Crown

10 In so far as this Act requires the taking of proceedings in the court for the recovery of possession or confers any powers on the court it shall (except in the case of section 4(10)) be binding on the Crown.

Application to Isles of Scilly

11(1) In its application to the Isles of Scilly, this Act (except in the case of section 5) shall have effect subject to such exceptions, adaptations and modifications as the Secretary of State may by order direct.

(2) The power to make an order under this section shall be exercisable by statutory instrument which shall be subject to annulment, in pursuance of a resolution of either House of Parliament.

(3) An order under this section may be varied or revoked by a subsequent order.

Consequential amendments, etc

12 [*Not reproduced*]

Short title, etc

13(1) This Act may be cited as the Protection from Eviction Act 1977.

(2) This Act shall come into force on the expiry of the period of one month beginning with the date on which it is passed.

(3) This Act does not extend to Scotland or Northern Ireland.
(4) References in this Act to any enactment are references to that enactment as amended, and include references thereto as applied by any other enactment including, except where the context otherwise requires, this Act.

Criminal Law Act 1977 ss6, 7, 12, 12A

PART II: OFFENCES RELATING TO ENTERING AND REMAINING ON PROPERTY

Violence for securing entry

6(1) Subject to the following provisions of this section, any person who, without lawful authority, uses or threatens violence for the purpose of securing entry into any premises for himself or for any other person is guilty of an offence, provided that–

(a) there is someone present on those premises at the time who is opposed to the entry which the violence is intended to secure; and

(b) the person using or threatening the violence knows that that is the case.

[(1A) Subsection (1) above does not apply to a person who is a displaced residential occupier or a protected intending occupier of the premises in question or who is acting on behalf of such an occupier; and if the accused adduces sufficient evidence that he was, or was acting on behalf of, such an occupier he shall be presumed to be, or to be acting on behalf of, such an occupier unless the contrary is proved by the prosecution.]

(2) [Subject to subsection (1A) above,] the fact that a person has any interest in or right to possession or occupation of any premises shall not for the purposes of subsection (1) above constitute lawful authority for the use or threat of violence by him or anyone else for the purpose of securing his entry into those premises.

[...]

(4) It is immaterial for the purposes of this section–

(a) whether the violence in question is directed against the person or against property; and

(b) whether the entry which the violence is intended to secure is for the purpose of acquiring possession of the premises in question or for any other purpose.

(5) A person guilty of an offence under this section shall be liable on summary conviction to imprisonment for a term not exceeding six months or to a fine not exceeding [level 5 on the standard scale] or to both.

[...]

(7) Section 12 below contains provisions which apply for determining when any person is to be regarded for the purposes of this Part of this Act as a displaced residential occupier of any premises or of any access to any premises [and section 12A below contains provisions which apply for determining when any person is to be regarded for the purposes of this Part of this Act as a protected intending occupier of any premises or of any access to any premises].

Amendments

Section 6(1A) was added by Criminal Justice and Public Order Act 1994 s72(2). The words in square brackets in s6(2) were inserted by Criminal Justice and Public Order Act 1994 s72(3). The words omitted in s6(3) were repealed by Criminal Justice and Public Order Act 1994 s72(4). The words in square brackets in s6(5) were substituted by Criminal Justice Act 1982 s46. The words omitted in s6(6) were repealed subject to transitory provisions specified in 2005 SI No 3495 art 2(2) by Serious Organised Crime and Police Act 2005 Sch

7 para 19(2). The words inserted at s6(7) were inserted by Criminal Justice and Public Order Act 1994 s72(5).

Adverse occupation of residential premises

[7(1) Subject to the following provisions of this section and to section 12A(9) below, any person who is on any premises as a trespasser after having entered as such is guilty of an offence if he fails to leave those premises on being required to do so by or on behalf of–

(a) a displaced residential occupier of the premises; or

(b) an individual who is a protected intending occupier of the premises.

(2) In any proceedings for an offence under this section it shall be a defence for the accused to prove that he believed that the person requiring him to leave the premises was not a displaced residential occupier or protected intending occupier of the premises or a person acting on behalf of a displaced residential occupier or protected intending occupier.

(3) In any proceedings for an offence under this section it shall be a defence for the accused to prove–

(a) that the premises in question are or form part of premises used mainly for non-residential purposes; and

(b) that he was not on any part of the premises used wholly or mainly for residential purposes.

(4) Any reference in the preceding provisions of this section to any premises includes a reference to any access to them, whether or not any such access itself constitutes premises, within the meaning of this Part of this Act.

(5) A person guilty of an offence under this section shall be liable on summary conviction to imprisonment for a term not exceeding six months or to a fine not exceeding level 5 on the standard scale or to both.

[…]

(7) Section 12 below contains provisions which apply for determining when any person is to be regarded for the purposes of this Part of this Act as a displaced residential occupier of any premises or of any access to any premises and section 12A below contains provisions which apply for determining when any person is to be regarded for the purposes of this Part of this Act as a protected intending occupier of any premises or of any access to any premises.]

Amendments

The whole of s7 was replaced by Criminal Justice and Public Order Act 1994 s73. The words of s7(6) were repealed subject to transitory provisions specified in 2005 SI No 3495 art 2(2) by Serious Organised Crime and Police Act 2005 Sch 7 para 19(2).

Supplementary provisions

12(1) In this Part of this Act–

(a) 'premises' means any building, any part of a building under separate occupation, any land ancillary to a building, the site comprising any building or buildings together with any land ancillary thereto, and (for the purposes only of sections 10 and 11 above) any other place; and

(b) 'access' means, in relation to any premises, any part of any site or building within which those premises are situated which constitutes an ordinary means of access to those premises (whether or not that is its sole or primary use).

(2) References in this section to a building shall apply also to any structure other than a movable one, and to any movable structure, vehicle or vessel designed or adapted for use for residential purposes; and for the purposes of subsection (1) above–
   (a) part of a building is under separate occupation if anyone is in occupation or entitled to occupation of that part as distinct from the whole; and
   (b) land is ancillary to a building if it is adjacent to it and used (or intended for use) in connection with the occupation of that building or any part of it.

(3) Subject to subsection (4) below, any person who was occupying any premises as a residence immediately before being excluded from occupation by anyone who entered those premises, or any access to those premises, as a trespasser is a displaced residential occupier of the premises for the purposes of this Part of this Act so long as he continues to be excluded from occupation of the premises by the original trespasser or by any subsequent trespasser.

(4) A person who was himself occupying the premises in question as a trespasser immediately before being excluded from occupation shall not by virtue of subsection (3) above be a displaced residential occupier of the premises for the purposes of this Part of this Act.

(5) A person who by virtue of subsection (3) above is a displaced residential occupier of any premises shall be regarded for the purposes of this Part of this Act as a displaced residential occupier also of any access to those premises.

(6) Anyone who enters or is on or in occupation of any premises by virtue of–
   (a) any title derived from a trespasser; or
   (b) any licence or consent given by a trespasser or by a person deriving title from a trespasser,
   shall himself be treated as a trespasser for the purposes of this Part of this Act (without prejudice to whether or not he would be a trespasser apart from this provision); and references in this Part of this Act to a person's entering or being on or occupying any premises as a trespasser shall be construed accordingly.

(7) Anyone who is on any premises as a trespasser shall not cease to be a trespasser for the purposes of this Part of this Act by virtue of being allowed time to leave the premises, nor shall anyone cease to be a displaced residential occupier of any premises by virtue of any such allowance of time to a trespasser.

[(7A) Subsection (6) also applies to the Secretary of State if the tenancy or licence is granted by him under Part III of the Housing Associations Act 1985.]

(8) No rule of law ousting the jurisdiction of magistrates' courts to try offences where a dispute of title to property is involved shall preclude magistrates' courts from trying offences under this Part of this Act.

Amendments
   S12(7A) was added by Government of Wales Act 1998 Sch 16 para3(3).

Protected intending occupiers: supplementary provisions
[12A(1) For the purposes of this Part of this Act an individual is a protected intending occupier of any premises at any time if at that time he falls within subsection (2), (4) or (6) below.

(2) An individual is a protected intending occupier of any premises if–
   (a) he has in those premises a freehold interest or a leasehold interest with not less than two years still to run;

(b) he requires the premises for his own occupation as a residence;

(c) he is excluded from occupation of the premises by a person who entered them, or any access to them, as a trespasser; and

(d) he or a person acting on his behalf holds a written statement–

    (i)   which specifies his interest in the premises;

    (ii) which states that he requires the premises for occupation as a residence for himself; and

    (iii) with respect to which the requirements in subsection (3) below are fulfilled.

(3) The requirements referred to in subsection (2)(d)(iii) above are–

(a) that the statement is signed by the person whose interest is specified in it in the presence of a justice of the peace or commissioner for oaths; and

(b) that the justice of the peace or commissioner for oaths has subscribed his name as a witness to the signature.

(4) An individual is also a protected intending occupier of any premises if–

(a) he has a tenancy of those premises (other than a tenancy falling within subsection (2)(a) above or (6)(a) below) or a licence to occupy those premises granted by a person with a freehold interest or a leasehold interest with not less than two years still to run in the premises;

(b) he requires the premises for his own occupation as a residence;

(c) he is excluded from occupation of the premises by a person who entered them, or any access to them, as a trespasser; and

(d) he or a person acting on his behalf holds a written statement–

    (i)   which states that he has been granted a tenancy of those premises or a licence to occupy those premises;

    (ii) which specifies the interest in the premises of the person who granted that tenancy or licence to occupy ('the landlord');

    (iii) which states that he requires the premises for occupation as a residence for himself; and

    (iv) with respect to which the requirements in subsection (5) below are fulfilled.

(5) The requirements referred to in subsection (4)(d)(iv) above are–

(a) that the statement is signed by the landlord and by the tenant or licensee in the presence of a justice of the peace or commissioner for oaths;

(b) that the justice of the peace or commissioner for oaths has subscribed his name as a witness to the signatures.

(6) An individual is also a protected intending occupier of any premises if–

(a) he has a tenancy of those premises (other than a tenancy falling within subsection (2)(a) or (4)(a) above) or a licence to occupy those premises granted by an authority to which this subsection applies;

(b) he requires the premises for his own occupation as a residence;

(c) he is excluded from occupation of the premises by a person who entered the premises, or any access to them, as a trespasser; and

(d) there has been issued to him by or on behalf of the authority referred to in paragraph (a) above a certificate stating that–

    (i)   he has been granted a tenancy of those premises or a licence to occupy those premises as a residence by the authority; and

    (ii) the authority which granted that tenancy or licence to occupy is one to which this subsection applies, being of a description specified in the certificate.

(7) Subsection (6) above applies to the following authorities–

   (a) any body mentioned in section 14 of the Rent Act 1977 (landlord's interest belonging to local authority etc.);

   (b) the [Regulator of Social Housing]; [...]

   [(ba) a non-profit registered provider of social housing;

   (bb) a profit-making registered provider of social housing, but only in relation to premises which are social housing within the meaning of Part 2 of the Housing and Regeneration Act 2008;]

   [...]

   [(d) a registered social landlord within the meaning of the Housing Act 1985 (see section 5(4) and (5) of that Act).]

(8) A person is guilty of an offence if he makes a statement for the purposes of subsection (2)(d) or (4)(d) above which he knows to be false in a material particular or if he recklessly makes such a statement which is false in a material particular.

(9) In any proceedings for an offence under section 7 of this Act where the accused was requested to leave the premises by a person claiming to be or to act on behalf of a protected intending occupier of the premises–

   (a) it shall be a defence for the accused to prove that, although asked to do so by the accused at the time the accused was requested to leave, that person failed at that time to produce to the accused such a statement as is referred to in subsection (2)(d) or (4)(d) above or such a certificate as is referred to in subsection (6)(d) above; and

   (b) any document purporting to be a certificate under subsection (6)(d) above shall be received in evidence and, unless the contrary is proved, shall be deemed to have been issued by or on behalf of the authority stated in the certificate.

(10) A person guilty of an offence under subsection (8) above shall be liable on summary conviction to imprisonment for a term not exceeding six months or to a fine not exceeding level 5 on the standard scale or to both.

(11) A person who is a protected intending occupier of any premises shall be regarded for the purposes of this Part of this Act as a protected intending occupier also of any access to those premises.]

Amendments

The whole of section 12A was inserted by Criminal Justice and Public Order Act 1994 s74. Subs(7)(b) was substituted by Housing and Regeneration Act 2008 (Consequential Provisions) Order 2010 SI No 866 Sch 2 para 14(a). Section 12A(7)(c) was repealed by Government of Wales Act 1998 ss140, 152 and Sch 18 Part VI. Subss(7)(ba) and (7)(bb) were added by Housing and Regeneration Act 2008 (Consequential Provisions Order 2010 SI No 866 Sch 2 para 14(b). The words of subs(7)(d) were substituted by Housing Act (Consequential Provisions) Order 1996 SI No 2325 Sch 2 para 8.

Housing Act 1988 ss27 and 28

CHAPTER IV – PROTECTION FROM EVICTION

Damages for unlawful eviction

27(1) This section applies if, at any time after 9 June 1988, a landlord (in this section referred to as 'the landlord in default') or any person acting on behalf of the landlord in default unlawfully deprives the residential occupier of any premises of his occupation of the whole or part of the premises.

(2) This section also applies if, at any time after 9 June 1988, a landlord (in this section referred to as 'the landlord in default') or any person acting on behalf of the landlord in default–

   (a) attempts unlawfully to deprive the residential occupier of any premises of his occupation of the whole or part of the premises, or

   (b) knowing or having reasonable cause to believe that the conduct is likely to cause the residential occupier of any premises–

      (i) to give up his occupation of the premises or any part thereof, or

      (ii) to refrain from exercising any right or pursuing any remedy in respect of the premises or any part thereof,

   does acts likely to interfere with the peace or comfort of the residential occupier or members of his household, or persistently withdraws or withholds services reasonably required for the occupation of the premises as a residence,

and, as a result, the residential occupier gives up his occupation of the premises as a residence.

(3) Subject to the following provisions of this section, where this section applies, the landlord in default shall, by virtue of this section, be liable to pay to the former residential occupier, in respect of his loss of the right to occupy the premises in question as his residence, damages assessed on the basis set out in section 28 below.

(4) Any liability arising by virtue of subsection (3) above–

   (a) shall be in the nature of a liability in tort; and

   (b) subject to subsection (5) below, shall be in addition to any liability arising apart from this section (whether in tort, contract or otherwise).

(5) Nothing in this section affects the right of a residential occupier to enforce any liability which arises apart from this section in respect of his loss of the right to occupy premises as his residence; but damages shall not be awarded both in respect of such a liability and in respect of a liability arising by virtue of this section on account of the same loss.

(6) No liability shall arise by virtue of subsection (3) above if–

   (a) before the date on which proceedings to enforce the liability are finally disposed of, the former residential occupier is reinstated in the premises in question in such circumstances that he becomes again the residential occupier of them; or

   (b) at the request of the former residential occupier, a court makes an order (whether in the nature of an injunction or otherwise) as a result of which he is reinstated as mentioned in paragraph (a) above;

and, for the purposes of paragraph (a) above, proceedings to enforce a liability are finally disposed of on the earliest date by which the proceedings (including any proceedings on or in consequence of an appeal) have been determined and any time for appealing or further appealing has expired, except that if any appeal is abandoned, the proceedings shall be taken to be disposed of on the date of the abandonment.

(7) If, in proceedings to enforce a liability arising by virtue of subsection (3) above, it appears to the court–

(a) that, prior to the event which gave rise to the liability, the conduct of the former residential occupier or any person living with him in the premises concerned was such that it is reasonable to mitigate the damages for which the landlord in default would otherwise be liable, or

(b) that, before the proceedings were begun, the landlord in default offered to reinstate the former residential occupier in the premises in question and either it was unreasonable of the former residential occupier to refuse that offer or, if he had obtained alternative accommodation before the offer was made, it would have been unreasonable of him to refuse that offer if he had not obtained that accommodation,

the court may reduce the amount of damages which would otherwise be payable to such amount as it thinks appropriate.

(8) In proceedings to enforce a liability arising by virtue of subsection (3) above, it shall be a defence for the defendant to prove that he believed, and had reasonable cause to believe–

(a) that the residential occupier had ceased to reside in the premises in question at the time when he was deprived of occupation as mentioned in subsection (1) above or, as the case may be, when the attempt was made or the acts were done as a result of which he gave up his occupation of those premises; or

(b) that, where the liability would otherwise arise by virtue only of the doing of acts or the withdrawal or withholding of services, he had reasonable grounds for doing the acts or withdrawing or withholding the services in question.

(9) In this section–

(a) 'residential occupier', in relation to any premises, has the same meaning as in section 1 of the 1977 Act;

(b) 'the right to occupy', in relation to a residential occupier, includes any restriction on the right of another person to recover possession of the premises in question;

(c) 'landlord', in relation to a residential occupier, means the person who, but for the occupier's right to occupy, would be entitled to occupation of the premises and any superior landlord under whom that person derives title;

(d) 'former residential occupier', in relation to any premises, means the person who was the residential occupier until he was deprived of or gave up his occupation as mentioned in subsection (1) or subsection (2) above (and, in relation to a former residential occupier, 'the right to occupy' and 'landlord' shall be construed accordingly).

The measure of damages

28(1) The basis for the assessment of damages referred to in section 27(3) above is the difference in value, determined as at the time immediately before the residential occupier ceased to occupy the premises in question as his residence, between–

  (a) the value of the interest of the landlord in default determined on the assumption that the residential occupier continues to have the same right to occupy the premises as before that time; and

  (b) the value of that interest determined on the assumption that the residential occupier has ceased to have that right.

(2) In relation to any premises, any reference in this section to the interest of the landlord in default is a reference to his interest in the building in which the premises in question are comprised (whether or not that building contains any other premises) together with its curtilage.

(3) For the purposes of the valuations referred to in subsection (1) above, it shall be assumed–

  (a) that the landlord in default is selling his interest on the open market to a willing buyer;

  (b) that neither the residential occupier nor any member of his family wishes to buy; and

  (c) that it is unlawful to carry out any substantial development of any of the land in which the landlord's interest subsists or to demolish the whole or part of any building on that land.

(4) In this section 'the landlord in default' has the same meaning as in section 27 above and subsection (9) of that section applies in relation to this section as it applies in relation to that.

(5) Section 113 of the Housing Act 1985 (meaning of 'members of a person's family') applies for the purposes of subsection (3)(b) above.

(6) The reference in subsection (3)(c) above to substantial development of any of the land in which the landlord's interest subsists is a reference to any development other than–

  (a) development for which planning permission is granted by a general development order for the time being in force and which is carried out so as to comply with any condition or limitation subject to which planning permission is so granted; or

  (b) a change of use resulting in the building referred to in subsection (2) above or any part of it being used as, or as part of, one or more dwelling-houses;

and in this subsection 'general development order' [has the meaning given in section 56(6) of the Town and Country Planning Act 1990] and other expressions have the same meaning as in that Act.

Amendments

The words in square brackets in s28(6)(b) were substituted by Planning (Consequential Provisions) Act 1990 Sch 2 para 79(1).

Protection from Harassment Act 1997 ss1–7, 12

ENGLAND AND WALES

Prohibition of harassment

1(1) A person must not pursue a course of conduct–
    (a) which amounts to harassment of another, and
    (b) which he knows or ought to know amounts to harassment of the other.
[(1A) A person must not pursue a course of conduct–
    (a) which involves harassment of two or more persons, and
    (b) which he knows or ought to know involves harassment of those persons, and
    (c) by which he intends to persuade any person (whether or not one of those mentioned above)–
        (i) not to do something that he is entitled or required to do, or
        (ii) to do something that he is not under any obligation to do.]
  (2) For the purposes of this section, the person whose course of conduct is in question ought to know that it amounts to [or involves] harassment of another if a reasonable person in possession of the same information would think the course of conduct amounted to [or involved] harassment of the other.
  (3) Subsection (1) [or (1A)] does not apply to a course of conduct if the person who pursued it shows–
    (a) that it was pursued for the purpose of preventing or detecting crime,
    (b) that it was pursued under any enactment or rule of law or to comply with any condition or requirement imposed by any person under any enactment, or
    (c) that in the particular circumstances the pursuit of the course of conduct was reasonable.

Amendments
Section 1(1A) was added by Serious Organised Crime and Police Act 2005 s125(2)(a). The words in square brackets in s1(2) were inserted by Serious Organised Crime and Police Act 2005 s125(2)(b). The words in square brackets in s1(3) were inserted by Serious Organised Crime and Police Act 2005 s125(2)(c).

Offence of harassment

2(1) A person who pursues a course of conduct in breach of [section 1(1) or (1A)] is guilty of an offence.
  (2) A person guilty of an offence under this section is liable on summary conviction to imprisonment for a term not exceeding six months, or a fine not exceeding level 5 on the standard scale, or both.
    […]

Amendments
The words in square brackets were substituted by Serious Organised Crime and Police Act 2005 s125(3). The words omitted in s2(3) were repealed by Police Reform Act 2002 Sch 8 para 1.

Civil remedy

3(1) An actual or apprehended breach of [section 1(1)] may be the subject of a claim in civil proceedings by the person who is or may be the victim of the course of conduct in question.

(2) On such a claim, damages may be awarded for (among other things) any anxiety caused by the harassment and any financial loss resulting from the harassment.

(3) Where–
   (a) in such proceedings the High Court or a county court grants an injunction for the purpose of restraining the defendant from pursuing any conduct which amounts to harassment, and
   (b) the plaintiff considers that the defendant has done anything which he is prohibited from doing by the injunction,
   the plaintiff may apply for the issue of a warrant for the arrest of the defendant.

(4) An application under subsection (3) may be made–
   (a) where the injunction was granted by the High Court, to a judge of that court, and
   (b) where the injunction was granted by a county court, to a judge or district judge of that or any other county court.

(5) The judge or district judge to whom an application under subsection (3) is made may only issue a warrant if–
   (a) the application is substantiated on oath, and
   (b) the judge or district judge has reasonable grounds for believing that the defendant has done anything which he is prohibited from doing by the injunction.

(6) Where–
   (a) the High Court or a county court grants an injunction for the purpose mentioned in subsection (3)(a), and
   (b) without reasonable excuse the defendant does anything which he is prohibited from doing by the injunction,
   he is guilty of an offence.

(7) Where a person is convicted of an offence under subsection (6) in respect of any conduct, that conduct is not punishable as a contempt of court.

(8) A person cannot be convicted of an offence under subsection (6) in respect of any conduct which has been punished as a contempt of court.

(9) A person guilty of an offence under subsection (6) is liable–
   (a) on conviction on indictment, to imprisonment for a term not exceeding five years, or a fine, or both, or
   (b) on summary conviction, to imprisonment for a term not exceeding six months, or a fine not exceeding the statutory maximum, or both.

Amendments
   The words in s3(1) were substituted by Serious Organised Crime and Police Act 2005 s125(4).

Injunctions to protect persons from harassment within section 1(1A)

3A(1) This section applies where there is an actual or apprehended breach of section 1(1A) by any person ('the relevant person').

(2) In such a case–
   (a) any person who is or may be a victim of the course of conduct in question, or
   (b) any person who is or may be a person falling within section 1(1A)(c),
   may apply to the High Court or a county court for an injunction restraining

the relevant person from pursuing any conduct which amounts to harassment in relation to any person or persons mentioned or described in the injunction.

(3) Section 3(3) to (9) apply in relation to an injunction granted under subsection (2) above as they apply in relation to an injunction granted as mentioned in section 3(3)(a).

Amendments

The whole of subsection 3A was added by Serious Organised Crime and Police Act 2005 s125(5).

Putting people in fear of violence

4(1) A person whose course of conduct causes another to fear, on at least two occasions, that violence will be used against him is guilty of an offence if he knows or ought to know that his course of conduct will cause the other so to fear on each of those occasions.

(2) For the purposes of this section, the person whose course of conduct is in question ought to know that it will cause another to fear that violence will be used against him on any occasion if a reasonable person in possession of the same information would think the course of conduct would cause the other so to fear on that occasion.

(3) It is a defence for a person charged with an offence under this section to show that–

(a) his course of conduct was pursued for the purpose of preventing or detecting crime,

(b) his course of conduct was pursued under any enactment or rule of law or to comply with any condition or requirement imposed by any person under any enactment, or

(c) the pursuit of his course of conduct was reasonable for the protection of himself or another or for the protection of his or another's property.

(4) A person guilty of an offence under this section is liable–

(a) on conviction on indictment, to imprisonment for a term not exceeding five years, or a fine, or both, or

(b) on summary conviction, to imprisonment for a term not exceeding six months, or a fine not exceeding the statutory maximum, or both.

(5) If on the trial on indictment of a person charged with an offence under this section the jury find him not guilty of the offence charged, they may find him guilty of an offence under section 2.

(6) The Crown Court has the same powers and duties in relation to a person who is by virtue of subsection (5) convicted before it of an offence under section 2 as a magistrates' court would have on convicting him of the offence.

Restraining orders [on conviction]

5(1) A court sentencing or otherwise dealing with a person ('the defendant') convicted of an offence [...] may (as well as sentencing him or dealing with him in any other way) make an order under this section.

(2) The order may, for the purpose of protecting the victim [or victims] of the offence, or any other person mentioned in the order, from [...] conduct which–

(a) amounts to harassment, or

(b) will cause a fear of violence,
prohibit the defendant from doing anything described in the order.
(3) The order may have effect for a specified period or until further order.
[(3A) In proceedings under this section both the prosecution and the defence may lead, as further evidence, any evidence that would be admissible in proceedings for an injunction under section 3.]
(4) The prosecutor, the defendant or any other person mentioned in the order may apply to the court which made the order for it to be varied or discharged by a further order.
[(4A) Any person mentioned in the order is entitled to be heard on the hearing of an application under subsection (4).]
(5) If without reasonable excuse the defendant does anything which he is prohibited from doing by an order under this section, he is guilty of an offence.
(6) A person guilty of an offence under this section is liable–
　　(a) on conviction on indictment, to imprisonment for a term not exceeding five years, or a fine, or both, or
　　(b) on summary conviction, to imprisonment for a term not exceeding six months, or a fine not exceeding the statutory maximum, or both.
[(7) A court dealing with a person for an offence under this section may vary or discharge the order in question by a further order.]

Amendments

The words in square brackets in the section title were inserted by Domestic Violence, Crime and Victims Act 2004 Sch 10 para 43(2). The words omitted in s5(1) were repealed by Domestic Violence, Crime and Victims Act 2004 Sch 11 para 1. The words in square brackets in s5(2) were inserted by Serious Organised Crime and Police Act 2005 s125(6). The words omitted in s5(2) were repealed by Domestic Violence, Crime and Victims Act 2004 Sch 11 para 1. S5(3A) was added by Domestic Violence, Crime and Victims Act 2004 s12(2). The whole of s5(4A) was added by Domestic Violence, Crime and Victims Act 2004 s12(3). Section 5(7) was added by Domestic Violence, Crime and Victims Act 2004 s12(4).

Restraining orders on acquittal

5A(1) A court before which a person ('the defendant') is acquitted of an offence may, if it considers it necessary to do so to protect a person from harassment by the defendant, make an order prohibiting the defendant from doing anything described in the order.
(2) Subsections (3) to (7) of section 5 apply to an order under this section as they apply to an order under that one.
(3) Where the Court of Appeal allows an appeal against conviction they may remit the case to the Crown Court to consider whether to proceed under this section.
(4) Where–
　　(a) the Crown Court allows an appeal against conviction, or
　　(b) a case is remitted to the Crown Court under subsection (3),
　　the reference in subsection (1) to a court before which a person is acquitted of an offence is to be read as referring to that court.
(5) A person made subject to an order under this section has the same right of appeal against the order as if–

(a) he had been convicted of the offence in question before the court which made the order, and

(b) the order had been made under section 5.

Amendment

The whole of s5A was added by the Domestic Violence, Crime and Victims Act 2004 s12(5).

Limitation

6 In section 11 of the Limitation Act 1980 (special time limit for actions in respect of personal injuries), after subsection (1) there is inserted–

'(1A) This section does not apply to any action brought for damages under section 3 of the Protection from Harassment Act 1997.'

Interpretation of this group of sections

7(1) This section applies for the interpretation of [sections 1 to 5A] .

(2) References to harassing a person include alarming the person or causing the person distress.

[(3) A 'course of conduct' must involve–

(a) in the case of conduct in relation to a single person (see section 1(1)), conduct on at least two occasions in relation to that person, or

(b) in the case of conduct in relation to two or more persons (see section 1(1A)), conduct on at least one occasion in relation to each of those persons.]

[(3A) A person's conduct on any occasion shall be taken, if aided, abetted, counselled or procured by another–

(a) to be conduct on that occasion of the other (as well as conduct of the person whose conduct it is); and

(b) to be conduct in relation to which the other's knowledge and purpose, and what he ought to have known, are the same as they were in relation to what was contemplated or reasonably foreseeable at the time of the aiding, abetting, counselling or procuring.]

(4) 'Conduct' includes speech.

[(5) References to a person, in the context of the harassment of a person, are references to a person who is an individual.]

Amendments

The words in square brackets in s7(1) were substituted by Domestic Violence, Crime and Victims Act 2004 Sch 10 para 44. Section 7(3) was substituted by Serious Organised Crime and Police Act 2005 s125(7)(a). Section 7(3A) was added by Criminal Justice and Police Act 2001 s44(1). Section 7(5) was added by Serious Organised Crime and Police Act 2005 s125(7)(b).

National security, etc.

12(1) If the Secretary of State certifies that in his opinion anything done by a specified person on a specified occasion related to–

(a) national security,

(b) the economic well-being of the United Kingdom, or

(c) the prevention or detection of serious crime,

and was done on behalf of the Crown, the certificate is conclusive evidence that this Act does not apply to any conduct of that person on that occasion.

(2) In subsection (1), 'specified' means specified in the certificate in question.

(3) A document purporting to be a certificate under subsection (1) is to be received in evidence and, unless the contrary is proved, be treated as being such a certificate.

Criminal Justice and Police Act 2001 s42A

PART 1: PROVISIONS FOR COMBATTING CRIME AND DISORDER
CHAPTER 3: OTHER PROVISIONS FOR COMBATTING CRIME AND DISORDER

Further provision about intimidation etc.

Offence of harassment etc. of a person in his home

42A(1) A person commits an offence if—

- (a) that person is present outside or in the vicinity of any premises that are used by any individual ('the resident') as his dwelling;
- (b) that person is present there for the purpose (by his presence or otherwise) of representing to the resident or another individual (whether or not one who uses the premises as his dwelling), or of persuading the resident or such another individual—
  - (i) that he should not do something that he is entitled or required to do; or
  - (ii) that he should do something that he is not under any obligation to do;
- (c) that person—
  - (i) intends his presence to amount to the harassment of, or to cause alarm or distress to, the resident; or
  - (ii) knows or ought to know that his presence is likely to result in the harassment of, or to cause alarm or distress to, the resident; and
- (d) the presence of that person—
  - (i) amounts to the harassment of, or causes alarm or distress to, any person falling within subsection (2); or
  - (ii) is likely to result in the harassment of, or to cause alarm or distress to, any such person.

(2) A person falls within this subsection if he is—

- (a) the resident,
- (b) a person in the resident's dwelling, or
- (c) a person in another dwelling in the vicinity of the resident's dwelling.

(3) The references in subsection (1)(c) and (d) to a person's presence are references to his presence either alone or together with that of any other persons who are also present.

(4) For the purposes of this section a person (A) ought to know that his presence is likely to result in the harassment of, or to cause alarm or distress to, a resident if a reasonable person in possession of the same information would think that A's presence was likely to have that effect.

(5) A person guilty of an offence under this section shall be liable, on summary conviction, to imprisonment for a term not exceeding 51 weeks or to a fine not exceeding level 4 on the standard scale, or to both.

(6) In relation to an offence committed before the commencement of section 281(5)of the Criminal Justice Act 2003 (alteration of penalties for summary offences), the reference in subsection (5) to 51 weeks is to be read as a reference to 6 months.

(7) In this section 'dwelling' has the same meaning as in Part 1 of the Public Order Act 1986.

Amendment

The whole of s42A was added by Serious Organised Crime and Police Act 2005 s126(1).

Notices to Quit etc (Prescribed Information) Regulations 1988 SI No 2201

1. These Regulations may be cited as the Notices to Quit etc (Prescribed Information) Regulations 1988 and shall come into force on 15 January 1989.
2. Where, on or after the date these Regulations come into force, a landlord gives a notice to quit any premises let as a dwelling, or a licensor gives a notice to determine a periodic licence to occupy premises as a dwelling (and the premises are not let or occupied as specified in section 5(1B) of the Protection from Eviction Act 1977), the information prescribed for the purposes of section 5 of the Protection from Eviction Act 1977 shall be that in the Schedule to these Regulations.
3. The Notices to Quit (Prescribed Information) Regulations 1980 are hereby revoked.

SCHEDULE: PRESCRIBED INFORMATION

1. If the tenant or licensee does not leave the dwelling, the landlord or licensor must get an order for possession from the court before the tenant or licensee can lawfully be evicted. The landlord or licensor cannot apply for such an order before the notice to quit or notice to determine has run out.
2. A tenant or licensee who does not know if he has any right to remain in possession after a notice to quit or a notice to determine runs out can obtain advice from a solicitor. Help with all or part of the cost of legal advice and assistance may be available under the Legal Aid Scheme. He should also be able to obtain information from a Citizens' Advice Bureau, a Housing Aid Centre or a rent officer.

Explanatory note

These Regulations prescribe the information to be contained in a landlord's notice to quit given on or after the 15 January 1989 to determine a tenancy of premises let as a dwelling, or a licensor's notice given on or after that date to determine a periodic licence to occupy premises as a dwelling. They do not apply to the premises specified in section 5(1B) of the Protection from Eviction Act 1977 (premises subject to excluded licences or certain excluded tenancies). These Regulations replace the Notices to Quit (Prescribed Information) Regulations 1980, which applied only to tenancies.

Legal Aid, Sentencing and Punishment of Offenders Act 2012 s144

Offence of squatting in a residential building

144(1) A person commits an offence if–

    (a) the person is in a residential building as a trespasser having entered it as a trespasser,

    (b) the person knows or ought to know that he or she is a trespasser, and

    (c) the person is living in the building or intends to live there for any period.

(2) The offence is not committed by a person holding over after the end of a lease or licence (even if the person leaves and re-enters the building).

(3) For the purposes of this section–

    (a) 'building' includes any structure or part of a structure (including a temporary or moveable structure), and

    (b) a building is 'residential' if it is designed or adapted, before the time of entry, for use as a place to live.

(4) For the purposes of this section the fact that a person derives title from a trespasser, or has the permission of a trespasser, does not prevent the person from being a trespasser.

(5) A person convicted of an offence under this section is liable on summary conviction to imprisonment for a term not exceeding 51 weeks or a fine not exceeding level 5 on the standard scale (or both).

(6) In relation to an offence committed before the commencement of section 281(5) of the Criminal Justice Act 2003, the reference in subsection (5) to 51 weeks is to be read as a reference to 6 months.

(7) For the purposes of subsection (1)(a) it is irrelevant whether the person entered the building as a trespasser before or after the commencement of this section.

(8) In section 17 of the Police and Criminal Evidence Act 1984 (entry for purpose of arrest etc)–

    (a) in subsection (1)(c), after sub-paragraph (v) insert–

        '(vi) section 144 of the Legal Aid, Sentencing and Punishment of Offenders Act 2012 (squatting in a residential building);';

    (b) in subsection (3), for 'or (iv)' substitute ', (iv) or (vi)'.

(9) In Schedule 10 to the Criminal Justice and Public Order Act 1994 (consequential amendments), omit paragraph 53(b).

Index